MW01531956

HOPE PERSONIFIED:
FRANCES
MASCHAL LANDERS

A Woman from Arkansas, A Priest from Haiti,
A Generation Changed through Education

Martha Abbey Miller

Martha Abbey Miller

WESTBOW
P R E S S®
A DIVISION OF THOMAS NELSON
& ZONDERVAN

Copyright © 2016 Martha Abbey Miller.

All rights reserved. No part of this book may be used or reproduced by any means, graphic, electronic, or mechanical, including photocopying, recording, taping or by any information storage retrieval system without the written permission of the author except in the case of brief quotations embodied in critical articles and reviews.

New Revised Standard Version Bible, copyright © 1989, Division of Christian Education of the National Council of the Churches of Christ in the United States of America. Used by permission. All rights reserved.

WestBow Press books may be ordered through booksellers or by contacting:

WestBow Press
A Division of Thomas Nelson & Zondervan
1663 Liberty Drive
Bloomington, IN 47403
www.westbowpress.com
1 (866) 928-1240

Because of the dynamic nature of the Internet, any web addresses or links contained in this book may have changed since publication and may no longer be valid. The views expressed in this work are solely those of the author and do not necessarily reflect the views of the publisher, and the publisher hereby disclaims any responsibility for them.

Any people depicted in stock imagery provided by Thinkstock are models, and such images are being used for illustrative purposes only. Certain stock imagery © Thinkstock.

ISBN: 978-1-5127-4999-1 (sc)
ISBN: 978-1-5127-5000-3 (hc)
ISBN: 978-1-5127-4998-4 (e)

Library of Congress Control Number: 2016911660

Print information available on the last page.

WestBow Press rev. date: 08/05/2016

By air, Haiti is ninety minutes and a world away from Miami, Florida.

For the faithful supporters of Haiti Education Foundation
who enlarge the footsteps of Frances Landers
up the mountainsides and down

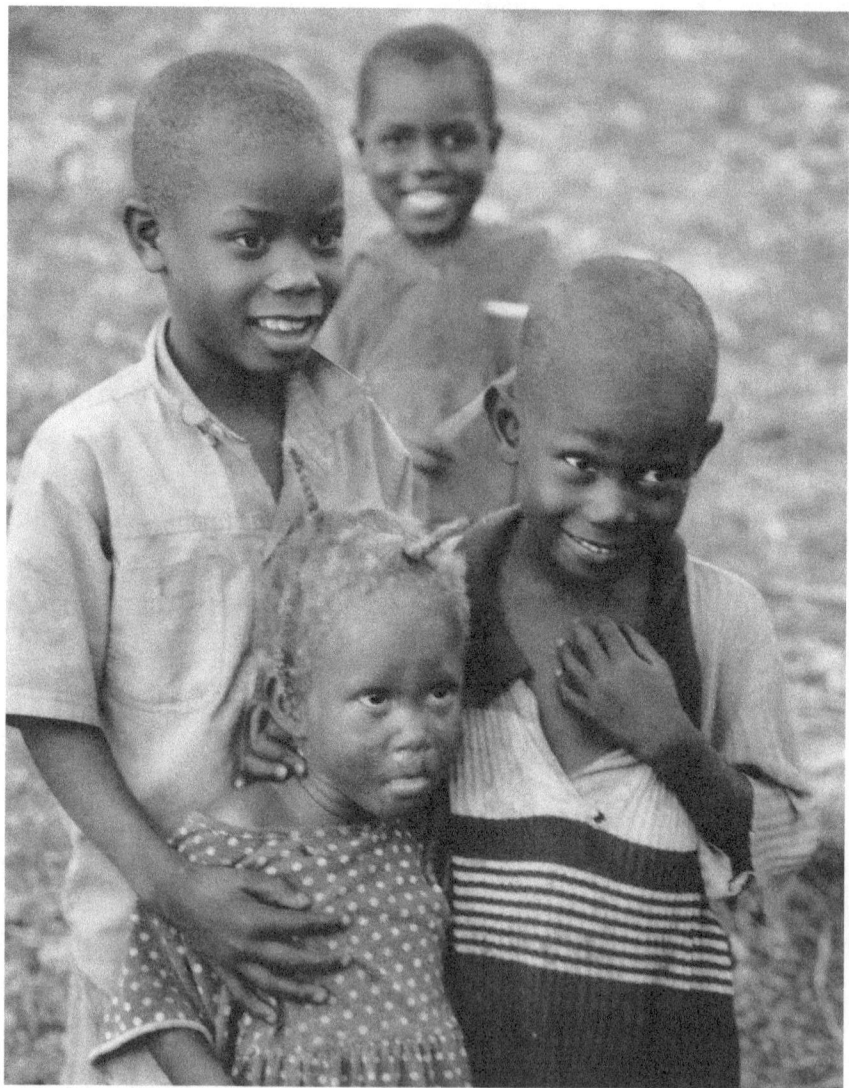

Haiti, a land where despair often obscures tropical beauty, is the poorest country in the Western Hemisphere. Most of its nearly eleven million people do not earn three dollars a day. In the mountains of Grande Colline, a rugged region southwest of the capital city of Port-au-Prince, farmers struggle to grow crops. They fight endless rocks, depleted soil, and insufficient rain. Families are large, meals are small, and schools are few. Illiteracy is the norm, the future bleak.

Years ago, two people began to change this.

Cherident, Haiti: May 1989

A tall, stately white woman and a much taller black man stood beside his battered Land Rover on a rutted trail that ended part way to the top of a treeless mountain. The two looked toward a simple mission church made of stone. Its chiseled cross, jade green, was more or less centered above an open wooden door painted to match.

The Haitian priest swept his long arms wide. He raised his animated voice, his English impressive though thickly accented. Hungry children stood nearby, clothes tattered, feet bare. Their curiosity—they had never seen a white woman—added a momentary sparkle to their ordinarily listless eyes.

One little boy stopped speaking Creole to listen, though he could not understand, as the priest finished his sentence.

"And that is my responsibility to God, to have a mission school beside each of my seven churches."

"But Pere Albert," the woman from Arkansas began her reply, for *pere* is French for "father." Her rich southern voice was poised but insistent. She looked with sympathy past the ragged children and up to meet the priest's piercing black eyes. "I can't possibly raise money for seven schools. Why, just look at this place." She gestured at the inhospitable terrain. "This is barely a road. And I'm already funding three schools."

"Frances," the Episcopal priest interrupted, his words booming and undaunted. "If *God* wants schools in the mountains, there *will be* schools in the mountains."

Contents

Frances Landers's hand-drawn map
pinpointed the location of her mountain village schools.

Preface

From Once Upon a Time to Happily Ever After

Once upon a time, in one of dozens of impoverished villages scattered across the barren mountains of southwestern Haiti, there was a young boy. At the first cry of the rooster before dawn, he rolled off his mat to fetch water for his mother. Barefoot, he ran two miles down the steep slopes to the dirty riverbed. On his return, he balanced a full, forty-pound, five-gallon bucket on his head. Careful. Don't spill a drop!

At daylight he joined his father to farm the rocky, difficult land. He never went to school. There was no school. Like his parents and grandparents, he could neither read nor write.

When not helping his family, he would play with his village friends, using makeshift toys. Rocks, most plentiful. A hoop and a stick. Perhaps string and plastic for a kite. By keeping active, he didn't hear his hungry, bloated stomach growl.

There were a few rainy days. Sometimes there was so much rain that mud swirled across the rugged road, so much wind that he feared his family's insufficient house would blow away. But some years there was not enough rain to keep his father's meager crops alive. And then the young boy's stomach would grumble all the more.

This was his life.

If asked about growing up, he'd shrug. He assumed he would get married someday and build a little hut close to his family's home, and his own illiterate children would crowd onto this exhausted plot of earth. Like his father, he would struggle daily to provide. He and his wife would worry when their malnourished kids got sick. Before fifty, bone tired and ready to pass this life down to his children, he would die.

This young boy was in for a surprise.

One January day in 1989, a very tall Haitian Episcopal priest moved to the young boy's mountains. Four months later, the priest brought to the village a stately American woman. He addressed her as Mrs. Landers.

Yes, in 1989 this young boy's life was destined to change.

In 2005 Pere Jean-Wilfrid Albert (pronounced "Al-bear") was exhausted, but not from years of bending over to plant beans or remove another rock or milk a scrawny goat. No, he was tired—mostly in a good way—from sixteen years of bending over backward to be the spiritual father to thousands (including the young boy) in this region called Grande Colline.

Endlessly, Pere Albert preached the gospel and implored his people to live with hope. He recruited local crews to construct schools, hired Haitian principals and teachers, and oversaw their curriculum. And he smiled through the years as he watched the young boy and thousands of other children scamper happily across the mountains to—finally—go to school.

Pere Albert was justified in being tired. Cancer ravaged his fifty-six-year-old body.

His work was far from done. Too many adults still knew the darkness of Haitian *vodou* and not the light of the Lord. His parish had sparse water, hardly any electricity, no doctors or nurses, too many coffins, and too little food.

And too many children still without a school.

Though Pere Albert had a large vision and a larger faith, on the third of July that year, the cancer won.

In 2010 Frances Maschal Landers was tired. On the fourteenth of September, five years after the death of Pere Albert—a man like a son to her—Frances was ready to leave her Haiti Education Foundation in the hands of those who loved her. At ninety-three she had devoted the final third of her life to the children of Haiti. She ended illiteracy for thousands of boys and girls and for their siblings, parents, and grandparents.

Frances funded her first school for Pere Albert in 1981. Ultimately, she built schools in forty Haitian villages. Pere Albert and Frances would educate (and her Haiti Education Foundation continues to educate) tens of thousands of children like the young boy.

To the end, Frances was gallant and gracious, faithful and focused. She personified hope.

Pere Albert and Frances Landers knew that educating Haiti's youngest generation was the only answer for this struggling, impoverished country. Together, one of them living in Haiti and the other in Arkansas, they answered God's call to give hope through education. They led and they inspired. They prayed and cajoled. They laughed. And they cried.

These partners changed the life of that young boy and countless thousands of others in Haiti and in the United States.

When Pere Albert and Frances Landers closed their eyes for the last time, they were each richly rewarded. They saw God reach out His arms. They felt His strong, loving grip. They heard Him thank them for all they had done. They smiled as He welcomed them home.

And they lived happily ever after.

The story of Frances Landers and her work with Pere Albert will take us across the United States and south over the Caribbean Sea. We will travel down to the depths of despair over the endless challenges that Haitians endure, and then up denuded mountain slopes to the region of Grande Colline, to dozens of poor but joyous villages. Our journey will fill in all of the important gaps between the young Haitian boy's "once upon a time" and the "happily ever after" that rewarded Pere Albert and Frances Landers.

Thank you for wanting to read this book.

At its core, this is a story of Christ our Lord moving through ordinary lives to accomplish miracles.

At its heart, this is a story about the life-changing value of education.

At its soul, this is a story about love's powerful hope, a hope personified by Frances Landers.

Would Frances have wanted a published biography?

In 2003 this author asked her, "Is anyone in your vast network writing the story of you and Pere Albert and this miracle in Haiti?"

Her answer was prompt.

"No one is writing the story of Pere Albert and this miracle in Haiti. It would be wonderful if you could do this, Martha. You know the work from so many angles."

Ah, an endorsement. But look at Frances's response: "the story of Pere Albert and this miracle in Haiti." She took the reference to herself out of her reply.

So here we are, more than ten years later, and I raise the question again: would Frances have wanted *her* biography written?

Probably not.

Frances would stand pat that this story is not about one woman but about thousands of people, most very young, with dark skin, growling stomachs, and appetites equally hungry for learning. She would contend that this story is more about a tall Haitian priest with an index finger that reached halfway to heaven than it is about her.

It's easy to picture Frances, thinking of the stature of Pere Albert and all that he initiated for the children in his impoverished mountains. With a lilt to her voice, Frances would insist that she should not be this book's main character, or even be center stage.

"I am willing to be *on* the stage, yes," she would say, pausing on the word "yes" and expanding it to two syllables. "But I must share it with every person who supports Haiti Education Foundation. And with every Haitian child who's been in school. I will stand behind our beloved, towering Pere Albert, which won't be hard," she'd say with a laugh. "You can surround me with the children, of course, and their families, teachers, principals, and the other priests. I'll stand beside my own family, our board of directors, the church, and a thousand other friends and donors and partners. But you mustn't forget. This story isn't about *me*. Make it a big stage. Leave room on it. This is a long-term adventure for Haitians and supporters still to come.

"And one more thing," Frances would begin and then stop, knowing that what she was about to say was obvious to all who are invested in her sort of work. But she would finish her thought, just the same. "This story isn't about any of us *on* the stage at all. It's about He who presides *over* it."

As Frances would have wanted, the stage set in this book is large and well populated. She is as often the director as the lead player.

In the beautiful but difficult land that is Haiti, maintaining hope is essential. Frances Landers radiated enormous hope. May ours be strengthened by her story.

PART I

DISCOVERY

As a young woman, Frances Landers did a little fashion modeling.

Chapter 1

Better Than a Victrola

My dad told me that there was a lot to learn that was not in books.
—Frances Landers, El Dorado, Arkansas, 2004

Outside First Presbyterian Church of El Dorado, Arkansas, the fall evening air was cool and crisp. Inside, the lights in the meeting room were warm and welcoming, the chairs more than half full.

Dr. and Mrs. Gardner Landers and their family occupied a handful of those chairs. On this night in 1977, churchgoers listened to an update on international medical mission projects.

Keith McCaffety of Medical Benevolence Foundation was the speaker. MBF, a nonprofit in suburban Houston, Texas, partnered with churches to bring healing to impoverished people around the world.

Gardner and Frances periodically wrote checks to MBF. They had come that evening to hear how their money was being spent.

"MBF operates a little hospital, Sainte Croix, in Léogâne, Haiti," Keith said. He described a rudimentary clinic that served thousands, insufficiently. Sainte Croix employed a Haitian medical staff, but expertise from the United States was always needed.

"We need American doctors to come down and work," Keith said.

Gardner, El Dorado's ophthalmologist, leaned over to his wife. "Sounds like they need internists and general surgeons. They don't need eye specialists like me."

Keith overheard the remark and was quick to reply.

"Oh, no. Our greatest need is ophthalmologists. Many adults in Haiti are blind from cataracts. Unless they come to a mission hospital when an eye surgeon visits from the United States, they are blind for life. Children are even born blind from cataracts."

Frances caught her breath. Removing cataracts was quite straightforward. Her eyes met her husband's. Imagine being able to heal the blind and not doing so. Impossible.

They looked over to their sons. Jim had followed his father into ophthalmology. His practice was in Little Rock, two hours north of El Dorado. Bill was an optometrist, and Mike was a young lawyer, both in El Dorado.

Gardner asked, "A worthwhile cause?" All three sons nodded.

"This is something we can do," Gardner told Keith, "to make a difference in a few people's lives. We will go Thanksgiving week."

Gardner, Frances, and Jim were immunized for third-world travel, and they packed their bags and surgical instruments. After an early Thanksgiving dinner with all the trimmings, they bought a frozen turkey for the staff at Sainte Croix.

On Saturday, November 19, 1977, the trio (with the turkey) left Little Rock for Miami, Florida. The flight across the Caribbean Sea to Port-au-Prince, Haiti, took an hour and a half.

Frances was sixty and Gardner sixty-four. They had not been looking for a mission field the night they heard Keith McCaffety speak. Certainly, they were not looking to change their lives.

God, however, had other plans.

At a time in life when many people think of slowing their pace, Frances Landers began an incredible journey, an adventure that would fulfill and challenge her for over thirty years.

She ventured deep into the impoverished nation of Haiti. She reached deep into her time, money, and Christian faith. And deep was the impact that she had on tens of thousands of lives.

In 1899 the Atchison, Topeka, and Santa Fe Railway completed a line south from Kansas into northeastern Oklahoma. The fertile prairie was home to Cherokee Indians and homesteading settlers. Rich topsoil and bluegrass graced the surface of the plains. Beneath them, coal beds spread wide. Coal mining was prosperous, as were oil and gas drilling and agriculture.

When Oklahoma became a state in 1907, fewer than a thousand people lived in Collinsville. Rail traffic was brisk. John Maschal had a good job with the Santa Fe as Collinsville's station agent.

John Henry Maschal was born in 1881. His wife, Ethel Faye Paine, always called Faye, was born in 1887. They had their first child, Marjorie Paine, in

1911. Two years later, John Howard arrived. Then on March 5, 1917, Faye's doctor came to the family home to usher Frances Lucile into the world.

The family was thrilled with the new arrival.

Well, perhaps not John Howard.

On the blessed day of Frances's birth, her four-year-old brother, whom the family called Howard, shared the news with neighbors. The couple, eager for their own baby, offered to trade their Victrola for Howard's newborn sister. Howard was elated. He would love a Victrola to play phonograph records! He had no use for another sister.

The trade was never made. Despite Howard's misgivings, it became apparent that Frances was going to stay.

Frances included this anecdote in a small, untitled memoir that she began on June 2, 2004. It is easy to imagine Frances, then eighty-seven, telling aloud this delightful tale. Her southern voice, like music, ran up and down the scale, ranging several octaves.

Her voice was richly accented but clear and melodious. On specific words she added emphasis, like a whole note or a dotted half. They could be persistent words or inspirational ones, spoken seriously or fringed with humor. Often she expressed great wonder and appreciation, and sometimes impatience. But always Frances's words were musical.

Perhaps Frances Lucile was more like that Victrola than John Howard had ever imagined.

When Frances typed her unpublished memoir into the computer she acquired late in life, she used her favorite font, Lucinda Handwriting. In this book, that font represents her writing.

> *When things didn't go MY WAY, I would climb into a big soft chair and imagine I was DEAD and all the family was CRYING because their baby sister had died. After enjoying this for a while, I would get up and be HAPPY again.*

Frances used capital letters for emphasis, mirroring the way she elongated certain words when speaking. In her customized verbal dictionary, "my way" stretched out for several seconds ("maahh wayyy"), and "dead" had two syllables ("day-ed").

The Great Depression that gripped the nation in the late 1920s did not spare Collinsville. When the local bank closed, Frances lost her twelve dollars in savings and thought she'd never trust a bank again.

*My friend could not go to the basketball game
because the ticket was ten cents and her dad did
not have a job.*

The Maschals were fortunate. The Santa Fe still steamed through Collinsville. John's job was secure enough for the family to purchase a new home with four bedrooms and two baths. It cost $3,500.

John and Faye encouraged their children to help with expenses. Frances, eleven, delivered telegrams and bought fabric with the money she earned. Marjorie, a good seamstress, sewed dresses for herself and Frances.

Faye instilled courtesy and humility in her children. John was an attentive father. Telegrams came into the railroad depot, so Frances spent a lot of time at her father's office. Because John taught Frances to read and understand numbers at an early age, she skipped two elementary school grades. John also took time to talk with his daughter about "adult things."

*He talked about MONEY and RESPONSIBILITY, and
PAYING BACK for our good fortune by helping others.
He explained that when we CHARGE at a store, the
bill needed to be paid ON TIME. He showed me the
fine print on the utility bills and why they had
the right to penalize customers for being late with
payments.*

In her senior year at Collinsville High School, Frances and her classmates wrote term papers on people of historical importance. Of all the people across the globe, Frances Maschal picked a Haitian general, Toussaint Louverture. In the early nineteenth century, Louverture helped black slaves win their freedom from France.

What did an Oklahoma teen know about Haiti, this Caribbean island nation south of Cuba, and its turbulent racial past? Frances had not traveled much outside of Collinsville and had little knowledge of third-world countries.

"Our family always marveled that Mother chose to write about Haiti," her son Mike told me.

Frances, sixteen, had no idea how prophetic it was that she chose a Haitian general as her subject. She could not have imagined that forty-four years later, Haiti would begin to dominate her life.

"Mother certainly did not know what was in store for her, but she developed such a love for this place," Mike said. "In 1933 God began to prepare the way for Mother's dedication to Haiti."

All three Maschal children attended the University of Oklahoma in Norman, 140 miles southwest of Collinsville. In Marjorie's junior year as a business major, Howard came on campus. He majored in electrical engineering and then joined AT&T.

When he was young, he subscribed to Popular Mechanics and that was about all he read. Howard studied at MIT, something to do with national security that he said I would never understand.

Marjorie met Ardell Young in college. After graduation he began law school, and she returned to Collinsville to teach. The couple later married.

In the spring of 1933 Frances wrapped up her term paper on Toussaint Louverture and graduated as salutatorian, second in her class. That fall, midway through her sixteenth year, she began college. Frances thought that teaching was the only option for a woman, so she enrolled in education. Her mother arranged for her to live with a family close to campus.

There were three women who were amateur actresses and real PHONIES. I was SO miserable.

The family routinely got up late. Frances rushed to campus with no breakfast, in a panic because she couldn't find the right building. Decades later, despite all her accomplishments, she still had bad dreams of being late to class.

Within two weeks Frances considered leaving school. Fortunately, Marjorie's sorority, Alpha Xi Delta, asked Frances to pledge. Since she had not chosen a sorority during campus rush week, she needed permission from the dean of women. After hearing Frances's story, the dean said yes.

That saved me from being a dropout.

Frances became captain of the rifle team and president of Alpha Xi Delta. Howard got a job at the sorority house, waiting tables and taking care of the furnace.

John Howard resented that Dad paid for me to join a sorority when he had to work ... especially at the same sorority.

But there was an upside for Howard. Van Autry also worked in the sorority house. His sister, Callie Jane, became Howard's wife. Callie Jane and Van were cousins of Gene Autry, the famed cowboy singer and actor.

Frances dated during college, but Ardell Young kept close watch. If Frances dated someone in law school, he would tell Marjorie.

She would write and tell me what a DUD that person was, and that I DIDN'T want HIM ... so I would drop him and try again.

Alpha Xi Delta wanted to start a chapter at the University of Arizona in Tucson. The sorority offered Frances a semester scholarship in the spring of 1937, if she would meet with young women and assess their interest.

When the University of Oklahoma's registrar confirmed that Frances could take her final thirteen credit hours in Tucson, she boarded a train.

I had made no arrangements about enrolling or a place to live. How dumb could I be?

There were no vacancies in the dorms. A taxi took Frances from one boarding house to another, until she found two girls looking for a roommate. Her contagious enthusiasm helped spark the eventual founding of an Alpha Xi Delta chapter at the University of Arizona. The sorority's goal was to nurture intellectual and personal growth, solid ethics, and community responsibility. Frances took these values seriously at the time, and she relied on them heavily throughout her challenging mission work forty years in the future.

Frances returned to Norman, Oklahoma, and graduated. But she wasn't satisfied with her grade point average in either high school or college.

My Dad told me that there was a lot to learn that WAS NOT in BOOKS, so I should not think I had to make a four point. I took him at his word and did NOT make a four point or anything near.

I was salutatorian of my high school class. The valedictorian was Mildred Andrews. She made perfect grades and practiced the piano four hours each day. She also went to O.U., became an organ professor, and had a building on campus named for her. Quite a contrast.

Perhaps. But when Frances typed this story in 2004, she neglected to mention that a rather impressive school building had been constructed some years earlier, with her own name carefully painted on its upper story. Her school was in the mountain village of Cherident, Haiti.

By age twenty, Frances had a degree in education tucked under her arm. Her first interview was with the school superintendent in Owasso, halfway between Collinsville and Tulsa.

I thought he was SO INSULTING. He was a real NERD. He tried to make me believe I didn't know anything. I was told NOT to stay out late or be seen with undesirable people. Before the end of the interview, I knew I would NOT be teaching in OWASSO. I wanted to tell him (you know what).

Frances wisely held her tongue and was hired to teach mathematics and civics at Collinsville High School. She could handle the civics but needed help with the math.

I had the funniest little girl named MILLIE. She was a WHIZ at MATH. When we came to a difficult problem, I would ask MILLIE to come to the board and show the class. She could ALWAYS do it. She was so skinny, never smiled, but worked the problem and returned to her seat without saying a word. MILLIE PAYNE got me through that year.

The next fall, Frances was asked to teach English literature at Collinsville High School for eighty dollars a month.

I was twenty-one. A nineteen-year-old student (a preacher's son) would write me love notes and leave them in my desk drawer. I was careful not to be alone with him after school. All he did was WRITE NOTES.

Frances lived at home and paid her parents for room and board. On occasion, she was a fashion model. It was not surprising that the preacher's son found this beautiful young brunette appealing. So did Kermit Alexander, the principal of Collinsville High School.

He was the only person in Collinsville to date. He was single and I was single. We depended on each other for our social life. He was also the football coach.

After two years, John Maschal cornered his daughter. "Mr. Jones asked if you and Kermit are going to get married."

"What did you tell him?"

"I told him that you were too smart for that."

Frances never dated Kermit again. Mature at twenty-two, she knew it was time to extend her independence and her social life. In the summer of 1939, she moved to Fort Worth, Texas, where Marjorie taught and Ardell practiced law. Ardell would become a brilliant military and trial attorney, part of a United States team that prosecuted Nazi war criminals after World War II at Nuremberg, Germany. Later, Ardell was a respected Texas district judge.

Ardell and Marjorie offered Frances their apartment daybed.

Frances's employment hunt didn't last long. Her competence and character were a good fit for Leonard's Department Store. Marvin Leonard hired Frances for the Women's Ready-to-Wear department, where she worked ten-hour days for eighteen dollars and ninety-five cents a week.

John Marvin and Obadiah Paul Leonard had founded Leonard's in 1918. The store prospered. The brothers, known as Mr. Marvin and Mr. Obie, attributed their success to the company slogan, "More Merchandise for Less Money."

Pleased with her employer, Frances turned her attention to housing more permanent than Marjorie's daybed. She met two girls whose apartment building was within walking distance of the store. One had a cousin who was coming to town and needed an apartment mate.

Her name was Cleta Bell Dodgen. She was a good-looking blonde and had a federal job of some kind. We agreed to share an apartment.

Fort Worth was working out just fine. Frances lived close to her sister and brother-in-law. She had a good job and a place to live. Now, about finding the ideal young man …

After four college years of dating no one in particular, a school year of unwanted love notes from the preacher's son, and two years of football games with Kermit Alexander, Frances Lucile Maschal's romantic life was about to take a positive and lasting turn.

Chapter 2

More Handsome Than
a Red Packard

We have had no reason to regret the decision to move to Arkansas.
Our lives in El Dorado have been enjoyable and satisfying.
—Gardner Landers, El Dorado, Arkansas, 2004

In the fall of 1941, army life still accommodated simple pleasures, like a shiny new convertible.

Two officers from Camp Bowie in Brownwood, Texas, drove the diagonal 130 miles northeast to a Fort Worth car dealership. The passenger, a dark-haired young man, was almost twenty-eight. The driver, about the same age, wanted to trade in his car for a new red Packard convertible. He did.

Grinning, he challenged the salesman. "Now we need dates!"

"Well, I know a blonde, Cleta Bell Dodgen. I'll see if she has a friend."

When the apartment telephone rang, Frances, twenty-four, was putting in another long day at Leonard's. Cleta Bell was home. She answered, listened, and smiled through the receiver at the salesman.

"Yes, we will be there."

Cleta Bell had agreed to meet the army officers at the corner diner. Impatient, she waited to share news about the blind dates with Frances.

"Absolutely not," Frances said. "I am too tired."

"Just come and say hello," Cleta Bell said. "You don't have to go on a date." Reluctant, Frances agreed.

That was where I saw Gardner for the first time.

Frances, who loved letters, wrote one to celebrate Gardner's ninety-first birthday on November 12, 2004. Sixty-three years had passed since that "first time." Frances thought back to the day she met her future husband.

> *When I joined the table, I saw two officers. At that moment, I decided Cleta Bell could have the red convertible. I would take the good-looking officer with the black curly hair. His name was Gardner.*

Now ninety-one, Gardner wanted to preserve his own memories. While he reminisced, Frances typed. The document's title was without fuss: "The following has been written by Gardner Hayden Landers." It continued, "This is an effort on our part to leave an account of some of the experiences we have had. I hope there will be no confusion in our relating these events, as we will be doing some of them together."

For over six decades, Frances and Gardner blended their lives. This chapter blends their memories, allowing us to share in their rich marriage.

Jeffrey Hayden and Nell Gardner Landers had two sons. Earl was three when Gardner was born on November 12, 1913. The family farm in the northern Arkansas town of Melbourne was three hundred acres.

Gardner's grandfather ran one of three mercantile stores in the area that were referred to by townsfolk as Landers, Miller, and Billingsley. Gardner said, "Of course, the Landers store was the best."

For years Earl and Gardner helped stock the store's shelves. In a mule-drawn wagon, they rode for hours along a rutted trail to pick up goods from river barges and freight trains. Eventually a blacktop highway replaced the trail. A Ford pickup truck replaced the mules.

Gardner played basketball during high school and was what he called "a flunky" in the Landers store. The summer before college, he also cashiered in a bank. In 1931 he entered the University of Arkansas in Little Rock for premed studies. Earl was on campus studying agriculture.

An excellent student, Gardner began advanced studies in 1933. When he graduated with his medical degree in 1938, he joined the 36th Division of the Texas National Guard. While on reserve status, he interned at Hurley Hospital in Flint, Michigan, and then began a surgical residency in Mt. Holly, New Jersey.

Military tensions heightened. Several months into Gardner's residency, he learned that his National Guard unit would be activated. To be ready, he moved to Texarkana, Texas, bought a little gray Buick, and worked at Cotton Belt Railroad Hospital. His unit was called up on November 25, 1940.

As Gardner dictated, his bride of sixty-two years typed away. "That is when my Army service began. It would end five years later with a loving wife and wonderful family. I'm profoundly grateful." Military service agreed with Gardner. He became an officer in the United States Army and was stationed at Camp Bowie.

However, at this point in his story he was seated in a Fort Worth corner diner. His buddy's new red Packard convertible was parked outside. The young men waited for blind dates.

Cleta Bell Dodgen bounded in, followed by the work-weary Frances Maschal. When she saw the handsome young doctor with the curly black hair, her spirits brightened. She brushed aside her fatigue and enjoyed her date.

Gardner called the next week. Frances was rested up and eager to date him again. And again. "The 36th Division remained long enough in Brownwood, Texas, for me to fall in love with a beautiful girl. On my third date, we were attending a small party when we heard a message announcing Pearl Harbor on the radio. All Army personnel were told to return to base."

> *On December 7, 1941, Gardner and other officers from Camp Bowie were in Fort Worth. They rented hotel rooms to have a place to gather with friends. Suddenly, that Sunday afternoon, news from Pearl Harbor began coming over the radio. Officers were ordered to return to their bases. But arriving back in camp, Gardner and the others found no activity, just military men looking at each other, not knowing exactly what would happen next.*

It soon became clear that Gardner might be ordered to another base, and possibly overseas, at any time. "There was no question that I was going to ask her to marry me. The question was whether it would be before or after I left for overseas. Frances said, BEFORE."

Note that as Frances typed her husband's memoir, she used her convention of capital letters to drive home a point she felt pertinent.

> *After only a few dates, we began talking about getting married. I decided to ask my Dad what he thought. I wish I could find that letter, but this is what it said: "Dear Frances, I have three things to say about getting married. One, look at the man, not the uniform. Two, don't let anyone talk you into it. Three, don't let anyone talk you out of it."*

Frances followed her father's advice. She and Gardner picked their wedding date: February 7, 1942, two months after the attack on Pearl Harbor. Marvin Leonard was the only person who tried to talk Frances out of marriage, since she had known Gardner such a short time.

Despite his fatherly misgivings, Mr. Marvin gave Frances a few days off, and Gardner obtained permission to leave Camp Bowie. The couple drove to meet each other's family.

Gardner's gray Buick made a journey of thirteen hundred miles. Picking up his fiancée in Fort Worth, Gardner continued north to Collinsville, Oklahoma. He gained John and Faye Maschal's immediate approval.

The Buick logged over four hundred miles that day and three hundred the next as the couple drove east to visit the Landers clan in Batesville and Melbourne, Arkansas. Hayden and Nell were impressed with Frances.

The return trip to Texas, nearly six hundred miles, gave Gardner and Frances plenty of time to talk about their wedding.

Frances went back to work in Fort Worth. Gardner made wedding plans in Brownwood and was appointed commander of Hospital Company H. In his new role, he oversaw doctors and other personnel from national guard units across East Texas.

The big day arrived.

When we got to the church, there were other couples waiting to get married. The church was decorated with flowers for ALL OF US.

"Benny Clark was my best man. He was tall, a former member of Baylor's football team, and an officer in Company H. Many of my fellow officers and enlisted men attended. At the close of our wedding ceremony, all were respectfully quiet. After the ceremony, a group of enlisted men from the ambulance company used about twenty Army gurneys, forming a triangle under which we were to walk as we left the church."

The new Dr. and Mrs. Landers, recently back from that triangular driving route to become part of each other's family, began their life together by walking through an archway of the same shape.

And so, against the backdrop of World War II, Gardner and Frances, having dated infrequently across ten weeks, became newlyweds.

On their sixtieth wedding anniversary in 2002, the couple sent a check to First Baptist in Brownwood, Texas, as a thank you for taking care of them decades earlier. A young couple at the church was delaying marriage until they accumulated enough money. The church staff gave them the gift from the long-married Dr. and Mrs. Gardner Landers.

The honeymoon was short: two nights at a motel in the shadows of Camp Bowie. Monday morning, Gardner reported to base and learned that his 36th Division would leave within days for Camp Blanding in north Florida.

Frances drove the gray Buick to Fort Worth and returned to Leonard's. But Gardner, separated from his wife of one week, had ample time to think as he rode for days in an Army vehicle. He called Frances as soon as he could.

"Come to Gainesville."

I quit my job, packed my worldly belongings into that gray Buick, and started on a Sunday morning toward Florida. I thought I could make it to Shreveport, Louisiana, but it started to snow and I wasn't sure I would EVER make it. I did get to a hotel in Shreveport about dark.

Late the next day, Frances rolled safely into Gainesville, gleeful to be out of the Buick and back in Gardner's arms.

Gardner and Charles Richardson, fellow captains, needed a place for their wives to live. Jane Richardson, like Frances, had just joined her husband. The men rented a house for their brides, and the couples became good friends.

Before long, the 36th Division was ordered to North Carolina and then to Cape Cod for further training. Jane and Frances drove separate cars but met each night to find a hotel.

We spent a few months in Charlotte and then Cape Cod. That was my first time to drive through Washington, D.C. and New York. I wasn't sure I could do it, but I DID! After a few months, Gardner was ordered back to Florida, but Charles was in the group going overseas.

"We left Cape Cod before cold weather and moved to Tallahassee, Florida, where landing exercises continued on the coast."

Another stint back at Camp Bowie followed. In Brownwood, William Hayden was born. Gardner was away from base on maneuvers when Bill arrived. "My unit moved many times. The next move was to California. Frances and the baby were in Palm Springs, and I had the privilege of visiting them on some weekends. Our desert training was at Twentynine Palms. A scene that I will never forget was watching Frances and Bill depart in that little gray Buick. With no trees in sight, I watched them go down the road to the highway about three miles away, and head east. It gave me an empty feeling at camp."

Overseas deployment was imminent. Gardner's unit headed by troop train to Fort Dix, New Jersey. Frances and young Bill returned to Collinsville. Seven months later, she gave birth to James Howard. "Frances was alone when Bill was born in 1943, and alone again when Jim was born in 1944. Mike was born in 1946 in Roanoke, Virginia. Frances has told me that I have been forgiven for not making these three great events, but maybe it made her life stronger."

On April 6, 1944, Gardner boarded a British vessel and began a two-week voyage across the Atlantic Ocean. The waters were rough and dangerous. "We had to form convoys on several occasions and hoped the navy could prevent submarine attacks. Ours was a moderate-sized troop ship, one of twenty-two in the convoy. We saw two ships attacked and destroyed. This was, I suppose, my first observance of warfare."

Ten days at sea, Gardner learned that the ship was bound for Southport on England's south coast for a final month of training.

Gardner's unit, Fifteen (or XV) Corps, Third Army, crossed the English Channel on June 4, 1944. It landed at Omaha Beach two days after D-day, the assault of one hundred sixty thousand Allied troops along a fifty-mile coastline stretch of Normandy, France. Thousands were killed or wounded, but one hundred thousand—including Dr. Gardner Landers, XV Corps Assistant Surgeon—marched across Europe to begin to end World War II. "D-day landing was just over, for which we were very thankful, but the devastating results remained. Many infantrymen were lying in fields behind the hedgerows in the countryside of Normandy."

Gardner served in Normandy, Northern France, Rhineland, and Central Europe. He earned three ribbons, including the Bronze Star Medal, and participated in liberating the concentration camp at Dachau, Germany. Commended for his bravery, skill, and judgment, Gardner was relieved of active duty on January 5, 1946. He returned to his young family with pride.

At thirty-three, Gardner accepted a residency to specialize in ophthalmology at Gill Memorial Hospital in Roanoke, Virginia. He and Frances bought a home using the GI Bill. There, Michael Richard was born. All her life, Frances had fond memories of the family home in Virginia—and the yard with its clothesline full of diapers.

Dr. Gill asked Gardner to join the hospital staff, but he and Frances wanted to return closer to their families. When the sole ophthalmologist retired in El Dorado, Arkansas, Gardner accepted the invitation to take over the practice. The children were young (Bill was five, Jim four, and Mike two), and Gardner and Frances welcomed the new adventure. "We decided that this was a good location. We moved to El Dorado in 1948 in the little gray Buick that I purchased in Texarkana in 1940."

It was the same little gray Buick that Frances had driven in 1942 back to Fort Worth as a lonely bride of one week; the one she had driven during a snowstorm en route to Florida; the car she'd driven northeast through the Carolinas, Massachusetts, and New York; and later, down a dusty California road from Twentynine Palms with an infant son.

In that little gray Buick, Frances clocked many miles in support of her husband's military service. John Maschal had known what he was doing when he'd taught his daughter to drive at age twelve.

In El Dorado the couple attended First Presbyterian Church. Frances joined an established church group, Presbyterian Women. The next year, she was asked to become president. Honored, she said yes.

The women gave their new leader a warm reception. Mrs. Bart Mahony, a long-time member of Presbyterian Women, hugged Frances. "My dear, you are a perfect example of zeal without knowledge," Mrs. Mahony said. "But I will pray for you every day."

Frances rarely lost her zeal for doing the Lord's work, but she certainly gained knowledge. She went on to serve as an elder and trustee, both officer positions within the Presbyterian church.

Gardner was a respected ophthalmologist and also a church leader. He and his family led a comfortable life.

"I grew up in First Presbyterian," Susan Oliver Turbeville told me. As a little girl, Susan did not know how Frances's life and her own would intertwine. "I was very young when I first noticed Mrs. Landers at church. We Olivers sat in a pew on the left. Dr. and Mrs. Landers sat on the right. Frances Landers was a beautiful woman. I admired her greatly. I always looked forward to seeing her in church, wondering what she would be wearing."

Susan continued, "She was fashionable, enjoyed society, and in every regard was a doctor's wife. That changed when she became involved with Haiti. She'd wear a simple denim jacket and skirt most every time she went there."

Mike concurred. "Mother and Dad did a lot of entertaining. Mother had all the dishes, different tablecloths, and placemats. She had elaborate parties and kept track in notebooks of the menus, guest lists, and how the table was set. After going to Haiti, Mother largely changed how she applied her time and organizational skills. It was Haiti that was important to her."

Frances always joked that although Gardner was not easy to catch, she was smart enough not to let him get away. In his 2004 birthday letter, she reminded him again.

> *Because I worked so hard, you are celebrating your ninety-first birthday with me. Aren't you glad you didn't run too fast?*

Frances ended the letter with a sentiment and then a postscript.

Happy Birthday … I love you, Frances.

I may not be able to fry bacon, but there are things in life better than CRISP BACON.

No doubt one of the better things on Frances's mind that day was changing the lives of thousands of children in the long-struggling country of Haiti.

Chapter 3

Four Hundred Years of Struggle

Cushioned amid the white-sand, palm-fringed beaches and warm,
sapphire-hued waters of the Caribbean lies the island nation of
Haiti—once a lush, tropical sanctuary, now a paradise lost.
—*Former US Senator Mike DeWine, Ohio,*
Devastation, Destruction, Desperation, 2009

Fifty miles southeast of Cuba is Hispaniola, an awkwardly shaped horizontal landmass. The Dominican Republic occupies the eastern two-thirds of Hispaniola. The western third is the Republic of Haiti.

A jaw-like formation distinguishes Haiti's western coastline. Two jagged peninsulas, the larger one to the south, give the impression that Haiti tries to ensnare in its mouth its own nugget-sized island of La Gonave—or with greater aggression strains upward to take a bite out of southern Cuba.

Cuba and Hispaniola block the sparkling waters of the surrounding Caribbean Sea from spilling east into the Atlantic Ocean or merging indiscriminately with the Gulf of Mexico to the north.

To its west and south, the sea splashes warm, frothy waves onto the shores of Central and South America. The northern and eastern waters lap over the sands and coral of ten thousand landmasses. These reefs, islets, and islands are grouped into two chains: the Greater Antilles and the Lesser Antilles. Cuba and Hispaniola are the largest islands of the Antilles.

Cuba actually consists of twenty-three islands, and Jamaica twenty-six. The Netherlands, United Kingdom, and France own Caribbean territories. So does the United States: Puerto Rico comprises one hundred forty-two islands, and the Virgin Islands total eighty-one.

The Antilles and the Commonwealth of The Bahamas were originally named the West Indies. The Bahamas is a disorganized jumble of seven hundred islands and islets scattered off the southeastern coast of Florida.

One hundred miles off Florida's southern tip, a much tidier island parade begins a graceful arc of two thousand miles. Cuba heads the procession of the Greater Antilles, followed by Hispaniola, Cayman Islands, Jamaica, and Puerto Rico. Sprinkled like afterthoughts are the smaller islands of the Lesser Antilles: Martinique, Barbados, Grenada, and dozens more, trailing off gently as they near South America's northern coast.

Today the West Indies is called the Caribbean, a region that includes the sea, its island chains, and the coastlines of Central and South America.

Haiti is well known as the poorest nation in the Western Hemisphere. Its capital, Port-au-Prince, is ninety minutes by air from Miami, Florida. Slightly smaller than Maryland, Haiti is home to nearly eleven million people, all but five percent black. Most live on a few dollars a day.

With ninety-five percent of its tropical mountainsides deforested, eighty percent of its population unemployed, eighty percent living in poverty, fifty percent illiterate, and a mere twenty percent of its land arable, the obvious question is, why? On so many levels, why?

The answer requires a review of colonialism, slavery, and greed.

Christopher Columbus and the Taino Indians

On August 3, 1492, Captain-General Christopher Columbus set sail from Spain. Ninety men were aboard his ships: the *Niña*, *Pinta*, and *Santa Maria*. After a month's delay on one of the Canary Islands to repair the rudder of the *Pinta*, the fleet crossed the Atlantic Ocean in five weeks.

Spain's King Ferdinand and Queen Isabella, who financed the expedition, shared Columbus's belief that a western sea route to the Far East would glean new territory and wealth. And, appealing to the pious queen, explorers could share the Christian gospel along the way.

Columbus had been unsuccessful generating interest in the adventure from his native Italy. But a fellow Italian, Marco Polo, influenced him greatly.

In the late 1200s, Marco Polo spent twenty years exploring the East Indies of Persia, India, and China by land and sea. But these trips east stopped short of the destination of his dreams: Japan, then called Çipangu.

Two hundred years later, Columbus convinced Spain's monarchy that if he sailed *west*, he would discover the sea route to Çipangu.

On his four western voyages, two errors skewed Columbus's thinking. First, he believed Marco Polo's faulty premise that a large ocean separated Mainland China from Japan. Second, he accepted Polo's estimate that the Asian continent was far wider than it actually was. Had these assumptions been correct, only a small ocean would lie between the western coast of Europe and the islands of Japan.

Since Columbus followed Polo's lead, he calculated the distance between the Canary Islands and Çipangu as a manageable 2,400 nautical miles. This was a gross error. Eleven thousand miles of sea and land separate the Canary Islands from Japan. Columbus was off by a factor of nearly five.

Neither Marco Polo in the 1200s nor Christopher Columbus in the 1400s imagined the existence of the Western Hemisphere of North, Central, and South America.

On October 12, 1492, Columbus's men spotted lush land 2,400 miles from the Canary Islands. Ah, Çipangu!

Spain's king and queen had promised Columbus a new title, Admiral of the Ocean Sea, if he reached the East Indies. Certain that he had, Admiral Columbus proclaimed the title for himself and the island for Spain. A landing party rowed across azure water and unfurled a royal Spanish flag.

Columbus erected a cross in honor of Jesus Christ and named the island San Salvador. He called the natives Indios. Later, they would be called Indians, or Amerindians.

Admiral Columbus reasoned that he was on an island north of Çipangu's largest landmass, in the waters of the today's Pacific Ocean. For three months, his ships navigated an island maze in search of the biggest island, today's Mainland Japan.

The fleet was actually in The Bahamas, half a world away.

Columbus found an unmatched splendor of trees, flowers, and fish—not at all how he imagined the East Indies. By the time he reached (and named) Cuba, Columbus was unable to reconcile his measurements. Believing no island could be as large as Cuba, he speculated that he was on Mainland China.

The explorers did not sail enough coastline to discover that Cuba was, after all, an island. On December 5, 1492, they moved on.

Winds carried the *Niña*, *Pinta*, and *Santa Maria* southeast. For two weeks the ships sailed the northern coast of another landmass.

On December 21, Columbus and his men stepped ashore on today's Haiti. The admiral claimed the island for Spain and named it La Isla Española. A thousand cheerful Taino Indians greeted the ninety explorers.

Eight hundred years earlier, when the Tainos migrated north from today's South America, they named the island Ayiti (Land of High Mountains).

Guacanagarix, the Taino leader, seemed to confirm that gold was nearby, though Columbus's men found none.

On Christmas Eve, the *Santa Maria* drifted onto a coral reef near today's Cap-Haitien and began to sink. Tainos helped the explorers save their supplies. With the timbers of the *Santa Maria*, sailors built a simple fort on La Isla Española's northwest point. Columbus named the settlement Villa de la Navidad. Guacanagarix gave permission for thirty-nine men to stay.

The rest of Columbus's expedition boarded the *Niña* and *Pinta* and set sail for Spain. Columbus was confident that in the following year, his men at Navidad would hand him the gold he sought.

In 1492 Columbus's exploration was one of discovery. In 1493 his voyage was all about colonization. Seventeen ships held provisions for six months. Amid a cacophony of sounds and smells, pigs, horses, cattle, goats, sheep, chickens, and dogs shared space with twelve hundred men. Women were not allowed.

The fleet sailed smoothly. Anticipation was high. But when Columbus anchored at Navidad on the island's north coast, he was shocked. His settlement was destroyed, all thirty-nine sailors murdered. Guacanagarix blamed Indians from another island.

Columbus's dream of peace between natives and settlers was replaced with lasting mistrust and violence.

With Navidad in ruins, Columbus began another settlement, La Isabela, but he later determined that it was not suited for long-term growth. His brother Bartholomew built a new capital city, Santo Domingo, on the island's southeastern coast. Gradually the eastern two-thirds of La Isla Española also became known as Santo Domingo.

Spain, Portugal, England, France, Italy, and Holland competed for control of the Caribbean. As more westerners settled on La Isla Española, Tainos—with no immunity to Old World diseases—died in massive numbers. Others were murdered. The rest were enslaved to work the fields of sugarcane that Columbus's men had planted.

Sugar production rose in proportion to the brutality inflicted on Taino slaves. Historian Bartolomé de Las Casas criticized the Spaniards, calling them extraordinarily cruel. Ironically, he recommended enslaving African men instead. As early as 1501, ships sailed to Africa to forcibly bring blacks to the Caribbean island.

In 1492 a million Tainos lived on La Isla Española. By 1504 there were only twenty-nine thousand, perhaps the most rapid demise of any indigenous people in the Americas. Tainos were virtually extinct by 1550.

Admiral Christopher Columbus's discoveries included the Atlantic Ocean, the Bahamas, Cuba, Hispaniola, and Central and South America. But in 1506 he went to his grave not knowing that he had found an entirely new land. He believed he had sailed west to Marco Polo's East Indies.

When Spain's rulers realized the error, they added "West" to "Indies" to distinguish the region from the East Indies in the Pacific Ocean.

Over time, the West Indies became known as the Caribbean.

Spain and France in Hispaniola

In 1510 Bartolomé de Las Casas shortened La Isla Española's name to Española. Twenty years later, historian Peter Martyr d'Anghiera called the island Hispaniola, a spelling that would last.

For decades Hispaniola was the jewel of the Spanish empire. Then, hungry for greater territory and wealth, settlers began heading to other regions of the Americas and to Mexico. Hispaniola's growth slowed, especially outside of the southern region of Santo Domingo.

In the early 1600s, Spain's king mismanaged control of Hispaniola. Irate because his colonists were illegally trading with the Dutch, he decided to isolate them from other countries' merchants. The king's troops destroyed the northern settlements and forced colonists south to Santo Domingo. Spain essentially abandoned Hispaniola's north.

Consequences were disastrous. Half of the resettled Spaniards died from disease and starvation. Slaves escaped. Thousands of cattle roamed free. French settlers moved in and named the northern region Saint-Domingue.

France also occupied Tortuga, a small island off Saint-Domingue's north coast, named by Christopher Columbus for its resemblance to a sleeping tortoise. Tortuga was home to ruthless buccaneers who plundered Spanish ships and hunted wild cattle.

In 1665 Bertrand D'Ogeron became governor of Saint-Domingue and Tortuga. He cared little what the buccaneers did on the seas as long as they obeyed him on land. D'Ogeron was ambitious. His French population grew to four thousand, setting the stage for conflict between Spain, which had claimed Hispaniola in 1492, and France, which acted like the northern region was hers.

Tensions erupted. In May 1697 thirteen French ships and four thousand men attacked Spain's port city of Cartagena in Columbia, South America. The city reeled under bloodshed and looting.

Defeated, Spain signed France's 1697 Treaty of Ryswick. Under its terms, Spain kept the eastern two-thirds of Hispaniola (Santo Domingo) but ceded the western third (Saint-Domingue) to France.

Slavery in Saint-Domingue

In Saint-Domingue and on Tortuga, land was lush and plentiful, as were slaves to work it. French colonists built sugar, tobacco, and indigo plantations. Slaves planted, harvested, and processed the crops. They made barrels and served their masters' families.

No longer a luxury, sugar became a staple of European diets and was by far Saint-Domingue's largest and most lucrative export. Plantations created an insatiable demand for slaves. During the seventeenth and eighteenth centuries, one and a half million blacks were captured in the jungles of Africa and funneled into Saint-Domingue.

The grim reality began on the horrific ocean voyage, the Middle Passage, from Africa to the Americas. Tens of thousands died, their bodies thrown overboard. The rest began brutal lives of enslavement.

Saint-Domingue's different languages, religions, and traditions of slave communities reflected the regions of Africa from which natives were kidnapped. Blacks born in Saint-Domingue were called creoles. Haiti's language, Creole, is an evolutionary blend of African and French dialects.

Half of black children on the plantations did not live to adulthood. Half of the adults died within a few years. Most white plantation owners, also called masters or planters, found it cheaper to replace slaves rather than treat them well enough to prolong their lives.

On large plantations, overseers—at the bottom of the hierarchy of white society—monitored the slaves in the fields.

Below the overseer—at the top of the black hierarchy—was the slave driver who gave orders and inflicted whippings. Drivers walked a fine line: loyal to their masters but with close ties to fellow blacks.

Some slaves escaped. Some earned freedom. The vast majority toiled six days a week to bring wealth to their owners. The hierarchical gap between master and slave could not have been wider.

In the middle of the sociological ladder between whites and blacks were mixed-race mulattoes, also called free people of color or free-coloreds. Though they could own land and hold jobs, free-coloreds had limited political rights and could not vote.

French laws dictated how slaves were to be fed, clothed, housed, worked and rested, and punished and rewarded. Most slave owners flagrantly disregarded the rules. Violent torture was widespread, as documented in gritty but important books of history.

Saint-Domingue had a reputation for turning French colonists into rich men. Many fortune seekers brought coffee beans, an ideal crop for the sixty percent of Saint-Domingue that was mountainous and not suited for sugar cultivation. Coffee exports added to the colony's enormous wealth.

In the Western Province, slaves worked 3,500 plantations, and in 1751, Port-au-Prince became the colonial capital. The city was notable for its attractive government buildings and an active port, but it lacked the appeal of its larger neighbor, Le Cap, in the Northern Province.

By 1789 the city of Le Cap had gardens, a theater, public bathhouses, and fifty-six well-ordered streets in a neat grid up against the surrounding mountains. Hundreds of ships docked in the port at any given time. The Northern Province had three thousand plantations and an unsettling ten-to-one ratio of blacks to whites.

The Southern Province, geographically isolated from the Atlantic shipping trade, had 1,400 plantations. Colonists in port towns like Jacmel found more affinity with Spain's Santo Domingo and England's Jamaica than with their own Northern and Western Provinces.

Across Saint-Domingue, in fact, colonists had more in common with Caribbean neighbors than with their homeland, France.

Revolt in France

Saint-Domingue now produced half of the world's coffee and sugar. The colony was France's most profitable possession. But imperial rulers and the colony's wealthy landowners disagreed about trade policy, pricing, managing slaves, and the rights of free-coloreds. Tensions escalated proportionally to the growing dependence France had on her slave-based money machine, Saint-Domingue.

There was also angst inside Saint-Domingue. New discriminatory laws enraged the twenty-eight thousand free-coloreds. This further worried the forty thousand white landowners already in fear that their half-million black slaves would revolt.

Back in France, earlier wars had bankrupted the country. Taxation was inequitable, the economy was a disaster, harvests were poor, and people were hungry and angry.

In 1789 the period known as the French Revolution began. Marked by struggles for leadership and massive violence, it would last ten years.

With insurmountable budget problems, the beleaguered King Louis XVI needed help. He dusted off the Estates-General, a consultative body of clergy, nobility, and common people. Inactive for seventy-five years, its relevance satisfied no one. Controversy swirled.

Delegates representing the commoners took advantage of the confusion. They created their own National Assembly, rewrote the French constitution, and crafted a statement of principles, the *Declaration of the Rights of Man and the Citizen.*

Saint-Domingue's planters, knowing slavery would be a contested topic of the Estates-General, wanted representation. A delegation of colonists with a vested interest in slavery sailed uninvited to France. The contingent arrived to find that the Estates-General had dissolved and that the National Assembly was in control. Colonists wrangled six delegate seats.

Abolitionists were shouted down and discussion on slavery ended. But an ominous cloud loomed: the threat of a slave rebellion.

In August 1789 the *Declaration of the Rights of Man* was adopted. It declared that all men were born with rights and remained equal in them. Saint-Domingue's delegates sent urgent letters home, warning ship merchants and postal clerks to control news flowing in from France. The slaves must not learn about the declaration.

Revolt in Saint-Domingue

In Saint-Domingue, animosity was as thick as the tropical humidity. Hate simmered between whites and blacks, whites and free-coloreds, blacks and free-coloreds, and colony and homeland. The period later named the Haitian Revolution was about to begin.

Across the Northern Province, clusters of slaves hid in sweltering jungles. At these late-night meetings, Creole voices were low. Black slaves were planning a revolt against their white owners.

On August 20, 1791, the meetings ended, undetected. Hundreds of slaves slipped back to their plantations, dark bodies moving in silence through the dark night. They waited in suspense and anticipation for the most subtle and unsuspecting gray of daylight. Hearts pounded with the obligation of centuries of ingrained retaliation.

At the first hint of predawn sky, hundreds of slaves rose from their sleepless beds to do their part to change history.

The rebels carried out coordinated, terrifying attacks, exercising role reversal with the same unthinkable torture that slave owners used on them. They beat and murdered plantation masters in their beds, torched buildings and fields, and strangled and stabbed overseers who tried to flee.

White children were not always saved.

When the sun rose, the first of the carnage that would last twelve years shocked those who had, for now, escaped. Though plantation owners had long feared a slave uprising, they were astounded when one actually occurred.

The revolt spread. The slave army grew to twenty thousand in four days. Soon, much of the Northern Province was engulfed in orange flames and drenched in red blood.

Dutty Boukman was the most visible leader during the first days of the revolt. The night before the attacks, this slave driver gathered his men deep in the jungle outside Le Cap—so deep that outsiders could not hear the eerie ceremony. So deep that no one could listen to Boukman's motivational chants.

Deep enough that no white man in the Northern Province saw the squealing pig, or witnessed its sacrifice, or saw the black men drinking its blood.

Chaos spread to Saint-Domingue's Western and Southern Provinces. France's colony was reeling. Though few slaves could read, they carried *The Rights of Man* in their pockets.

By September, insurgents from Saint-Domingue's sugar, coffee, and indigo plantations numbered perhaps eighty thousand: men, women, African, Creole, free-coloreds, overseers, slave drivers, field-workers, and house servants.

These eighty thousand people were of disparate race, background, culture, language, religion, status, ability, and intellect. But they had one common cause: human freedom. Using violence against a violent system, the eighty thousand destroyed in short order the economy of one of the richest areas in the world.

Shocked and scared, some slaves wanted to return to plantation life under better conditions. Others stayed loyal to their masters. But most were committed to destroying the whites.

Many slaves who had been fighting civil wars in Africa when they were abducted were experienced warriors. Thanks to free-coloreds and Spain's military, they now were armed. Frightened masters fled to France, Cuba, or North America. Their slaves declared ownership of the plantations and settled on in.

Many blacks were freed to protect their plantation owners. Saint-Domingue's tightly woven institution of slavery had unraveled.

An ocean away, the National Assembly finally granted mulattoes the right to vote and assume positions of influence. Was the motive altruistic? No. The assemblymen sensed that ending slavery was inevitable, but in the meantime, the free-coloreds were the only force that could prevent a slave revolt. Perhaps the National Assembly was right, but it was eight months too late.

French officials, led by chief commissioner Léger Félicité Sonthonax, sailed to Saint-Dominique to create new, racially integrated assemblies. Sonthonax was shocked at the raging violence.

The commissioners had brought six thousand troops to end the slave revolt. The military was no match for tropical disease, poor food, and armed slaves. Half of the men died in two months. The revolt continued.

In 1793 King Louis XVI and Marie Antoinette were guillotined in Paris, and French revolutionaries began a civil war of terror. Imperial wars erupted too. France was under attack by Spain, Britain, and Austria.

France's enemies did not limit their battlegrounds to Europe. Spain was still annoyed that Hispaniola's western third had slipped into French hands a century earlier. Spanish fighters offered Saint-Domingue's slaves freedom if they would join the battle against French forces. The British, also wanting Saint-Domingue, aligned with nervous white masters.

Across the colony, chaos mounted. Slaves joined Spain's fight. Planters joined Britain's. The economy was at a standstill.

Something had to give. It did.

When a white colonial official presented a petition on behalf of the slaves, the battered Commissioner Sonthonax gave in. It was time for the oppressed blacks to be recognized within *The Rights of Man*.

Emancipation and Toussaint Louverture

On August 29, 1793, the Northern Province emancipated its slaves and gave them French citizenship. By the end of October, the decree was applied to the Southern and Western Provinces.

All Africans and their descendants, and all born or yet to be born in the colony, were free citizens of France. *The Declaration of the Rights of Man and the Citizen* was translated into Creole and posted across the provinces.

Was this the end of the story? Hardly. Though Paris legislators ratified the abolition of slavery on February 4, 1794, it was in many ways just another beginning of the black man's struggle for equality.

It's not surprising. The ruling was unprecedented. The slaves freed in Saint-Domingue could look nowhere in the world to learn from earlier experience. In the United States, the terrible injustice of slavery would not end for seventy years.

In Saint-Domingue there was no transition between slavery and freedom. Most blacks were illiterate and did not understand how to handle liberty. Some wanted to return to plantation life and be paid. Others did not.

Slavery may have ended on paper for the blacks, but a clear path for their future had not been scribed. They needed a leader. Toussaint Louverture, the subject of Frances Maschal's term paper, emerged.

On August 29, 1793, the same day Léger Sonthonax abolished slavery in the Northern Province, Toussaint Louverture announced that he was the true, independent defender of liberty.

Fifty years earlier, Louverture had been born in Saint-Domingue. His father was an enslaved African prince. His godfather, a free black who was schooled by missionaries, sponsored Louverture's Jesuit education. A coachman and keeper of his master's livestock, Louverture earned freedom in the mid-1770s. He acquired a slave and farmed a coffee plantation before turning to his real passions: politics, military leadership, and preserving freedom for his people.

A tall, feathered hat added stature to Toussaint Louverture's short frame and cheered up his homely face. During the slave revolt, he was a negotiator between the black army and white colonial administrators. For a time, convinced that France would never abolish slavery, he joined the Spanish army. But when he learned that France had ratified *The Rights of Man*, he returned to his prior allegiance and battered Spanish forces for two years.

Finally, in 1794 a war-weary Spain signed a peace treaty and retreated to its two-thirds of Hispaniola, Santo Domingo.

Only one imperial enemy now remained in Saint-Domingue: the stubborn British, who attempted to re-instill slavery in the regions they controlled. At age fifty-one, General Toussaint Louverture took on the fight. His ragged, hungry, and poorly compensated army did not drive Britain to a negotiated peace treaty until 1799.

As the 1790s drew to a close, Louverture persuaded Léger Sonthonax to return to Paris. Now able to rule the colony as he saw fit, Louverture added "Governor" to his title.

Governor-General Toussaint Louverture, shrewd and tenacious, was known as the Bonaparte of the Antilles. His Saint-Domingue was an economic shambles. Louverture knew that for the black population to have a long-term say about its future, the colony must be financially secure. He stressed that the sugar and coffee plantations were an economic necessity, and he urged ex-slaves to return to their plantations. Many resisted. Though they were paid for their work, they saw little difference between their old lives and their new ones.

Believing that liberty needed to be defended at all costs, Louverture created a virtual police state. He earned many enemies in the colony, even as he made remarkable progress reviving its shattered plantation economy.

In early 1801 Governor-General Louverture wrote a constitution for Saint-Domingue, declaring that slavery was permanently abolished. All who lived in Saint-Domingue now would be born and would die free and French.

It was no surprise that Governor-General Louverture's constitution granted him power to sign all laws, oversee trade agreements, make appointments, and in every other way exert full control for the rest of his days.

Napoleon Bonaparte

Louverture, the Bonaparte of the Antilles, made a strategic misstep. He neglected to seek alignment with the First Consul of France, the actual Napoleon Bonaparte, who had led a coup of the French parliament in 1799. Bonaparte intended to restore Saint-Domingue as a vastly profitable French colony. Its economy, of course, would rely on slavery.

Bonaparte had watched as Louverture rose in power, declared himself governor, and had the gall to author a constitution for Saint-Domingue. Beyond annoyed, Napoleon Bonaparte drew up a plan to retake control of the island, depose Louverture, and reinstate slavery.

Across eighteen months, Bonaparte's brother-in-law, General Charles Leclerc, brought eighty thousand soldiers to Saint-Domingue. In January 1802, the first forty thousand landed. Leclerc expected a quick victory, but he underestimated the fierce armies of freed slaves led by Generals Henri Christophe and Jean-Jacques Dessalines. No, the blacks were not happy with Toussaint Louverture's oppression, but they despised even more Bonaparte's threat of a return to slavery.

After months of bloody fighting, General Leclerc promised that slavery would never be reinstated. Christophe, Dessalines, and Louverture laid down their arms.

The promise was a ruse. Leclerc simply wanted to deliver the pesky Louverture to his brother-in-law. Louverture was imprisoned in a cold, damp fortress in the French Alps. Half starved and virtually alone, Toussaint Louverture died there on April 8, 1803. He was fifty-nine.

Louverture's dream of freedom for the blacks did not die with him, nor did the stamina of his armies, which reenergized to complete his legacy.

With Louverture gone, Bonaparte anticipated that his military would control Saint-Domingue before summer. His miscalculation cost tens of thousands of lives. A plague of yellow fever swept over unacclimated French troops. Men staggered to gruesome deaths at the rate of one hundred a day. General Leclerc, age thirty, was not spared. He died of yellow fever on Tortuga.

Leclerc's successor was Lieutenant-General Donatien-Marie-Joseph de Vimeur, Vicomte de Rochambeau, a name longer than his time in power. His forces struggled against General Jean-Jacques Dessalines's ragged army.

As 1803 drew to a close, Emperor Napoleon Bonaparte waited in France for news from Saint-Domingue. Word came. General Dessalines's fighters, those tired but tenacious former slaves, had won. Bonaparte had lost.

Twelve calamitous years after Dutty Boukman led the slaves' first revolt against their white masters, Saint-Domingue became the world's first black republic.

Gone was Emperor Bonaparte's dream of a burgeoning treasury amassed from the plantations of a re-enslaved Saint-Domingue—and much more.

Bonaparte had counted on his vast Louisiana territory in North America to supply food for his prospering, slave-based Caribbean island colony. After the defeat, Bonaparte sold the land to United States president Thomas Jefferson for fifteen million dollars—a few cents an acre.

The Republic of Haiti

On January 1, 1804, the victorious General Jean-Jacques Dessalines signed a feisty declaration of independence. He stated that it was insufficient to have expelled the barbarians who had bloodied Saint-Domingue for two hundred years. He called for all of the people in Saint-Domingue to renounce France forever and be willing to die rather than live again under her rule.

The indigenous Tainos had called their land of high mountains Ayiti. General Dessalines renamed the newly independent Saint-Domingue: Haiti.

To eliminate distinctions of color, Dessalines decreed that all Haitians would be known as blacks. Whites who chose to reject France and the slavery it had inflicted could change their official identity. They would be embraced as blacks.

Such generosity notwithstanding, Dessalines murdered many white people believed to be his enemies.

Issues of equality and trust would not be leaving Haiti anytime soon. Haiti was now an independent nation, but that did not correlate with its being a peaceful one.

Jean-Jacques Dessalines was assassinated in 1806. The young nation was again embroiled in civil war. Alexandre Pétion, who ruled the south, defeated Henri Christophe in the north to become president.

In 1821 President Jean Pierre Boyer succeeded Pétion. When colonial Santo Domingo declared independence from Spain, President Boyer sent Haitian forces across the border, seized the territory, and renamed it Spanish Haiti. He ended slavery but ruled as a dictator until 1844. That year, Spanish Haiti regained its freedom and established a new identity: the Dominican Republic. The DR, as the country is called, withstood decades of assaults by Haiti and imperial Spain.

Haiti had its own struggles to maintain independence.

In 1825 King Charles X of France sent a fleet to recapture Haiti. Unwilling to engage in more bloodshed, President Boyer signed a costly treaty. France would recognize Haiti's independence if the black republic paid the cost—one hundred fifty million francs—of achieving it. In 1938 the amount was reduced to ninety million. Still, the sum was staggering. Haiti was in debt to its former homeland until 1947. France was no friend of its former colony.

Indeed, Haiti had few friends.

Most nations, being prejudiced, isolated Haiti and shunned the black republic from import and export businesses. Its scant economy worsened.

President Thomas Jefferson, fearing unrest from fellow slave owners, reversed the United States position of befriending Haiti. Diplomatic ties between the two nations did not resume until 1862.

Over the next one hundred fifty years, relations between the governments of the United States and the Republic of Haiti would be tested again and again.

Yet one thing is abundantly clear. Governments aside, the people of Haiti and the people of the United States have great love for each other. While Haiti struggles mightily to this day, her citizens would suffer far more if not for the care and generosity of people from many nations.

Especially from the nearby United States. Especially from people like Frances Landers.

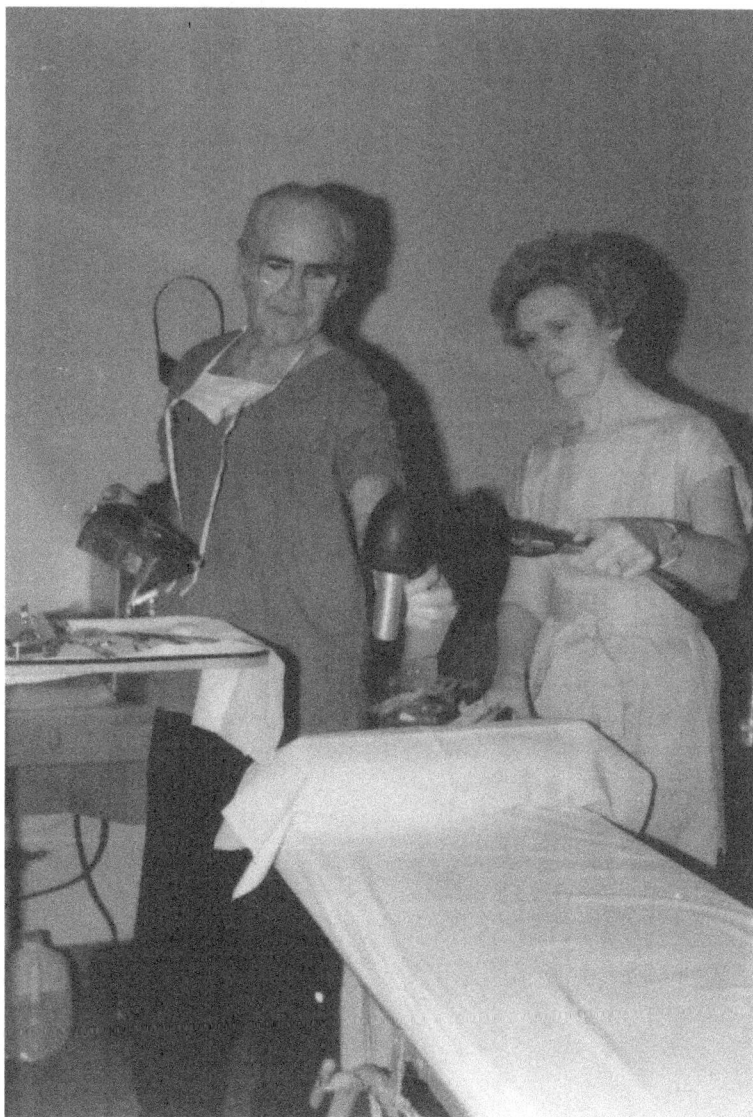

For twelve years, Dr. Gardner Landers partnered with his wife on medical mission trips to Sainte Croix Hospital in Léogâne, Haiti.

Chapter 4

We Were Only Going to Go Once

I'd probably be sitting in a home somewhere,
rocking and staring at the wall, if this hadn't happened.
—*Frances Landers, El Dorado, Arkansas, 1989*

Mike Landers remembers well the fall evening of 1977 when Keith McCaffety talked to El Dorado's First Presbyterian Church about Medical Benevolence Foundation.

"It was a typical Wednesday church program," Mike told me. "Our whole family was there. Haiti has been part of our lives since that evening. I was the non-doctor in the family. Haiti hit a chord with me, as it did with my brothers and our parents."

Keith McCaffety's message about the plight of cataract sufferers did strike a chord with the Landers family. And more, it reshaped their lives.

In the early 1970s, Medical Benevolence Foundation, wanting to begin mission projects in Haiti, had looked for a partner that knew the country's needs. MBF found Église Episcopalé d'Haiti, the Episcopal Church of Haiti. A collaboration between Episcopalians and Presbyterians held great promise.

A Haitian-American partnership was also fitting. In 1861 Reverend James Theodore Holly had come to Port-au-Prince from Connecticut to form Haiti's first Episcopal church. Reverend Holly believed fervently that churches were responsible for educating the country's children.

In 1974 MBF's Episcopal-Presbyterian team was ready to tackle its first project. A woefully inadequate hospital in the city of Léogâne needed attention. With three small rooms for outpatient care, the clinic could scarcely be called a hospital. American Presbyterians first constructed a small ward so a few patients could stay overnight, and then they added a small apartment for the medical director and missionaries.

Haitians knew the clinic by its local name, L'Hôpital Sainte Croix. Some Americans called it Holy Cross. Under any name, its condition appalled Gardner, Frances, and Jim when they arrived in late November 1977.

At a time when Léogâne's population totaled two hundred thousand, the one-room ward accommodated thirty patients. On bare ground outside, family members prepared food for their sick relatives and then moved inside as darkness fell to sleep under patients' beds and assist during the night.

Gardner and Jim squeezed into a poorly lit room and opened their instrument bags. News spread that American eye surgeons were at the hospital. Haitians with good eyesight led their blind friends and relatives across the countryside for miles. For hours. Even days.

Jim said, "We were extremely busy. Working through interpreters, we talked with patients and we operated. It was gratifying."

"It was so rewarding," Frances often said. "Some had been blind for ten years and didn't have a thing wrong with them except a cataract. Now, I shouldn't use the word 'simple' to describe cataract surgery, but it is routine."

Working thirteen-hour days, Gardner and Jim gave sight to astonished Haitians, treated other eye diseases, and distributed eyeglasses.

The exhausted team was upbeat as it packed to return to Arkansas.

"We were only going to go once," Frances would say. "We would accomplish something and then get back on the golf course."

Then Jim and his parents walked out of the hospital. They were stunned. Across the compound, hundreds of blind Haitians waited.

Gardner was pragmatic. "We will come back the week after Easter to finish." They came back. More people, more eyeglasses, more surgeries. Time ran out. Untreated Haitians remained.

Again Gardner said, "We'll come back Thanksgiving week."

Twice a year, Thanksgiving and Easter, they came, until Gardner retired. A scrub nurse and family members assisted Gardner. Frances, not trained in medical work, described herself as "sort of the organizer and the errand girl."

Explaining medical procedures was laborious, since patients had little education and did not speak English. Interpreters translated each direction or explanation from English to Creole and back.

Sometimes surgery could not restore a Haitian's eyesight.

"Gardner made a rule," Frances said. "Before he told anybody he couldn't help them, he asked the entire family to come in. I'm not very emotional, but I never told this story in my talks because I'd choke up.

"One day, a man came in. He was blind from glaucoma, and there was nothing Gardner could do. Gardner told him to ask his family in. The man said, 'I do not have a family.' Gardner asked, 'Well, are you alone?' In his blindness, he looked up and said, 'No, I am not alone. Jesus is with me.'"

Jim recalled, "We examined a child who had lost one eye and had an infection in the other. She needed an operation I could do to save the eye. We were all set to do the surgery, but the family was gone. I asked where they went and was told that the family had decided to take her to a witch doctor."

Frances couldn't believe it. She had no patience for *vodou*, the correct spelling for the Haitian-specific practices that are part of the broader ritual traditions of voodoo. Frances once said, "I think all of us, if we could understand vodou, would understand darkness. This is the deepest darkness that people can live in."

Vodou emerged hundreds of years ago in Saint-Domingue. A blend of Taino, African, and European spiritual practices, it is centered on belief in a distant, unknowable god named Bondye (Good god). The pagan rites of vodou include witchcraft, magic, and serpent worship.

Superstitious vodou followers cannot approach Bondye directly. They rely on intermediary spirits, the Ioa, each responsible for an aspect of life. Peasants present offerings they can ill afford to give to the spirit of agriculture, the spirit of love, the spirit of rain, and the like.

Vodou priests and priestesses lead elaborate ceremonies in gaudy temples. The cult followers try to entice the Ioa to take possession of them and direct their speech and actions.

Dutty Boukman's vodou ceremony on the night before the uprising of 1791 still inspires Haitians. But as Frances walked the villages and saw houses with colorful, jagged glass on roofs and walls to ward away evil spirits, she subconsciously fingered the large silver cross she wore around her neck.

Gardner's teams generally had great success. Babies and toddlers, blind from congenital cataracts, came through surgery well. Frances's most dog-eared photograph was of a grinning little boy. For the first time in his eighteen-month-old life, he could see.

"We kept them overnight after surgery," Frances said in an interview. "Then we took the bandages off and put on thick cataract glasses. This was before lens transplants."

Frances broke into an up-and-down-the-musical-scale sentence.

"Of course, they were blind when they came in, and their families would be so excited. They all wanted to gather around, because there were grandchildren they hadn't seen. It was a very emotional time for all of us. I would take my Kleenex with me, you know, and dry my eyes.

"One morning we had a large Haitian man. We heard him say to other people in the beds, 'Tomorrow I'm gonna see!' Well, the next day, Gardner took the bandages off of his eyes and slipped the glasses on him. He looked up at Gardner and said, 'You're white!' Gardner said, 'I just happen to be.'"

One August an elderly woman was found in a ditch. She was blind, malnourished, and diabetic. For three months she stayed in a hospital bed to recover and wait for an ophthalmologist from Arkansas to care for her eyes.

The cataract surgery was successful. The next morning the woman smiled up at the kind doctor. Gardner, satisfied, smiled back.

Gardner's teams had problems getting surgical supplies through customs at Port-au-Prince's airport without paying a duty. This changed when an airport security official brought his blind mother to Léogâne.

Jim said, "My father operated on her and had good results. From then on, it smoothed the way every time we went through security. When we started, Sainte Croix's eye care was almost nonexistent. Eventually, it improved. But the story is really the role my mother has played in getting schools."

And what a story it is.

Frances had taught mathematics, civics, English, and Sunday school. At age sixty, there was a lot of schoolteacher left in her when she made that first trip to Haiti.

Presbyterians were funding a trade school in Port-au-Prince. Curious, Frances arranged a visit. While Gardner and Jim tackled cataracts, a driver took Frances to the school, where she met missionary Rhine Fecho.

Frances did more than take a tour. She gained a friend. For years she kept in touch with Rhine by mail, in between the return visits to Haiti that she'd never thought she would make.

Two years later, Thanksgiving week of 1979, Gardner's medical team was back in Léogâne for a fifth round of cataract surgeries. He and Frances opened the door of Sainte Croix Hospital. They heard a Haitian talking in another room, a man's voice they did not recognize. His words were loud and authoritative, insistent but not harsh.

"I wonder who that is," Frances said to Gardner, her voice low. "He sounds ... well, tall."

A very tall man, indeed, came around the corner to meet the eye surgeon and his wife, about whom he had heard many good things.

Jean-Wilfrid Albert was born October 30, 1948, in Thomazeau, north of Port-au-Prince. Like most in Haiti, the Albert family, Roman Catholics, had no money. Of the ten children, Jean-Wilfrid was chosen to go to school. Each afternoon he came home and taught his family all that he had learned.

The Alberts lacked more than money and education. Food was scarce. All his life, Jean-Wilfrid remembered his mother crying as she boiled leaves for a meal.

Intelligent and inquisitive, Jean-Wilfrid built kites as a youth and then studied tailoring. Perhaps his height, six foot five inches, made it easier for him to sew his own blue jeans than to find those that would fit.

When Mrs. Albert lost her job, which paid eight dollars a month, Jean-Wilfrid was angry. He wrote to a preacher, claiming that there must not be a God. The preacher sent a Bible to the young man, who, in disgust, threw it on the ground. A friend, watching, told the tall boy that the Bible was a gift from God. Jean-Wilfrid picked it up, began to read, and was never the same.

At age twenty, certain that God had spoken to him in a dream, Jean-Wilfrid entered the Episcopal seminary in Port-au-Prince, studied theology, and learned of Reverend Holly's conviction that the church must educate its young. Mrs. Albert brought her son his meals in a basket on her head.

Jean-Wilfrid dedicated his life to God. He never married.

The tall man's black hair was cropped short off a wide forehead. The hint of a mustache and beard framed his mouth.

His welcome was authentic. Piercing eyes exuded warmth, and a wide smile lit up his dark-skinned face. Enormous hands on long arms gripped Frances's shoulder and shook Gardner's hand at the same time.

Father Jean-Wilfrid Albert, a new priest with a faithful impatience for all things good, was thirty-one. Several months earlier he had graduated from seminary; now he was Sainte Croix Hospital's chaplain. At the hospital, American missionaries Day and Blanche Carper trained the young priest.

Pere Albert (*pere* is the French word for "father") was a towering presence. His height—some Americans were convinced he was six foot eight—further elevated a booming voice that erupted in raucous laughter as often as it gently comforted the sick, or demanded that some wrong be made right. He spoke his native Creole, of course, and fluent French, and English that was far better than fair.

Laughing needs no language, and this too Pere Albert did exceptionally well. His loud and hearty laughter rained down, replenishing all who were near him, like a sudden downpour nourished the thirsty Haitian soil.

Each day, the young chaplain led worship and prayed with patients. He spent weekends riding a shabby bicycle into rural villages to spread God's love.

That Thanksgiving week, he engaged Frances in conversation every spare moment. Pere Albert impressed upon her the tragedy of illiteracy. He explained that the government did not fund public schools in much of his country. Private schools were out of the question for poor families.

"It does not matter how many people can see," Pere Albert said. "What Gardner does is good. Very good. But without knowing how to read, the Haitian people will never make progress."

In 1980, right after Easter, Gardner's medical team returned to Léogâne. Pere Albert began again a spirited conversation with Frances about education. One afternoon he asked her to go with him to a nearby village.

The priest used the hospital's vehicle and took Frances five miles down a bumpy and marginally drivable road to Mercery.

"I want you to see a village where no one can read or write."

He stopped the car to point out a garish temple. The vodou priest was Mercery's leader. Since the people brought him their produce, he was the only person in the village who was not hungry.

Next to the brightly painted temple stood a small chapel. Plain, with weathered blue and white paint, it had been boarded up for years.

"God has called me to preach the gospel here," Pere Albert said, shaking his large index finger in the chapel's direction as if to start brushing away years of disuse.

There was no school in Mercery. Hundreds of impoverished children with bloated bellies roamed about. Frances saw hopelessness in the children's bulging, expressionless eyes. But she saw conviction in the eyes of her tall companion who had relinquished his life to God.

Back home in Arkansas, Frances was captivated with the idea of combating poverty with education. But how should she begin? Where?

Before long, she received direction.

It took three weeks for mail to travel from Haiti to Arkansas. Twenty-one days after Gardner and Frances returned to their home at 1801 West Block Street in El Dorado, a letter from Pere Albert was in their mailbox.

The priest wrote that the children of Mercery wanted a school. Pere Albert would use his little chapel as a weekday schoolroom. He needed money for a teacher.

Frances, a great storyteller, inspired friends at El Dorado's First Presbyterian to give enough money for a teacher's salary. Boys and girls contributed their vacation Bible school offering of fifty dollars. With the funds, Pere Albert hired a teacher and built benches for the chapel.

Enfolded in the loving care of Haiti's Episcopal Church and shepherded by Pere Albert, the chapel schoolroom opened in early October 1980. Children crowded onto each bench to learn to read.

The priest imagined Frances's radiant smile when, in November, he would bring her to the first school in Mercery's illiterate history.

Pere Albert and Frances and Gardner had known each other ten and a half months—not long, but long enough to take the first step on a journey of hope that, despite the eventual deaths of all three, continues to this day.

On the Sunday after Easter in 1981, Frances watched a little girl approach Pere Albert in Mercery's chapel to ask him something. He bent down, his massive frame nearly doubled in half, to hear her soft Creole voice.

Pere Albert began his reply with a recognizable word. *Non.*

The young child turned away, her eyes downcast.

Frances said, "What did she ask you?"

"She asked if she could enroll in our school. I had to tell her no. There is no room for any more students in the little church."

"Call her back. I want to take her picture."

The incident inspired Frances to do something to ensure that the priest could say yes—*wi*—to any child who wanted to go to school.

"I took a picture of the little girl," Frances would say. "I went to the mission committee at our church and asked for money to build a school."

First Presbyterian opened an account called the Haiti Fund in its mission budget and contributed $25,000. The Landers family and their friends added another ten. When a check for $35,000 arrived in Léogâne, Pere Albert let out a hearty laugh and praised the Lord. He had plans drawn up for an eight-room primary school for four hundred children.

The Landerses' church continued its support of the Haiti ministry. Learning that Gardner's medical teams slept in spare hospital beds or in the chapel, the congregation funded an apartment-like guesthouse.

Sainte Croix's medical director, Dr. David McNeeley, was thrilled. New accommodations would attract more missionaries.

Thanksgiving week of 1981, Gardner and Frances brought to Léogâne an engraved silver plaque, nine inches by twelve, mounted on mahogany:

VISITING DOCTORS' QUARTERS
GIVEN TO HONOR
DR. AND MRS. GARDNER H. LANDERS
BY
FIRST PRESBYTERIAN CHURCH
EL DORADO, ARKANSAS
1981

The plaque was hung on the guesthouse wall.

In 1982 four classrooms of Mercery's school were built. Pere Albert hired a principal and teachers, enrolled as many children as the rooms could hold, and waited impatiently for Thanksgiving week to roll around.

When it did, the beaming priest took Frances and her daughter-in-law Susan to the new school. With their tall host, Frances and Susan visited each class. Not one child whispered or fidgeted or misbehaved; they were intent on capturing every nugget of education they'd never thought they would receive. The children smiled, first shyly and then broadly.

Pere Albert led the dedication of Mercery's new primary school. Hundreds of excited villagers attended. Next to the school, a makeshift canopy was erected from a patchwork of bedsheets that Frances's family had donated. Haitians crowded in the shade next to Frances and Susan. More villagers spilled into the sunshine.

As Pere Albert presided over the ceremony, Frances and Susan looked up. Familiar linens, formerly used in their households, gently flapped in the warm breeze.

A wave of satisfaction that could have carried Frances back to El Dorado swept over her, a feeling of accomplishment she would still talk about twenty-five years later.

"The children started on the same level," she said. "None of them could read. As they progressed, we divided them into classes by age and ability. We had two kindergartens and grades one to six. We also had a kitchen: a black iron pot over charcoal."

In three years, Mercery's educational system evolved from nothing, to a makeshift chapel school, to a concrete building that overflowed with teachers and children and learning. When students could read, they were given a Creole Bible to take home and teach their families.

Villagers believed that a miracle had occurred. A significant, one-time gift of $35,000 had increased the hope and faith of the entire community.

But the school, of course, needed ongoing commitment. Mercery's parents relied on a small Arkansas church to sustain their dreams.

Pere Albert and Frances knew they owed their supporters and the Lord a high degree of accountability as they did His work. They settled on a budget. Fifty-five dollars for each student, collectively, funded the teachers' and principal's salaries, supplies, and a nutritious daily meal. The fifty-five dollars was, in effect, an annual scholarship for one child.

Frances routinely said, "This is sixteen cents a day. That's all it takes. It's just sixteen cents a day to send a child to school. That's all we need."

That's all. Her message was relentlessly simple.

Scholarships for four hundred children totaled twenty-two thousand dollars—each year. The ophthalmologist's wife became a fundraiser.

Powered by raw enthusiasm, Frances packed her bags, her thirty-five-millimeter slides, a projector, and a small woven basket to hold donations. She paid her own travel expenses and drove across Arkansas and Louisiana to churches and civic groups.

"Educating the children is the hope of Haiti," Frances said, eyes sparkling. Her beaming smile and happy voice were infectious.

Raising two thousand dollars a month took effort. But for Frances, fueled by her love of the Haitian children, it was not that difficult.

One afternoon Frances and her daughter-in-law Lynn rode with Pere Albert to check on Mercery's busy school. They stopped to visit the vodou priest. He was irritated with Pere Albert.

"I am going to leave the village because I do not have a following," he said. "The people are going to church. My wife has been going to church, and she wants to stay so the two children will be able to attend school. Would you let my little boy, André, enroll in your school?"

Pere Albert said, "We would love to have him."

Recalling this story, Frances added, "Lynn and I ran over to take a picture of André. We thought that to have the witch doctor's son in school was really something."

The vodou priest had one more comment for Pere Albert. "I must go somewhere that you have not been, so I can start another vodou temple."

"He did just that," Frances said.

In 1986, when Mercery's school graduated its first class of students with a sixth-grade education, Frances was the guest of honor. On this trip was Dr. Bruce Henderson, an ophthalmologist from Shreveport, Louisiana.

"When it was time to give the diplomas, one little girl was missing," Frances said. "She lived about a mile from Mercery, and she had told her teacher the previous day that she would like us to come to her village. She wanted us to see something and suggested that we bring her diploma.

"When we got there, the child, probably around eleven, showed us a roll book and materials. She had enrolled fifty illiterate adults and had begun to teach them herself."

The adults emerged from doorways with books and tablets. They held their work up to show Frances and Bruce the letters they had learned.

Frances looked at her companion. They were both nearly in tears.

"Their need to learn was so great that they somehow found things to write with," Frances later said. "The men and women came out of huts with dirt floors, but this sixth-grade child was teaching them. I tell Dr. Henderson so often that if he had not been with me, I still would not believe it."

Firsthand, Gardner and Frances experienced the nearly miraculous improvement in the lifestyle of Mercery's families. Because children like the little girl taught adults to read, they could get jobs at the hospital.

"There has been so much progress," Frances said in 1987. "On our first visit, we saw no books. Now it seems that everyone has a Bible, a prayer book, and a hymnal. The atmosphere in the village is entirely different."

Mercery's school started a music program. One year the children gave a small concert, which Frances described to supporters.

> *We stood in an open field as they played their violins and sang. Their music brought tears to our eyes. They would like choir robes; therefore, this is another priority we undertake in the near future.*

They would *like* choir robes, *therefore*, this *is* another priority.

Whatever the children needed, Frances tried to provide. Increasingly, she realized the faith she would need month to month to maintain persistence and focus. Mercery's children no longer wandered aimlessly. The school was a triumph. But musical instruments? Choir robes? What next?

Improvements in Mercery caught the attention of neighboring villages. The priest-in-charge at a nearby parish wanted two primary schools. On his colleague's behalf, Pere Albert turned to Frances. When she and Gardner came to Léogâne in November 1988, they brought funds for small schools in La Colline and nearby Colin. Both would start midterm in January.

Had Pere Albert remained chaplain of Sainte Croix Hospital, there is no telling what more he and Dr. and Mrs. Landers would have accomplished to lift the hope of those living in and around Léogâne. The three were a powerful team. Eyesight. Education. Worship. Music.

But in January 1989, God would lead the tall, energetic Episcopal priest to a higher calling—literally and geographically—farther up into the mountains. Would Frances and Gardner—figuratively—go too?

Chapter 5

Banished

Pere Albert wrote to my mother, "Come and see." So she came and she saw.
To be with Mother and her friends, to see her interact with the children,
to see how the Haitians dearly loved her ... this has been a wonderful part of my life.
—*Judge Michael Landers, El Dorado, Arkansas, 2012*

On November 12, 1988, Gardner turned seventy-five. His El Dorado ophthalmology practice was vibrant. Across a dozen years, his teams had performed perhaps a thousand cataract surgeries in Léogâne.

The golf course beckoned.

"It is time for me to retire," he said to his wife.

Thanksgiving week, Gardner and Frances told the hospital staff that they would not return. But to the tireless Pere Jean-Wilfrid Albert, the concept of retirement reflected its biblical interpretation. There is no reference to retirement in the Bible.

Pere Albert was determined to intrigue the eye surgeon and his wife. The night before Gardner and Frances left, he talked with them.

"Living inside this compound is luxury in Haiti. There is a parish in the mountains of Grande Colline that needs a priest. God has called me to go there. There are no schools. Will you visit me?"

The region of Grande Colline, southwest of Léogâne, is rugged and remote. Its mountains are dotted with small, isolated villages and too few trees. The hillsides are largely barren.

For hundreds of years, farmers with hungry families have had no option but to destroy the forests, a process called slash and burn. They cut stands of trees to clear the land for meager crops and then slowly burn the trees and turn them to charcoal, Haiti's principal source of fuel.

There is always a market for charcoal.

If rainfall is favorable, farmers get two years of subsistence harvest. Then the tenuous hillside is depleted of nutrients. The exhausted land must lie dormant for fifteen years to heal. Farmers destroy the next stand of trees.

The deforestation of Haiti's mountains has severe consequences. Rains slide down denuded mountains. In streams that are too few in number and too divided in purpose, sheets of topsoil and grit choke the fish. This affects water for the animals, water for washing clothes, water for bathing, and water for drinking.

In many ways, Grande Colline is breathtaking. Mango trees are loaded with yellow-orange fruit. The air is scented. Bright crimson hibiscus plants grow beside a worn path that winds down to a murky stream. An orchid with spiked violet flowers peeks from behind taller foliage.

A Hispaniolan Emerald hummingbird darts toward the deep-red bracts of a poinsettia. Seeking the higher shelter of a leafy green tree, a yellow-breasted, curved-bill Bananaquit flits by.

This extravaganza of nature goes largely unnoticed by women in the mountains. Six or seven hours each day, the women fetch water for their families, walking the paths with little time or inclination to enjoy the scenery.

Primitive thatched houses are no match for brutal seasonal storms. Slightly more substantial wooden houses of two rooms are vividly painted, or at least they were before time and sun faded the color. A small goat and thin mule are tethered. A rooster ambles by, pecking at something that resembles food but is a pebble instead.

Rocks, in fact, appear to be the dominant crop in the mountains. Thousands of farmers live moment-to-moment with an insufficiency of food, water, income, education, and medical care, and little of anything else—except rocks.

The Episcopal parish in the region of Grande Colline needed a priest-in-charge to replace one who retired. Bishop Luc Anatole Jacques Garnier, leader of Église Episcopalé d'Haiti, chose Pere Jean-Wilfrid Albert.

Across Grande Colline's mountains, vodou temples were ample. The fledgling Christian presence of St. Matthias Parish included only a small church in one village and little worship huts in six others.

"Will you visit me?"

Pere Albert repeated his question before reminding Gardner and Frances that God talked to him in his dreams. "The job He has given us is to put schools next to that church and each of those worship stations."

Gardner and Frances did not know what to say.

Back in El Dorado, Gardner retired and increased his golf games. He and his wife continued to mull Pere Albert's plan to go to the mountains of Grande Colline and his passion to educate its children.

In late January 1989, a thin envelope from Haiti arrived at 1801 West Block Street. Its size surprised Frances. Pere Albert usually wrote several pages, praising God and thanking Frances for the money she raised. Then he would raise the ante with a new request or two. Or three.

This time Pere Albert could not have been more to the point: "Just come and see. Your son, Jean-Wilfrid Albert."

That was it. Frances asked Gardner if he wanted to go back.

"No, I really don't. Would you be afraid to go alone?"

She replied, "No. I have to go."

Gardner headed for the golf course. When he came home, he tossed his golf cap on the bed.

"I've changed my mind. I'm going with you."

Frances smiled. "I have always known God talks to you on the golf course."

Gardner and Frances scheduled one more surgical trip to depart on April 6, 1989. They would "just come and see" Pere Albert in the mountains. But on April 4, Dr. McNeeley sent a shortwave radio message to friends in Florida.

"Please alert Gardner Landers that his team should not come."

An uprising in Haiti's cities had shut down the airport in Port-au-Prince.

Frances told Haiti Fund supporters, "After I recovered from the depression of not getting to go, I resumed my talks and letter writing."

Pere Albert had told Gardner and Frances that living in the hospital compound was a luxury and that God had called him to the mountains. Both of these reasons for leaving Léogâne were likely true.

They were just as likely incomplete.

Pere Jean-Wilfrid Albert had no time for bureaucracy or protocol, even from the Episcopal Church that he loved. He was headstrong. Did Bishop Garnier have a motive in transferring the priest to the very remote region of Grande Colline?

Well, Pere Albert's long-time supporters never hesitated to replace "transferred" or "reassigned" with "banished."

The full story may never be clear. One thing was: Pere Albert's superiors did not intend to make his life easy. Presumably at the bishop's direction, Dr. McNeeley dispatched Pere Albert from Sainte Croix Hospital to the mountains without the Land Rover that Frances's Haiti Fund had purchased for him some years before.

Pere Albert was assigned seven churches, miles apart across steep and rugged terrain. He was able to go from place to place only by horseback, bicycle, or on foot.

Frances found out about the Land Rover.

Furious, she could not cross off the days on her calendar fast enough.

On May 10, Gardner and his wife traveled to a slightly safer Haiti. Frances wanted to check on Mercery's school and visit the new ones in Collin and La Colline. Pere Albert had opened another school in the village of Jean-Jean. Frances did not know how it was being funded, and she wanted to find out. She also felt compelled to see the priest's seven mountain villages.

Most importantly, she intended to get Pere Albert's Land Rover back.

Gardner brought no medical team, surgical instruments, or eyeglasses. For the first time, he and Frances went to Haiti outside of their Easter and Thanksgiving regimen.

A new chapter of the Haiti adventure had begun.

Frances and Gardner flew to Miami and then across the Caribbean Sea to Port-au-Prince. The jet had barely touched down when the woman from Arkansas deplaned, her husband behind her. They found their way to Léogâne and walked into David McNeeley's office at Sainte Croix Hospital.

Hearing determined footsteps, the doctor looked up. He was beyond surprised.

Frances sat down and glared at him. She did not utter one word. After an awkward silence, David spoke. "I guess I know what you're here for."

Pere Albert and Frances had evenly matched tenacity.

The priest got a ride to Léogâne, met Frances and Gardner at the hospital, collected his Land Rover, and drove his American friends up jarring roads into the mountains of Grande Colline to show them what God had in store for him.

On the jostling drive, Gardner looked out the front window at the deep-blue sky, brown treeless mountains, and remnants of a tropical paradise. He appreciated this view of Haiti outside of the operating room.

His eyes swept across countryside peppered with shanties and shacks. Women walked to market along the rutted road, baskets of produce on their heads. Farmers in tattered clothing slung machetes in the fields. A large circle of boisterous peasants allowed a partial view of a dirt arena. In the center, two angry brown cocks fought for their lives. Children were plentiful, shoes negligible.

The contrast between the beautiful hills and valleys of Haiti and the poverty of its people was jarring.

Four months earlier, Pere Albert had arrived. He had started reaching out to struggling parents, most of whom were immersed in vodou. At one time there had been in the region a small school that cost very little to attend. Many parents sent their children, though teachers were unqualified and did not know how to follow Haiti's national education system.

One young boy, Nicolas Michael, had spent six years in the school but learned almost nothing. Michael was twelve when Pere Albert arrived. The priest promised Michael's parents a proper school—soon. He made the same commitment to the parents of a bright-eyed, peppy little girl named Viergela.

As Pere Albert drove, Michael and Viergela were on his mind. He turned his head toward Frances in the backseat and chuckled.

"Here in the mountains I walk all over to look for children to invite to school. The parents say, 'My kids do not speak yet, Father.' They think I am crazy. I tell them, 'If they can say papa or mama, even if you do not have money, I will have a place for them. God will do the rest.'"

Frances was speechless. Later, she wrote:

> We visited the seven mountain villages where Pere Albert has churches. Some of the villages are so remote there are no roads, only footpaths or a riverbed, but the four-wheel drive made it with me holding on until my hands were bruised.
>
> When we arrived at each village, the parents had the children clean and dressed in their one nice garment that is reserved for church and very special occasions. I took pictures of each child so those who want to sponsor a child can have a picture.
>
> I can see the hope of Haiti shining in their black faces.

Pere Albert had his work cut out for him.

> There was one church building and these six stations and no schools. He lived in a little house with an outdoor kitchen and an outhouse down the road. And that was it.

The village where Pere Albert so sparsely lived was then called Grande Colline, the same name as the surrounding geographic region. Later, the village was renamed. For clarity, this book refers to Pere Albert's home village as Cherident, as it is known today.

As Pere Albert's congregations grew, he knew Bishop Garnier would fund small churches. Schools were a different matter. Reverend Holly may have wanted schools, but in rural areas like Grande Colline, the Episcopal Church rarely funded them.

Pere Albert got to the point. He asked Frances to raise money for seven shelter schools, which, like worship stations, were made of woven cornstalks and palm leaves. Concrete block buildings would come later.

Frances was insistent. "Pere Albert, I can't possibly raise money for seven schools. Why, just look at this place. This is barely a road. And I'm already funding three schools."

The impassioned priest interrupted her with a hearty laugh and words that have become near folklore to his friends in the United States.

"Frances," Pere Albert said. "If *God* wants schools in the mountains, there *will be* schools in the mountains."

"What are we going to do, Gardner?"

The couple was back home, looking at each other but saying little, unwilling to dismiss Pere Albert's challenge yet unable to reconcile it.

Gardner, this retired eye surgeon who had skillfully met challenges on the battlefields of World War II, was thoughtful. "Write the Presbyterian Women's organizations in Louisiana and Arkansas. Ask if you can speak. Don't talk for more than eighteen minutes. Tell them you will pay your own expenses. All they have to do is listen."

Frances was daunted by the thought of raising funds for seven more schools and then supporting ten schools each year. But she was inspired by Pere Albert's faith and Gardner's support. She followed her husband's advice.

The kitchen table became Frances's office.

"Poor Gardner," Frances was fond of saying. "For years he ate his lunch standing up."

She called the presidents of Presbyterian Women in Shreveport, Louisiana, and Hot Springs and Little Rock in Arkansas. A woman from Hot Springs's Westminster Presbyterian was receptive.

"They had sixty women for lunch," Frances said in an interview. "I had my slides, and I told my story. I thought, well, maybe I'll get a little bit. I saw money being put in my little basket, and I thought, oh, I am going to have a few hundred dollars."

As Frances packed her things, a lady came up to her.

"Our family foundation is behind in our giving. I think my sister would be interested in this. She's the president. I would like some material to send to her in New Orleans. That's where the foundation is."

"I came home so excited," Frances said. "I said to Gardner, 'I bet I'm going to get my first thousand dollars. You just wait. I know I am.'"

A few weeks later, an envelope from New Orleans arrived at 1801 West Block Street. Ten thousand dollars had been awarded to the Haiti Fund.

Frances sent the money to Pere Albert. His spontaneous, appreciative laughter reverberated against the mountains. Then he squeezed his eyes shut. He raised his face toward the sky and profusely thanked the Lord, who did, indeed, want schools in the mountains.

Chapter 6

Meanwhile

On our recent trip to Haiti, I received many times what I gave.
To walk and work among the poor of the world is to receive a gift of grace.
—*Pastor Dawkins Hodges, Hedgesville, West Virginia, 1984*

In the 1980s, a thousand miles north of Arkansas, mission-minded people in the Shenandoah Valley began accumulating their own stories about Léogâne and its Sainte Croix Hospital.

Pete and Fran Hobbs were members of Windy Cove Presbyterian in Millboro, Virginia. Fran traveled to Haiti twenty-seven times. The inspiration for her first trip came from Flo Boggs, who worshiped with her husband Harry at West Virginia's Keyser Presbyterian. Windy Cove and Keyser were part of Shenandoah Presbytery, a group of churches in geographic proximity.

In 1982 Shenandoah Presbytery hosted a conference. There Flo Boggs updated attendees on the work of Medical Benevolence Foundation.

Fran Hobbs told me, "Flo's workshop inspired me to go on a mission trip and give hands-on help to people in need." Fran was interested in Haiti because she knew Harvey and Doris Ann Musser, missionaries at Sainte Croix Hospital.

Soon after the conference, Fran joined a Methodist team on an eleven-day work trip to Haiti. She met up with Harvey and Doris Ann, who took her to Léogâne. There, she met a tall, thirty-four-year-old Episcopal priest in his third year as chaplain. His name was Pere Jean-Wilfrid Albert.

Pere Albert drove Fran to Mercery and pointed out a school under construction, funded by an American woman named Frances Landers. Fran had not heard of her.

"Four rooms will be ready for the start of the fall term," Pere Albert said. "This is good. Education is Haiti's hope."

Mercery's villagers had practiced vodou before Pere Albert arrived with his message about the saving grace of Jesus Christ. Arches made of palm leaves framed many doorways.

"You see those palm branches," Pere Albert said to Fran, his long index finger pointing. "They announce that the man and woman have just been married. Frances Landers sends me wedding rings in several sizes."

Pere Albert explained that when Haitian couples converted to Christianity, they vowed to follow Jesus and no longer practice vodou. Though couples may have been "married" for years, Pere Albert officiated Christian weddings with the brides wearing inexpensive rings from Walmart.

Fran Hobbs returned home and shared her experiences with her church, Windy Cove, which helped support Harvey and Doris Ann Musser. Intrigued, Pastor Rob Sherrard thought, *Why send just money to the Mussers? Why not send a team?*

Pastor Rob spent months trying to assemble a group. Planning stalled after the Mussers' missionary assignment changed. Finally, ten people from nine churches formed Windy Cove's first mission team to Haiti. Fran Hobbs was first on the list. Pastor Rob Sherrard was second.

On September 16, 1984, the group set out. When Pastor Rob wrote of his first impressions, he mentioned his teammate, Pastor Dawkins Hodges.

"How can I describe the desolate feeling of being an alien in a foreign land? I felt that way in the Port-au-Prince airport. Dawkins said I looked as if I wanted to curl up in my mother's arms and be held secure."

The Americans maneuvered through the crowded, sultry airport. They retrieved luggage and navigated customs.

Pastor Rob wrote, "But then what? How were we to know where to go or what to do? As we walked out amid the pushing crowd, we saw a reassuring sign, 'Welcome, Frances Hobbs. USA.'"

In her trip journal, Fran added context. "We drag, push, and pull our luggage outside. Octa, my Haitian pastor friend whom I met last time I was here, has sent a minister friend to meet me. He has a sign with my name on it. He gets us with the people from the hospital who have come to meet us."

The hospital's driver held another sign: "Reverend Sherrard, Presbyterian Church." Luggage was loaded into a small pickup truck. A station wagon appeared for the travelers. The Windy Cove team set out.

Over thirty years later, little has changed for arriving mission teams. The Toussaint Louverture International Airport is air-conditioned now. It's a tad less chaotic and a little more secure. But for those arriving from Miami or Fort Lauderdale, Florida, or from New York, the question is the same. Now what?

Stepping outside the airport into the sweltering tropical climate, sensory overload is common. The sun is too bright, the sky backlit with too much haze, the humidity too thick—and the people, too many.

Eight of ten in Port-au-Prince are unemployed. Crowds hover outside the airport doors, their dark skins dusty and pungent. They push close to those arriving from other countries, seeking handouts. The crush of people obscures the view of waiting vehicles and drivers.

Offers to handle luggage abound. So many are the arms outstretched for a tip that unwise visitors who relinquish their baggage—even to those with good intentions—often lose sight of it.

Americans find their Haitian drivers and exchange warm greetings. Returning mission workers are gleeful to see old friends. Haitian smiles are wide. "Bonjou! Bonjou!"

Luggage is loaded onto a truck bed. Mothers with soulful brown eyes, carrying deformed or starving children, move close to press their case for sympathy. They rap on the windows to get the attention of those who have slipped inside their waiting vehicle.

Visitors feel uncomfortable. They try not to stare.

A crippled man hobbles over, then three more. One man uses his forearms to crawl, dragging his limp legs behind.

Visitors feel inadequate. They try not to cry.

Artisans come with coffee bean bracelets, clay sculptures, and paintings in vibrant colors. The sight of an American wallet brings a dozen more Haitians, further delaying the team's decision of who will sit where.

Some travelers squeeze into the cab of a pickup truck or into a car with neither enough space nor seatbelts. The rest perch on top of the luggage in the open bed of the truck. Sunglasses on, eyes alert, watches in their pockets, they keep their mouths shut for the grimy and unpredictable drive through Port-au-Prince.

In 1984 the Windy Cove team experienced much of this. Drivers loaded luggage into the truck. Eight of the Americans piled into the station wagon. Fran Hobbs and Pastor Ray Cobb crowded into the truck's cab. Both drivers told their passengers to lock the doors and keep the windows up.

The truck and car both started on the first try and outpaced the Haitians who followed on foot, some still rapping on the windows.

With worn tires and shot suspensions, the vehicles that carried the Windy Cove team had aged prematurely, much like the men and women in this difficult land.

The country's poverty sprawled on both sides of the road and into gutters awash with raw sewage. Vendors lined the streets, selling fruit that was too ripe, clothes that were too cheap, and junk that no one needed.

Everywhere there was squalor.

Windy Cove's team rode through the absurdly chaotic streets and sights of Port-au-Prince without incident.

Pastor Rob's reaction? "Windy, hot, so many people just sitting or idly walking, the smells, the buildings either half built or half falling down, the jumble of brightly colored vehicles."

As the station wagon and truck skirted Haiti's north central coastline, the atmosphere became more serene, though no less impoverished. The vehicles climbed into the hills and pulled up to Sainte Croix Hospital.

Windy Cove's first mission team had arrived.

Pere Albert greeted Fran Hobbs like an old friend. "It is good that you came back, Mrs. Fran," the priest said with an endless hug and a big laugh. "God is pleased with you."

The team painted walls and did repairs for Dr. McNeeley and the Jordans, missionaries who had replaced Harvey and Doris Ann Musser. Scott Jordan ran the depleted pharmacy. Edna coordinated visiting medical teams.

Daily the group attended a worship service led by Pere Albert, visited the patients, and doted on malnourished children. Pere Albert taught the Americans the Creole lyrics to a happy tune, "Come and Go with Me." The song continues, "To my Father's house, where there is joy, joy, joy." Haitian and American voices brightened the hospital corridors.

Children from Léogâne followed Fran everywhere. With little privacy and long hours, it was late at night before she could write in her journal. "We get in two vehicles for a tour of Mercery with Pere Albert. We visit his new school. I see the four rooms he had when I was here before. Extended to that is an L-shaped building made of cinderblock, chicken wire for windows, a tin roof, and a concrete floor. Everywhere we look there are shacks with dirt floors, naked children, and extreme poverty."

Back in Millboro, Pastor Rob updated his congregation. "It became clear that we are indeed one in the Spirit, one in the Lord. Jesus was there, teaching us through the smiling face of a hospital chaplain."

The mission team showed slides and told stories, prompting Windy Cove Presbyterian to plan a return trip the following summer.

Pastor Rob asked, "Are you interested? The Lord is moving. Maybe He wants you to come along!"

The Lord wanted Flo Boggs to come along.

After seeing the slides of Fran Hobbs's first trip, Flo said, "If you take a team to Sainte Croix Hospital and have room, I want to go."

Flo waited three years. In 1985 there was room for Flo to take her first of sixteen trips to Haiti. Fran, Flo, and seven others headed to Léogâne.

"Our mission team stayed at the guesthouse by the hospital," Flo told me. "On the wall was a plaque saying that the guesthouse was donated in honor of a Dr. and Mrs. Landers. I wondered who they were."

It would be five years before Flo and Frances Landers would meet.

Painting was on Windy Cove's agenda that year. One room was infested with mosquitoes. Fran and her partner, Sharon Fry, had no choice but to run their paint rollers right over the mosquitoes on the walls. The women didn't know whether to laugh or cry.

Emotions ran deep on this trip. In a fear-ridden vodou village, the Americans saw adults tying strings around their malnourished children's necks, hoping to ward off disease. They felt a surge of hope when beaming children at Mercery's school displayed their tattered schoolbooks.

Later Fran said, "There was such a difference in the atmosphere of Christian villages compared to those still in vodou. Pere Albert, for years with only a horse or bicycle, eventually converted the whole area."

In 1986 another Windy Cove team flew into Port-au-Prince. The tropical beauty of the shore lined with palms, oleanders, and poincianas stunned first-time travelers. So did the sights and smells of poverty.

Shanties—a combination of tin, concrete blocks, and cardboard—were small, filthy, and crowded together. Open sewage ditches ran along the streets. It was not uncommon to see people bathing in a ditch.

The Americans, as always, were glad to safely get through the slums of Port-au-Prince and into Léogâne to be greeted by Pere Albert. They unloaded boxes of donated medicines, supplies, and clothing.

Walking through the hospital ward, Fran Hobbs noticed an elderly woman, blind and malnourished, in the first bed. Fran asked about her.

"She was found by the side of a road," Pere Albert said. "The doctor is treating her for sugar diabetes. In November an eye doctor is coming from the United States. He will operate on her eyes."

Pere Albert was referring to Dr. Gardner Landers, whom Fran still did not know. Of the blind woman, she wrote: "As I look down at her staring into space, the distance between us seems so great … until we sing, 'Come and Go with Me.' She keeps time to the music with her foot and is singing along with us. My feeling of despair turns to hope."

The blind woman too was hopeful. She was safe and warm. She would wait in bed for one hundred days more until the doctor would come from Arkansas. He would look into her sightless eyes. Perhaps he could do something—she reasoned that it would have to be magic—to enable her to look back into his.

By 1987 more than thirty people from Virginia and West Virginia had visited Sainte Croix Hospital. To raise awareness for Pere Albert's fine work, Shenandoah Presbytery paid for him to come to the Virginias. Flo Boggs helped publicize Pere Albert's visit with a vivid description.

"Picture a pastor riding his bicycle through waving fields of sugar cane, looking for the destitute in Haiti's villages. Picture a village in bondage to the evil of vodou, hearing the gospel for the first time. Picture a teenage choir of one hundred, meeting twice a week for practice, and singing each Sunday."

On March 12, 1987, the Haitian priest bent down, lest he hit his head, and boarded a northbound airplane. One of twenty-five Episcopal clergy in Haiti, Pere Albert was headed for nine days in the Virginias.

With family in New Jersey, Pere Albert had been in the United States before, but this was his first time in snow. A thick, wet blanket of it prolonged winter, giving the priest a change from Haiti's humid, ninety-degree days.

On Sunday morning Harry Boggs pulled into the parking lot of Keyser Presbyterian with his wife Flo and Pere Albert. The priest wore a beige sweater vest over his clerical collar, and a loosely fitted brown suit over his lanky body. A mustache and full beard accentuated his large smile.

Pere Albert, half-a-head taller than the handsome Harry Boggs, grinned widely. He was happy to be with his American friends in their Sunday snow. The trio went inside and were handed worship bulletins.

"We are brothers and sisters in Christ," Pere Albert always reminded his friends. "We pray to the same God." To illustrate this, he had collected short Creole prayers from his worshipers in Léogâne and had translated them into English. Eleven were printed in the bulletin. Here are three.

"Lord, if we are alive today in spite of hurricanes, hunger, and sickness, we should say, 'Thank You, Lord.' We must be here for a purpose."

"Father, it takes a special kind of mirror to see if our faces are dirty. Your Word is this."

"Lord, there is a big devil called Discouragement. We ask You to send him away because he is bothering us."

Insightful, aren't they?

When time came for the sermon, Flo introduced her friend. Attractive and postured, Flo stood barely past Pere Albert's shoulders. She wore a rose-colored jacket to ward off the late-winter chill.

"This morning we greet a man who gives hope in Haiti. To village after remote village, Father Albert has taken the gospel of Jesus Christ. I've seen him work among his people as teacher, encourager, and champion, yet as a gentle comforter, pastor, and friend. Educated as a tailor before entering the ministry, he even makes his own blue jeans!"

Flo paused to let the congregation finish chuckling. She looked at Pere Albert sitting in a nearby pew.

"Father Albert, I've met your church family on two occasions. I'm so proud for you to meet mine. Thank you for coming to wintry West Virginia."

Pere Albert loped to the microphone with neither notes nor Bible. His sermon was sure to run long, for he remained on "Haiti time" where church lasted for hours and preaching was thorough.

His sermon was long, and it was thorough. He quoted Scripture. He extolled the congregation to do good work for the Lord.

"Your time on this earth is short. You need to live the same way now that you want to spend your eternal days in heaven," he said, raising overhead his right index finger.

Many who had spent Sundays with the priest commented, "You've never been preached to until you've been preached to by Pere Albert."

After the service, the priest collected the congregation's donations of soap, toothbrushes, and the like. Pere Albert never lost an opportunity to bring hope to his impoverished people. Toothpaste and shampoo were tangible pieces of hope.

Returning to Léogâne, he sent a prompt letter of thanks to his hosts. "I appreciate very much my stay in your country. Thank you very much for your patience to listen to my French accent. I believe that you were so patient because I was talking about God's word."

He brought home money, seeds, soccer shoes, musical instruments, and two little organs for choirs he had formed around Léogâne.

It was just a dent, but it was an important dent that left a lasting impression on hundreds of people in snowy Shenandoah Valley.

Pere Albert nurtured Sainte Croix Hospital's patients, relatives, staff, and visitors. But he was not built to stay indoors. His ministry was wherever the Lord sent him. When the hospital formed small clinics across the countryside, Pere Albert traveled to each, first on horseback, then by bicycle, and later in a Land Rover funded by Presbyterians from Arkansas.

Increasingly, Windy Cove teams heard the name of Frances Landers. Their thoughts flashed back to that silver plaque on the guesthouse wall.

In 1988 Pere Albert said to the Windy Cove group, "Now I will show you a place where families do not live. They just exist."

He drove to a small village, Jean-Jean, with no church, no work, no money, and no school—only lethargy. In Mercery, its school in operation for seven years, smiles graced the faces of those who took pride in their appearance.

"You see how the whole village changes when children go to school and families worship the Lord," Pere Albert said. "I think that you can raise money for a school in Jean-Jean."

For five thousand dollars, he explained, the Episcopal Church of Haiti would build a school and hire three teachers.

The mission workers came home, ready to meet the challenge. Within a month they sent $1,700 to Pere Albert, enough for the children in Jean-Jean to begin school under a palm-leaf shelter. Keyser and Windy Cove continued to raise money for a concrete school building.

Generous donations came in, including one thousand dollars to fund three young men on Windy Cove's next trip. Keyser's sewing group made sixty outfits. Others contributed medicine and clothing. Someone spread the word to Emmanuel Episcopal across Mineral Street that something invigorating was going on in the neighborhood.

Keyser's Episcopalians responded by raising four hundred dollars. The church rector, Reverend Leonard Gross, wrote Pere Albert, asking that he use $150 to buy a sow. Flo Boggs would bring the check on her next trip. She would also bring 130 small crosses made of local woods by a Keyser man, H. L. Wilkins.

It was a long time before Pere Albert got Reverend Gross's letter. Months earlier, January 1989, the faithful Haitian priest had been reassigned—or banished, depending on one's point of view—to the mountains.

Without his Land Rover, Pere Albert could not go to Port-au-Prince for his mail. He might have taken a *tap-tap*, a colorful truck or bus used as public transportation, but he was busy getting acclimated to his new parish.

Pere Albert had told Gardner and Frances about his upcoming move to the mountains. But his Shenandoah Valley friends did not know this. In April, when the priest sent a melancholy letter, they found out.

Letters in English from Pere Albert and other Haitians always contained spelling, grammatical, and style errors. Excerpts are presented as written in order to give an accurate picture to readers of the cultural and language barriers common in third-world mission work.

> You can't imagine how I love you. If I, being a simple man, feel such a love in my heart for you, what about God? What you are used to do for Haiti is very important and it happens that with your help we can start a grammar school in Jean-Jean. Father Racine who is in charge of that school has already received all the money you sent for the shelter and for the teachers' salary. I can't give you any more information because I have been transferred to an other place since January.

I work now in a mountain place where there is still a lot to do. I would like you to know that my work is still your work, and yours is mine. You are not supposed to let me alone in that mountain mission. People there are less educated than those in Léogâne area.

I would like you to come to see me when you come to Haiti next time. That place is at one hour and 15 minutes from the hospital.

Pere Albert mailed copies of the letter to Fran and Rob in Virginia and to Flo in West Virginia—and to an ophthalmologist and his wife in Arkansas. Reading the letter, each recipient felt the priest's isolation as he adjusted to living in "that place."

The priest needed his friends, all of whom did not yet know each other. As they held his letter in their hands, they couldn't imagine how people in Haiti's mountains could be "less educated than those in Léogâne area."

Frances read the letter, dated April 18, with particular dismay. Two weeks earlier, she and Gardner had cancelled their final medical mission trip because of civil unrest. Clearly, Pere Albert was disappointed that his special friends from Arkansas had not come to see him.

Pere Albert, the lone Episcopal leader in the expanse of Grande Colline, perhaps silently pleaded as he typed, "I would like you to come to see me when you come to Haiti next time."

Pastor Rob could not get that sentence out of his mind. His Windy Cove team was heading back to Léogâne. What about a day trip to Cherident?

Early Sunday morning, July 9, 1989, a driver took Pastor Rob's team up the mountains. Pere Albert was gleeful to see his American friends.

"Pastor Rob! You will preach. You will wear my robe."

Rob gave the sermon in English, and Pere Albert translated it into Creole. Over two hundred gracious Haitians made the nine Americans feel very much a part of the service.

Flo Boggs shared the story with her congregation, exaggerating Pere Albert's height.

"You will recall that Father Albert is six foot eight inches tall, and Rob is ... well, not six foot eight. A rope was tied around his waist, a lot of white material flounced up over that rope, and the sleeves were rolled several times. Father Albert gave Rob his most beautiful stole. He was elegant!"

Pastor Rob's sermon was from the New Testament, the fifth chapter of Luke. As he recited Jesus's instruction to Simon to drop his fishing nets, "Leave everything and follow Me," two chickens scurried down the aisle toward him.

"No matter the ill-fitting robe," Flo told her laughing church friends, "to us Rob is a spiritual giant. It's no surprise that even chickens respond to his message."

Flo gave Pere Albert the 130 small crosses that Dutch Wilkins had carved out of Virginia walnut, cherry, and cedar. She also gave the grateful priest four hundred dollars from Reverend Gross. Pere Albert would, indeed, use part of the donation to buy a sow.

After worship he took Rob's team to a hillside above Cherident's church. "This is where I expect to build a guesthouse," Pere Albert said. Rob was skeptical.

Bill Ack, Rex Broome, and John Parker, the students funded by Keyser Presbyterian, were great additions to the team. On July 23 back in Keyser, the young men gave an inspiring sermon. Then Flo said a few words.

"I call Billy, Rex, and John a triple-A success. They were adaptable to any situation. They were assertive in their work and friendships. And they were appreciative—not only of us older folks and the Haitians, but also home, parents, privileges, freedom, opportunity, and comfort."

Pere Albert's friends from Virginia and West Virginia had not been the first Americans to visit his mountaintop home.

Two months before Flo gave Pere Albert hand-carved crosses and Episcopalian money for a pig, Gardner and Frances had responded to Pere Albert's invitation to "just come and see."

The doctor and his wife had waited out the unrest in Haiti's cities, had reclaimed the Land Rover in Léogâne, and had gone with Pere Albert into the mountains of Grande Colline. On that memorable day at the side of the road, Pere Albert had asked Frances to fund seven more schools.

Windy Cove's annual trips never overlapped with those of the Landers family. For years, Windy Cove travelers knew Gardner and Frances only by a nine-by-twelve-inch plaque on the guesthouse wall and a scrapbook on the table.

"I looked at the scrapbook every time I went," Flo Boggs told me. "I kept seeing new pictures of this doctor and his wife."

Flo had no idea that she and Frances would become close friends.

Did Pere Albert have any idea of the fabric that Frances would weave with Flo, Pastor Rob Sherrard, Fran Hobbs, and hundreds more across the United States? Of course he did. The Lord had blessed Pere Albert with immense vision and unwavering faith.

Pere Albert also knew, deep, deep down, that God *did* want schools in the mountains.

Fran Hobbs, left, and Flo Boggs made many trips to Haiti.

Chapter 7

Continued Struggle

Duvalier had gone and Haiti was free.
—Elizabeth Abbott, Haiti: The Duvaliers and Their Legacy, 1988

Here's a scene familiar to those who go to Haiti. Picture the local drugstore. A few days before heading to Port-au-Prince, someone brings to the cash register several assorted travel-sized toiletries.

"Where are you headed?" asks the cashier.

"To Haiti," the mission worker says.

"Oh, how nice! A vacation in Tahiti." The cashier smiles.

"Not Tahiti. To Haiti."

The smile disappears. "You're going to Haiti? It's not safe. Is it?"

Life in Haiti certainly wasn't safe during four hundred years of colonial settlement, slavery, and rebellion. Circumstances didn't improve much during the next one hundred fifty. During the last half of the 1800s and beyond, Haitian rulers were overthrown with regularity. Deadly clashes between military and civilians were common.

Time and again, as political distress combined with droughts, epidemic diseases, capsized boats, monsoon rains, flooding, hurricanes, mudslides, and a monstrous earthquake, the struggling, impoverished nation slid into chaos.

Presidential Mishaps

From 1911 to 1915, shortly before Frances Landers was born, six Haitian presidents were assassinated, overthrown, or forced into exile. In these years prior to World War I, German immigrants wielded much economic power across Haiti's commerce, banking, utilities, and ports. Fears of German influence prompted American president Woodrow Wilson to send Marines to Haiti in 1915. They occupied the country for nineteen years.

The Marines were chartered to improve roads. The labor source? Haitians. An obscure, dusty law required peasants to repair roads in lieu of paying a tax. Haiti's roads increased from three usable miles in 1915, to 470 in 1918, but outraged blacks saw this forced labor as a return to slavery.

Believing they were fighting another Haitian revolution, incensed peasants battled the Marines in 1919 and 1920. Haitian casualties ranged from three thousand, as reported in US Senate investigations, to fifteen thousand, as estimated by historians. Twenty Marines lost their lives. History views the American occupation as self-serving, prejudiced, and often brutal.

In 1930 Stenio Vincent was elected Haiti's president. When he took office, most Marines left. Those who remained for a few more years helped establish a Haitian military, the Garde.

By 1935 President Vincent wanted absolute power. He appointed his own senate and judiciary and ruled by decree when the legislature was not in session. He was brutal with opponents, censored the press, and governed to benefit corrupt cronies and, mostly, himself.

One of Vincent's enemies was Rafael Trujillo Molina, dictator of next-door Dominican Republic. In 1937 Trujillo ordered his army to murder thirty thousand Haitian peasants living on the Dominican side of the Massacre River, a fitting name. Next, Trujillo rallied Haitian Garde officers to stage a coup against their president. It failed.

Evidence grew that the Garde's leader, Colonel Calixte, was on Trujillo's payroll. He was. When President Vincent generously exiled Calixte rather than kill him, the colonel accepted a commission in the Dominican army.

In 1941 Elie Lescot, a competent mulatto, succeeded President Vincent. Many common Haitians thought he'd be a compassionate leader. He was not. President Lescot's quest for power matched Stenio's. In January 1946 Lescot resigned amid various political mishaps.

Dumarsais Estimé, a cabinet minister, outlasted two opponents in a free election. One was Colonel Calixte, who had defected to the Dominican Republic. The other was the leader of Haiti's communist party.

Estimé renamed the Garde, calling it the Haitian Army. He began his term with some progressive changes, but his economic policies alienated both simple peasants and elite mulattoes. In 1950 his own Haitian Army led a coup that sent him into exile in Jamaica.

Paul Magloire won the next election. Haiti's living conditions improved slightly until 1954, when Hurricane Hazel devastated the country. In a continuing pattern of corrupt leadership, President Magloire built an imposing mansion, monopolized industries for his own gain, and misused Hurricane Hazel's international relief funds. In 1956 he fled to Jamaica.

Even by Haitian standards, the sixteen months between the fall of President Magloire and the election of François Duvalier were disastrous. One interim president resigned. Haiti's Army deposed two.

Papa Doc

François Duvalier grew up amid chaos and poverty. He experienced the nineteen-year oppression of the American Marines and felt shame that Haiti was incapable of managing its own daily life.

As a teen, François saw a mother scrub the open sores on her son's arms, trying to cleanse them from disease. The incident motivated him to become a medical doctor.

Dr. Duvalier, nicknamed Papa Doc, was President Estimé's Minister of Health. Haitians thought that he was an honest humanitarian.

But what followed his election was one of the most repressive, corrupt, and evil dictatorships in modern times. For fourteen years, Papa Doc condoned violence, murder, and rape. His knowledge of magic and sorcery was deep.

Papa Doc's police were the Tonton Macoutes, named for a vodou monster. The Macoutes shot, stabbed, bludgeoned, beheaded, and buried or burned alive tens of thousands. They tortured and beat hundreds of thousands more.

Haiti's economic problems, not surprisingly, deepened.

In 1964 President Duvalier amended the Haitian constitution to declare himself President-for-Life. As he neared death in 1971, a second amendment named his son the next President-for-Life.

Papa Doc's son, appropriately, was nicknamed Baby Doc.

Baby Doc

The obese Jean-Claude Duvalier was a pampered nineteen-year-old. He had no clue how to run a country, other than to encourage the Tonton Macoutes's treachery. Baby Doc was a playboy, albeit a chunky one. He lived off of the immense wealth his family accumulated through corrupt dealings.

Fortunately for Jean-Claude, his mother, Simone Ovide Duvalier, was happy to look after Haiti's interests. Mrs. Duvalier, the First Lady of the Republic, maintained a lot of clout after her husband's death.

Unfortunately for Simone Duvalier, in 1980 Jean-Claude married a fast-living divorcée, Michele Bennett, who wanted her mother-in-law's power. The wedding cost three million dollars, an example of Baby Doc's unfathomable spending as the leader of his wretchedly poor country.

First Lady Michele Bennett Duvalier forced Baby Doc to lose seventy pounds, publicly harangued his mother into leaving Haiti, and exiled ninety-six members of Simone Ovide Duvalier's family.

Jean-Claude and Michele routinely stole from the coffers of ten Haitian departments and lived a heaven-on-earth existence in the National Palace. Outside the gates, Duvalier's enemies were tortured and murdered. Most of the rest of Haiti's six million citizens lived a moment-to-moment, grind-it-out existence of poverty, hunger, illness, and illiteracy.

President-for-Life Duvalier was unprepared to handle one crisis after another. In 1981 Hurricane Allen did more damage than had Hurricane Hazel twenty-seven years earlier. The AIDS epidemic brought Haiti's cities to hysteria. A swine fever virus led to the slaughter of all Creole pigs, a principal source of income. School enrollment in the cities plummeted, as parents could not afford uniforms and notebooks. A severe drought left the hungry nation hungrier.

In 1983 Pope Jean Paul II visited Haiti amidst unprecedented fanfare. Duvalier's military had worked hard to clean up the route the papal motorcade would take, to hide the squalor of Port-au-Prince.

To Baby Doc and Michele's horror, the pontiff condemned the Duvaliers and incited the crowd. Pope Jean Paul's speech motivated Catholic priests to berate the dictator from their pulpits.

In 1985 human rights violations prompted international leaders to halt millions of dollars of aid. Hungry Haitians rioted. The death toll climbed.

Throughout January 1986, pressure rose for Baby Doc to resign. He sought help from vodou spirits and finally made his decision.

On February 1 at 2:00 in the morning, the government-run television station flashed an announcement. President Jean-Claude Duvalier was leaving the country. Soon two cars of officials and bodyguards drove from the National Palace. In the lead was General Henri Namphy. The Duvaliers followed in a second car driven by Colonel Prosper Avril, a long-time family advisor.

The United States Embassy learned that a plane was standing by at (what was then named) François Duvalier International Airport. A White House spokesman confirmed that Baby Doc was headed out.

News spread. People stood on rooftops to watch the jet climb into the sky, taking their oppressive, dictatorial leader far, far away. Jubilation erupted. Shortwave and ham radios crackled in the night.

Two predawn hours later, the National Assembly hastily declared a state of martial law. The morning news headlined that Haiti was in lockdown.

Bewildered citizens could not understand why. They had been liberated; certainly this was not cause for violence.

They were wrong.

As crowds celebrated Baby Doc's departure, euphoria turned to chaos. A group stormed the Duvaliers' opulent vacation home, stole everything, and then burned the place down. Mobs turned vengeful toward the Duvaliers' henchmen, the Tonton Macoutes, and hunted them down to torture and kill them. Attacks ignited counterattacks. The death toll was high.

Nowhere was the fighting more vicious than in the sugarcane fields outside of Léogâne. Hundreds of villagers destroyed Tonton Macoute homes. Two Jeeps arrived, filled with the Macoutes, who opened their machine guns on unarmed men and women, killed an estimated fifty, and injured scores.

Most families, not wanting to be associated with the violence, took their injured relatives into their huts to treat them as best they could. Twenty-four seriously wounded peasants were taken to nearby Sainte Croix Hospital. Dr. McNeeley and his medical team spent more than thirty hours trying to save them.

The dead were buried with no identifying markers.

It had been a horrible night. Haiti's citizens were confused and nervous. And things were about to get worse.

At noon the government-owned television station came to life. Sitting in the studio, President-for-Life Jean-Claude Duvalier looked directly at the camera. He was tired and strained but in command. He didn't blink.

"Since two o'clock in the morning, you have been told that I left Haiti. It is not true. I did not leave. The president is here, stronger than ever."

Six million impoverished, hopeful Haitians were shocked. The news rocked the world. It was unimaginable.

Riding to the airport ten hours earlier, Baby Doc had asked a question of his advisor, Colonel Avril. "Must I really leave?"

Fearful for his own safety once Baby Doc was out of power, Prosper Avril suggested that, probably, the President-for-Life could regain control.

Jean-Claude had heard all he needed. He ordered the plane to depart, empty, hurtling over the rooftops.

His motorcade headed back to the palace. Colonel Avril nearly hit another car. To prevent the driver and his female companion from reporting that they had seen Duvalier, a bodyguard machine-gunned the couple to death.

The destruction that had followed the earlier belief that Baby Doc had left did not compare to the violence after the television broadcast. In city after city, for four days, mobs were uncontrollable. Riots occurred day and night. Fires flared, streets were barricaded, and schools and churches were closed.

Enraged protestors took care to spare property belonging to private citizens, but they showed no mercy for cars, homes, buildings, or land owned by the government or Tonton Macoutes.

Many fearful Macoutes were brutally killed. Some committed horrific murders to look invincible. The rest tried to lay low.

Relentless pressure wore Baby Doc down. On February 5, the Duvalier and Bennett families agreed to leave.

But the presidential couple did not intend to go quietly.

Baby Doc had always believed that the Haitian people loved him. Delusional and full of ego, he had never seen the bitterness of the average peasant. But he had witnessed their joy at his false departure. His feelings were hurt.

President-for-Life Jean-Claude Duvalier wanted revenge.

The American and French embassies were happy to help Baby Doc leave. A plane was ordered. Baby Doc complained about being subjected to airport metal detectors, so embassy officials agreed to skip the screening.

A passenger list of thirty-six family members was drawn up. When Michele insisted on bringing all of her artwork, furs, clothing, and jewelry, her luggage allotment increased, and the passenger count decreased. Michele's aging grandparents were two of the twelve names she cut.

As Michele packed, her husband made a list of those who had let him down. Eager for his successor's failure, Baby Doc had his favorite vodou priest purchase two sickly baby boys from a nearby hospital and sacrifice them over the presidential bed.

The First Couple slept comfortably that night in another bedroom.

The next day Jean-Claude consulted his list and drew up a plan for his Macoutes to commit mass murder. With the plan in his pocket, he met with officials, including his successor, General Henri Namphy.

Behind closed doors, talk turned ugly. Baby Doc nearly shot Namphy, but someone grabbed his gun and slapped on handcuffs. Before Michele could scream to alert Tonton Macoutes in the hall, she was punched in the jaw and dropped to the floor, unconscious.

The murder plan stayed in Baby Doc's pocket. Michele nursed her sore jaw. The two accepted their fate and decided to host a midnight champagne party for friends.

It was a nice way to say good-bye.

The flight was to leave at 2:00 in the morning on February 7, 1986. By 2:30 American and French officials were nervous. Other passengers had arrived. The luggage was loaded. But the First Couple was nowhere in sight.

Finally, at 3:30, tipsy army officers, General Namphy, Baby Doc, and Michele appeared. With no screening, the Duvaliers' handguns went unnoticed. At 3:47 the American C-141 cargo plane rumbled down the lone runway, lifted off, and slowly disappeared into the black sky, headed to France.

Below in squalid Port-au-Prince, thousands cheered.

Duvalierism

François Duvalier International Airport was renamed Port-au-Prince International. Avenue Jean-Claude Duvalier became Avenue Jean-Paul II. The grounds of the National Palace were opened to citizens, and the government used only its administrative wing. President Henri Namphy slept at home, not in the presidential bed.

For the common Haitian, the joy of being rid of the Duvaliers was too soon replaced by grim reality. Haiti remained a disaster—with parched soil; poor food; few jobs, schools, and decent homes; and far too much crime.

The Duvaliers were gone, but Duvalierism remained. President Namphy was overwhelmed by his country's problems. The government was still corrupt. Communism rose. Ominous Tonton Macoutes kept too low a profile.

As drug trafficking and political violence increased, the cities were disrupted by insurrections and massacres. United States' officials warned Americans of possible danger when traveling to Haiti.

Possible danger?

Mission travelers never lost sight of the risks of being in the country at the wrong time. Too often, whether initiated by man or climate, "danger" and "Haiti" were synonymous. In 1987 the Windy Cove team cancelled its trip and went to Mexico instead.

A few months earlier, when Pere Albert thanked Keyser Presbyterian for its hospitality during his trip, his letter had ended with a request: "Please don't forget us in your prayer. We are going to organize election. We need a very good leader for Haiti."

A rare bright spot in 1987 was the promise of a free presidential election. There were no political parties, so nearly one hundred candidates vied for the job. Election Day was Sunday, November 29.

Even the visionary Pere Albert could not have predicted the outcome.

Voters, with ballots in their hands and dressed in their Sunday best, lined up in front of churches that doubled as polling stations. Out of nowhere, young Tonton Macoutes appeared, shrieking that their period of hiding was over. Several hundred innocent, would-be voters were murdered.

Namphy's military shut down the election. The nation grieved over this day, which became known as Bloody Sunday.

A new presidential election was scheduled on January 17, 1988. Sensing that the election would be rigged, and fearing for their safety, few of the earlier candidates tried again. Voter turnout was four percent.

The election's winner was Leslie Manigat. Three months later, Henri Namphy's military forced him out of power and regained control of the country.

Jean-Bertrand Aristide

On Sunday morning, September 11, 1988, over a thousand worshippers packed into St. Jean Bosco in Port-au-Prince. During the Roman Catholic mass, a commotion began outside. Angry armed men surrounded the church and began a three-hour assault.

Fleeing congregants received no help from the Haitian Army, though the church was near a military barrack. Port-au-Prince's mayor, a former Tonton Macoute leader, was spotted among the rebels.

More than a dozen people were killed and scores wounded. Before the church was burned to the ground, the priest was evacuated.

His name was Father Jean-Bertrand Aristide.

In 1986 Father Aristide's fiery sermons had helped spark the unrest that led to Jean-Claude Duvalier's overthrow. Aristide had a large following among common Haitians, but he had many political rivals. The Sunday attack was the latest in a half-dozen attempts to kill him.

A week later, when a coup ended Henri Namphy's military rule, a series of temporary presidents took power. Each did all he could to benefit himself before being overthrown and replaced with a new repressive leader.

The pattern of civil unrest continued.

In 1989 Gardner and Frances postponed their Easter visit by a month. When Port-au-Prince settled down in May, the couple retrieved Pere Albert's Land Rover in Léogâne and rode with him to his new Episcopal mountain parish, St. Matthias.

As rural areas generally were during times of turmoil in the cities, the village of Cherident was quiet.

Well, there was that one tumultuous moment at the side of the road when the priest asked Frances to fund seven more schools.

PART II

MOUNTAINS OF SCHOOLS

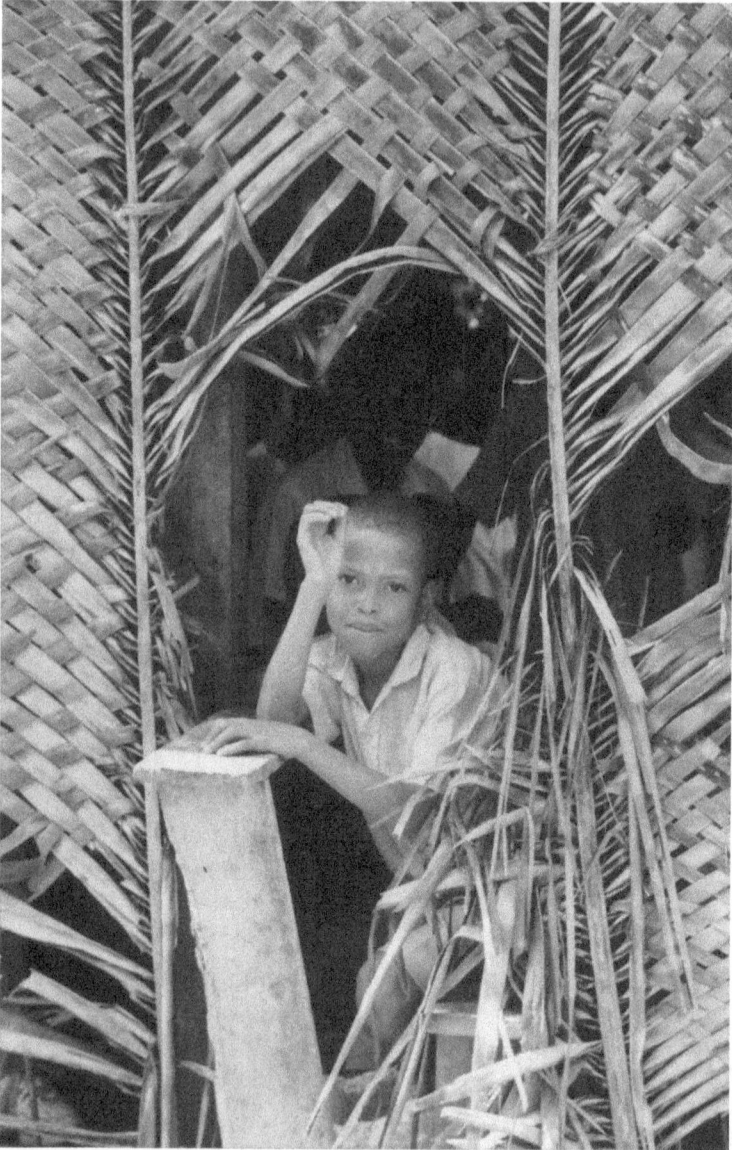

Shelter schools were constructed of sugar cane, woven cornstalks, and leaves from palm and coconut trees. Concrete block schools came later.

Chapter 8

More Schools, New Friends

*Each time a child reads the Bible and learns a trade,
his or her life gains dignity and God is pleased.*
—*Pere Jean-Wilfrid Albert, Cherident, Haiti, 1989*

In January 1989 Bishop Garnier gave a life-changing gift to thousands of impoverished villagers in the mountains. He sent them a feisty, forty-year-old priest who loved the Lord and believed in educating His people.

As priest-in-charge of St. Matthias Parish, Pere Albert had seven churches and fewer than one hundred Christians. He knew this would change. Across his parish, few could read or write. With Frances Landers's help, he would change this too. He prayed daily for Gardner and Frances to "just come and see."

In mid-May, they did.

The couple walked Cherident's dusty road and rode with Pere Albert to his other six villages. The Land Rover lurched across rocks, bounced over ruts, and struggled with nearly impassable streambeds. In each village, children lined up for Frances to photograph. Scrubbed and dressed in fresh clothes, they wanted their chance for scholarships so they could go to school.

Frances never understood how Pere Albert spread the word. How in the world did Haitian parents know, precisely, when she and her camera would arrive in their illiterate community?

Approaching his smallest village up a steep hillside, Pere Albert told Frances that eighty children wanted their pictures taken. The road was so poor that the priest's vehicle could not navigate it.

As Pere Albert turned his car around, Frances saw eighty gaily dressed children across the valley on another mountain. Before the Land Rover finished its descent, the children ran down their mountain and up the next one to meet Frances.

She photographed them on the spot.

Later she said, "These children were asking for the chance to move from darkness into light."

How could Frances not open her heart to all of the deserving children across Pere Albert's new parish home, St. Matthias? Frances brought home rolls and rolls of Kodak film. Her favorite photo finisher supplied slides and three-by-five-inch prints.

At the kitchen table, Frances wrote a thank-you note for each fifty-five dollar scholarship she received. She sorted her prints and tucked a picture of a grateful boy or girl in each card.

After sealing the envelopes for the afternoon mail, Frances put remaining prints in pink boxes and turned her attention to the slides. Her compelling slide show at a women's luncheon in Hot Springs, Arkansas, had prompted a gift of ten thousand dollars.

With the funds, Pere Albert paid workers to turn cornstalks and palm leaves into loosely woven walls. The villagers lay sugar cane roofs across the top. Carpenters made benches and desks for the shelter schools—a misnomer during the too-short rainy season when they provided no shelter at all.

Frances needed two thousand scholarships to pay the teachers Pere Albert had hired. A summertime letter updated her donors.

> *Our schools will include our Mercery School that we have supported for eight years, the three schools Pere Albert opened January 1, 1989, with money we took in November, and seven schools we hope to start at each of the mission churches. Does this seem impossible? I don't think so!*

To keep her message uncluttered, Frances did not explain that others, whom she did not know, funded one of "the three schools" near Léogâne. If she could provide scholarships for Jean-Jean's children, she was happy to help.

Two thousand scholarships totaled more than one hundred thousand dollars.

Frances took a deep breath and then mustered faith that approximated Pere Albert's. She booked speaking engagements, which she called "talks," in nearby states. She always paid her own expenses.

Her enthusiasm whenever she "talked" was contagious. So was her emphatic point that one hundred percent of Haiti Fund contributions would go directly to the work. The message, "No administrative expenses are deducted from your gift," was prominent in Frances's talks, letters, and, soon, fundraising materials.

A little brochure was indeed needed. Medical Benevolence Foundation offered to create one for Frances. It explained, "Mrs. Landers devotes most of her time raising support for the children. 'If Keith McCaffety hadn't come to our church, I'd probably be sitting in a room somewhere, rocking and staring at the wall!' Instead, she speaks to a different group nearly every week and spends hours writing letters, telephoning, and sending photos from the pink boxes on her kitchen table."

Frances exceeded her fundraising goal of one hundred ten thousand dollars.

In his seven villages, Pere Albert hired teachers and enrolled at least one child from each family. He told parents that once girls and boys started primary school, they would be guaranteed enrollment until they finished their sixth year. The priest wanted families to pay a little something, but those who could afford nothing were not turned away.

Pere Albert tested every child for placement at the right level. For example, twelve-year-old Nicolas Michael, who had had six years of ineffective schooling, was placed in Cherident's third grade.

When Haiti's 1989–1990 school year began, unmatched excitement filled the villages of Cherident, Trouin, Duny, Labiche, Moreau, Bois-neuf, and Bejin. Children in the mountains joined those in Mercery, Collin, La Colline, and Jean-Jean on a journey they had never imagined possible.

Two thousand children were in school.

During her latter days, Goldie Frances Campbell quietly made out her will and left her modest estate to her church, First Presbyterian of Sand Springs, Oklahoma.

In 1987 Goldie passed away. Her will directed First Presbyterian to fund global projects that helped children. The church selected ministries in Egypt and Africa.

Two years later, those overseeing the Campbell Trust met Frances Landers. Impressed with her dedication to educate Haiti's children, they added a third ministry: St. Matthias Parish. With a sizable donation that Pere Albert received from Goldie's estate, he began replacing the shelter schools with concrete block buildings.

Over the years, the Campbell Trust has donated generously to Pere Albert's children. Many in the congregation have visited the mountains. Reverend Tom Litteer shared his church's love of Haiti and developed deep friendships with Pere Albert and Frances.

Nine months after Pere Albert arrived in Grande Colline, his seven villages had schools. His ministry was unmistakably positive. But the villages around Léogâne felt the effects of his transfer to the mountains.

By early 1990 the school in Collin was closed. Frances sent money for the school in La Colline. The priest, Pere Racine, did not reply. Nor could she get information about Mercery's school.

Frances was frustrated.

In April she and Gardner visited retired missionaries Harvey and Doris Ann Musser in Michigan. Frances asked, "How can I get information from Pere Racine?"

"Contact Fran Hobbs," Harvey said. "Her church, Windy Cove, supports a little school in nearby Jean-Jean, also in Pere Racine's parish."

Frances wrote Fran and explained that Pere Racine did not respond to her letters. She asked if Fran had the same experience, and ended:

> *We made our last trip to Haiti in May '89 and since Gardner has retired, I believe my time can be better spent speaking at churches. Pere Albert needs the money I raise more than he needs me.*

She was wrong. She would return to Haiti thirty times.

Fran and Frances did not resolve communication problems with Pere Racine, but with this letter, the two women began a twenty-year friendship.

One morning Frances took a call from Leonard Gross of Emmanuel Episcopal in Keyser, West Virginia. Reverend Gross had learned that Frances worked with Pere Albert. He told her he had sent the priest a donation.

"If you told Pere Albert to buy a sow with part of the money, you can be sure that's exactly what he did," Frances said.

Reverend Gross followed up with another donation. Frances had a new ministry partner.

Another partner, Harriet Prichard from Apple Valley, California, was invaluable to Frances's fundraising.

Ten years earlier, Harriet had founded Alternative Gifts International, a nonprofit that helped people buy "authentic gifts" for others. Harriet selected projects that improved the lives of impoverished people worldwide and prepared an annual catalog of gift choices.

At Alternative Gift Markets, people purchased cows, chickens, goats, medical supplies, and more for family and friends. Those being honored received cards explaining that the gifts were given in their names.

When Harriet learned of Pere Albert's work in Haiti's mountains, she selected Frances's school scholarships for her 1989–1990 catalog.

On July 1, 1990, Windy Cove's team of eleven headed to Haiti. Flo Boggs and Fran Hobbs were on this trip, as were Harvey Musser and his brother Marshall. It was Harvey's first trip to Haiti since he and Doris Ann had left Sainte Croix Hospital years earlier. He was eager to travel to Grande Colline to visit his good friend Pere Albert.

The team did its usual work at the hospital and took a day trip to Cherident. On the drive, Flo thought again about the nine-by-twelve-inch plaque on the guesthouse wall.

She said, "Tell me about Dr. and Mrs. Gardner Landers."

Fran spoke first. "A few months ago, I had a letter from Frances Landers. She sounds like a wonderful woman."

Harvey said, "She is. Flo, you ought to call Frances when you get home. I think you and she are on the same wavelength. You have a lot in common. You're both Presbyterian. You each have three sons. Gardner was an ophthalmologist, and Harry is an optometrist."

Marshall added, "I'll give you her phone number when we get home."

In Haiti, Frances and Flo walked the same roads and sat in the same humble churches. They were each entranced by the beautiful Haitian children and their hardworking parents. The women both admired Pere Albert and routinely asked people to give them money to send to him.

But Frances and Flo did not know each other.

For months Frances's telephone number was on Flo's desk. Finally, on November 14, 1990, the phone in El Dorado rang. The conversation was delightful. Flo hung up, wondering why it had taken five years to get to know this gracious woman. Frances felt that she had known Flo for years.

The next day, Frances sent her new friend Flo a copy of a letter to Marshall Musser. Frances had written to Marshall,

> *It was so nice to hear that Old Stone and Windy Cove are planning to undertake a project for Pere Albert. I think our first need is for facilities where people can stay. Many would like to go when school is in session. If we expect this work to continue, we need to encourage teams to go and "see what God has done."*

Frances told Marshall about Pere Albert's seven schools, his desire to hire a nurse, and his need for new tires. The inhospitable roads and streambeds in Grande Colline chewed through tires within six months. Frances mentioned that she had met Flo Boggs by phone the previous day.

On Flo's copy of the letter, Frances penned a note.

To Flo - I enjoyed our telephone visit. I am going to send you a copy of my Christmas project.

The Christmas project was a fundraiser modeled after Harriet Prichard's Alternative Gift Markets. Donors could give a school scholarship and daily lunch (fifty-five dollars), a goat (twenty dollars), a school uniform (seven), a pair of shoes (six), or a Bible (four). Three dollars provided a Christmas gift for a child.

The Christmas project illustrated both the depth of need among Pere Albert's people and the breadth of Frances's volunteer job.

Always looking for every gentle angle to raise money, Frances added these sentences to the order form: "Would you like extra copies of this letter? How many?"

Frances kept track of each dollar. She sent donors a child's photograph for each scholarship. She mailed the precise quantity of extra order forms that were requested. Her kitchen table was piled high, and her hours "on the job" were many.

School buildings, scholarships, uniforms, Bibles, meal programs, goats, shoes, Christmas presents, medicine, a nurse's salary, a new set of tires: there was no end.

Frances shook her head at the irony. On that day at the side of the road, she had balked when *all* Pere Albert had asked for was seven more schools.

Year to year, Frances better understood the intertwined needs of the Haitian people: faith, education, medical care, food, clean water, shelter, clothing, and income. Yet more than once she felt ill-equipped to meet Pere Albert's massive expectations for St. Matthias Parish.

And the priest had not yet been there two years.

Chapter 9

Penmanship Matters

She'd never turn down a chance to show her slides and tell about Haiti.
Then she wrote those beautiful notes when she got back.
—Flo Boggs, Keyser, West Virginia, 2012

Unscarred by her experience as a young teacher receiving love notes from the preacher's son, Frances wrote tens of thousands of letters during her life. In one instance, a hand-addressed envelope was enough to begin a two-and-a-half-decade friendship.

In 1977 after Frances toured the Presbyterian-funded trade school in Port-au-Prince with missionary Rhine Fecho, she wrote him a thank-you letter. A few weeks later, with the unopened letter in his hand, Rhine walked into Pere Jean Monique Bruno's office. Pere Bruno was priest-in-charge of an Episcopal campus in Haiti's northern city of Cap-Haitien. The campus included a second vocational school sponsored by Presbyterians.

Rhine had unhappy news for Pere Bruno. It was the convention of the Presbyterian Church to withdraw funding after mission schools were up and running and to turn monetary responsibility over to the Episcopal Church of Haiti.

The time had come. Pere Bruno needed to seek funds elsewhere.

Rhine knew that he needed to have the uncomfortable conversation with the priest before he could enjoy reading the letter from his new friend, Mrs. Landers. But as he approached Pere Bruno's desk, the nervous Rhine distracted himself by opening the letter from Arkansas. He tossed the empty envelope into the wastebasket.

Pere Bruno was devastated at losing funding. He placed his head in his hands to pray. In the silence, Rhine left the room. As Pere Bruno raised his head, his eyes looked to the wastebasket. He reached down, picked up the empty envelope, and read the return address: Frances Landers, 1801 West Block Street, El Dorado, Arkansas.

Pere Bruno had no idea who this was, but he had the feeling that this was a person he should contact. When I received his letter I answered it immediately. I enclosed a modest check. That was the beginning of a lifelong friendship.

Pere Bruno had many connections in the United States who gave him financial support. But he was one of thousands influenced by Frances's letters.

She kept in touch with family, friends, pastors, and missionaries. She stayed connected with students and young people from Sunday school, congratulating them on life's triumphs and helping them through difficulties.

Once Haiti entered Frances's life, she spent hours writing letters nearly every day that she wasn't traveling. She answered inquiries, shared news, solicited donations, and offered support. When writing to a friend, Frances "thought out loud" and developed her ideas. And believing that each person who gave money should hear from her directly, she wrote thousands of notes of thanks.

Through pens and stationery, little Haitian note cards, typewriter ribbons and paper, envelopes and stamps, volunteer helpers, a fax machine in her seventies, a computer in her eighties, and always a rather messy address book, Frances's network of Haiti Fund supporters grew and grew.

People across the United States and Haiti smiled at Frances's distinctive handwriting when their mail arrived, knowing they were in for a treat. Her notes and letters, always on unlined paper, fascinated people by both their content and appearance. She selected her stationery with care. For thank-you notes, she preferred crisp white cards with hand-drawn Haitian art. Often her message included an explanation of the image or the artist.

Her written words matched her friendly and confident countenance: shining eyes with a bit of a twinkle and a dash of mischief, and a warm smile.

Not ornamental but bold and strong, her handwritten words were well spaced and decisive, straight up and down, nearly always in black ink. A blend of printing and cursive, most letters in any given word stood alone, not connected as in true script.

A handwritten letter from Frances conjured the image of perfect posture. If ever someone's handwriting had sit-up-straight, shoulders-back, chin-lifted posture, it would be hers.

With one look at the self-confidence of Frances's writing, who would not want to donate to the Haiti Fund?

Here are snippets from Frances's letters:

> *We have gone to Wilmington, NC, Asheville, NC, and Jackson, Michigan, ... also Chattanooga. These were all plane trips and we drive to Oklahoma, Texas, Louisiana, and Mississippi. I realize I am not going to be able to keep this up forever, but I can't retire now!!*

> *It is Tuesday, March 11. I am starting my day by writing you random information. During the day, I think of a dozen things I need to tell you...... Gardner has just informed me that this is WEDNESDAY, March 11. I am glad this 82-year-old has an extra day to get things done.*

> *Let's go back to Haiti ... that was so much fun!!*

> *I have used up my space without really thanking you for EVERYTHING ... but, Thanks ...*

Capital letters mirrored Frances's verbal elongation of certain words. Words underlined once or twice demanded to be read with extra emphasis. Frances would add three underscores when she really wanted to make her point. She was extravagant with exclamation marks.

She was also generous with those little dots that English majors call an ellipsis. In *The New Oxford Guide to Writing*, author Thomas Kane described the ellipsis as "a series of three dots, or, under certain conditions, four. It is never five or six or any other number."

It is evident that Frances did not read Kane's book.

That's okay. Sometimes enthusiasm trumps literary rules.

Frances's correspondence was impeccably neat. Her work surface was not. The kitchen table was covered, layers deep, and piled high with letters to read, checks to deposit, slides to sort, notes to write, photos to enclose, calendars to update, trips to schedule.

Some mornings, Frances hardly knew where to start.

But she was driven by the certainty that Pere Albert, in the same central time zone as El Dorado, had been up for hours.

She pulled out the chair at the kitchen table, sat down, and cleared a spot just large enough for some envelopes, note cards, her address book, and a cup of coffee. She rummaged underneath a stack of letters and found her pen.

First up was thanking donors.

Frances reached for a stack of small white envelopes and addressed them one by one. Then she wrote the accompanying notes, two rarely the same, and selected the pictures to include.

To augment the photographs she took in Haiti, Frances often asked others, in advance of their trips, to take pictures of charming boys and girls, brimming classrooms, teachers, and schools under construction. She was thrilled to receive negatives and prints for her pink photo boxes.

Frances was careful not to imply that a donor had sponsored a particular child. But a picture of a representative child was important, and she spent a lot of time looking through her pink boxes for darling faces.

When supporters funded classrooms or entire schools, Frances went to extra effort to send photos of children from that specific village.

There were a few Haiti Fund donors who expected to know the first and last names of their sponsored children as well as their levels in school. Frances would dig deeper on her kitchen table, find an enrollment roster she'd receive on occasion from Pere Albert, select a random child's name, and write it in ink on the back of a photo.

"It's the best I can do," Frances told friends. "After all, God knows these children's names."

She set aside the thank-you notes, stamped and sealed. Satisfied, she sipped her coffee. Caught up, she rewarded herself with newsy letters to family and friends. A long letter was nearly as good as a personal conversation.

Frances's productivity was amazing. Oh, there were a few slipups. She might forget to date her letters. She'd repeat a story, unsure if she'd already told it. Often, at the end of a two-page letter, she told the recipient she knew she had forgotten to mention *something*.

There was always next time.

Her enthusiasm bounded off the paper—a sort of invisible, contagious challenge to join the fun of educating Pere Albert's kids. By the hundreds—and then thousands—individuals, churches, and organizations across the United States joined in.

As she became busier, Frances used her typewriter as often as she wrote letters by hand. But she still wasn't happy with her speed.

"I should have invested in a computer with a printer and word processor many years ago," Frances wrote to Flo Boggs in 1992. "There is a limit to how much one person can do at the kitchen table!"

Ten years later, Frances gave in.

Who would believe that at 85, I got a computer? I wrote all day yesterday and was so tired my eyes were "swimming". I will confess that I really enjoy writing my own letters. I feel that I sometimes make them too personal, but I believe some of my monthly donors give to receive my letter. There are people who never receive a personal note of any kind.

In the latter half of her eighties, Frances became proficient with e-mail and appreciated the ability to send messages to multiple people. When she was younger, she thought nothing of driving to First Presbyterian to make photocopies of letters. In her later years, no longer driving, and conscious of making the most of every healthy day, Frances was pragmatic.

"I do what I can do."

Regardless of whether Frances wrote or typed her letters, whether they were stamped and mailed, faxed, e-mailed, or sent by computer, they closed with a sentiment such as, "Faithfully" or "Blessings" or "I appreciate you." As relationships deepened, she would say, "With love" or "I love you."

Then she ended each letter with her signature in stout black ink. Sometimes she printed her name with straight, strong vertical letters. But generally her signature was an elegant script, beginning with a large, confident, flowing *F* and ending in an equally sweeping, graceful, encouraging tail off of the *s*.

Frances was devoted to giving hope to the children in the mountains of Haiti. Her letters, personal and delightful, convinced each supporter that he or she was indispensible to the mission.

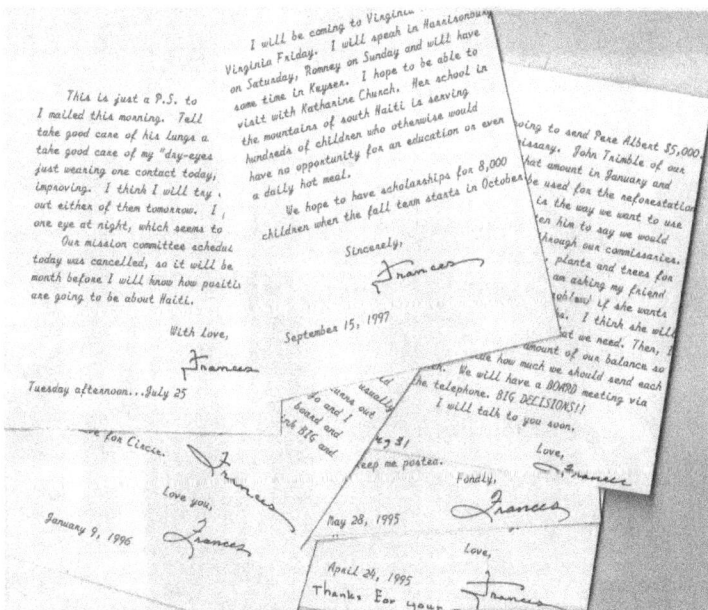

> I want to thank you very much for that. We appreciate that very much and we want to thank you again. What you have just done is for me a response to God's love when through His Son, He came to share with us the eternal life, the joy and the glory of His kingdom. I believe that through us God brings His love to those kids who experience it very soon. Praise the Lord for giving us the opportunity to manage well what He gives us and helping us to pass it onto those who don't yet meet Him so that they may taste Him and come to Him.

Written by Pere Jean-Wilfrid Albert, 1990.

> I found this card in a gift shop and thought it might be an idea for a Haiti card. If I could get an artist to do a black and white of a child, using the scripture — or a Haitian scene. I'm going to work on this when I get home.

Written by Frances Landers, 1992.

Chapter 10

Halfway to Heaven

There was never a time that
Pere Albert did not feel God's hand guiding this work.
—*Frances Landers, El Dorado, Arkansas, 1999*

Paper was scarce in the mountains. In his letters, Pere Albert fit twenty-five lines or more on a page. Like Frances, the priest used unlined paper and black ink, his pen having a very fine point. Unlike Frances, whose lines were perfectly straight across the page, his angled slightly uphill.

Pere Albert's handwriting was interesting. In the first word of each sentence, he separated the initial capital letter from the lowercase ones that followed. His script was fluid, like his thoughts. Rarely did he cross out phrases or choose his words again. If he noticed a misspelling, he inked over the errant word again and again before rewriting it correctly. When he had additional thoughts after ending his letter, which was often, the postscript beneath his name might contain several handwritten lines, small and close together.

Two years into his ministry in St. Matthias Parish, Pere Albert wrote Frances a five-page letter, illustrating his growing dependence on her. Most of the Americans who were fortunate to spend time with this giant of a man never saw this letter. But they heard him speak. Like Frances's voice, his ranged the musical scale, though an octave lower. Haitian male voices are deep and deliberate, lively and lyrical.

His "God" was pronounced "Gawd" and "good" was "gud."

And Pere Albert *was* good. Good at dreaming big. Good at keeping track of details and his budget, though he always wanted it larger. Good at telling it like it was. Good at giving God the glory, accentuating his message by pointing his long index finger what seemed to be halfway to heaven.

The priest was best at making those who worked with him want to do more. Frances always wanted to do more. Though she tried mightily to keep her fundraising limited to the elementary education of boys and girls, needs were vast in Haiti, and Pere Albert was *very* good at pointing this out.

Haiti January 14 / 1991

Dear Mrs. Frances,

Don't you just feel the Hand of God in your work, don't you? He wants to work with us. I am very pleased of that. God agrees with what we do, that is good for all of us. I have received before the trouble in Port-au-Prince the check of $3.000 for the nurse salary for one year and the $1.000 for tires. Thank you very much. I am going to write Pastor Charles Brown and our dear church of El Dorado. At any rate, I will not forget in my life how God makes miracles through you if we consider all that He has already realized through us.

God will remember you and all those who sent the $1.000 for tires. I can tell you that car is for God's work. We keep on doing pastoral work with it such as: going from villages to villages through mountains and bad roads to preach the gospel; taking people seriously sick to hospital and other emergency. I hope that this will be an encouragement for all those who contributed to send the gift.

I am also happy to see that thanks to God through you, we are able now to have a full time nurse in our mountain area. I thank you very much for all that you do with the help of God to help us realize that project. I have a black and white film to take pictures of the nurse and some patients to send to our church and explain the need. That will take some time until I finish the film before I mail it. Here is a plan of our health care project through all the villages where we can reach by car.

Medical care in the mountains was virtually nonexistent. Pere Albert was deeply concerned about this. He knew that a nurse was an important first step in developing improved health care for his villagers. He wanted the nurse to work in Cherident three days a week. Twice a week she would rotate among St. Matthias's six other villages.

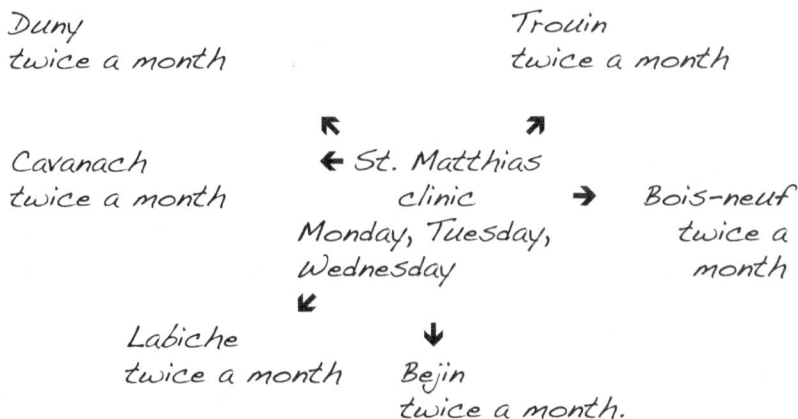

Duny
twice a month

Trouin
twice a month

Cavanach
twice a month

↖ ↗

← *St. Matthias*
clinic
Monday, Tuesday,
Wednesday

↙

→ *Bois-neuf*
twice a
month

Labiche
twice a month

↓

Bejin
twice a month.

As Pere Albert wrote out the nurse's schedule, he evidently concluded with Bejin. This village was the only one with a closing period. "Bejin twice a month." Period.

End of plan. Period.

"Frances," Pere Albert's voice boomed out through his hand-drawn health-care plan, "keep the nurse funded." Period.

The period, punctuating Pere Albert's determination, was not lost on Frances. She had worked with him for twelve years. She was used to his insistence and insatiable drive to better the lives of his people. Frances would make certain that the nurse was funded.

Pere Albert's letter continued—first about health care.

As you foresee it, we need to buy some medicine and supplies to start. According to a list I have received from the nurse, the estimation is about $1.500. If you have some possibility to help in this way, we will use it from the money we have for the nurse salary and you will replace it if possible.

People in mountains are so poor that we can't sell them the medicine we purchase in Port-au-Prince at the price we bought them. We are studying a way to receive something from them about $1.00 per patient. As you know, some of them will not be able to afford but we will not turn thanks to God anyone away. We will find thanks to Him a way *to spread His love. That contribution of $1.00 will permit us to keep the clinic running for some time.*

This is great, isn't it? The gift from Sand Springs Presb. Church. I am going to send them a thank-you note but I want first to wait for Old Stone Presb. Church to see if they are really engaged to build the clinic for us. They want to have an authorization from the bishop before starting. As you know, when the bishop has already approved a project he is not going to approve it again. I have seen him about that, he said that he would not permit me to build anything on the church land if he didn't approve it. I have already written Marshall about that. In the case where they will not go forward, we may use if you want the Sand Springs Presb. Church gift to build the clinic even in small size. If Old Stone Presb. Church decides to build the clinic we can use the gift to build 5 class rooms in Bejin where we have now 200 kids under a shelter made of palm tree and covered by coconut tree leaves. Next time, I will send a picture of that school to you.

Next, he wrote about the schools in Moreau and Bejin.

As I told you, in Moreau we need to build 3 class rooms. The estimation will be about $11.000. Musser agrees to send the balance for boss Alexis. You have already sent $4.000 for Moreau, the balance to send is $6.000 plus $650 for boss Alexis' salary. Total U.S. $6.650 or in Haitian money $15.600.

Now in Port-au-Prince and some other towns in Haiti schools are not in session. In mountains where thanks be to God we have peaceful life, we keep working because kids there are really late. We have thanks to God our budject on hand, we have no way to lose time.

When I am convinced that Old Stone Presb. Church will build the clinic, I will send a thank-you note to Sand Springs and tell them their gift will be used to build 5 class rooms at Moreau. I know that according to your last letter, we can have the money to finish the school at Moreau;

that means that we will have on balance $5.000 that we can use to build 5 class rooms at Bejin. I am not going to mention to them the village of Bejin but I will talk to them about Moreau because you have made the request on Moreau.

Regarding the wedding rings …

The rings you send are perfect. I can say that I have more than what I expect. As you know, I don't need expensive things but just something to help people to get married and be able to receive Holy Communion. They are nice but they are too small. Ladies in the mountains have big fingers. You may send size 7 and 8. That will be good if you can find them in a way where we can open them like that one I have sent to you. What you have just sent are better but I am afraid of having them too small or too big. Try to send some like size 7 and 8 so that I may try them on some fingers.

Pere Albert had some other needs too.

As I told you, Boss Alexis will be hired to build the school at Moreau. God approves what we do, this is why He is with you to help people open their heart to do His will. We want to educate our people and if we can use the balance of $5.000 to build five class rooms at Bejin, we will have to build three or four class rooms at Bois-neuf, the place where we turned around because was so bad and the kids came to you to have their picture taken. We would like the $3.000 you have just received to build 3 class rooms there. We need also 3 class rooms at Cherident because of kindergarten school. We have now 110 kids in kindergarten. Now people in mountain have to send their kids at 3 years old at school. I want to tell you also that before we have that kindergarten school, it didn't exist in our area. This year we have 425 kids at St. Matthias school. In spite of 4 new rooms we have, we still have 3 classes in the church building. We need 3 more class rooms. I would like to use the $1.000 you and Dr. Gardner gave and the ones *given by Mr. and Mrs. Chester Wood, and you have some opportunity to add $1.000, that will be an amount of $3.000 to build 3 more class rooms in Cherident. You may send a plaque for us to fix on your room. When we finish that phase, we will be able to pass on to another one. I am going to write all the people you mention in your letter.*

God loves you and more again because you and your dear husband gave your life to Him like He has given you your life. Please, when you have time read Matthew 19:27-29.

Keep contact with Him and keep on working for Him.

He will be with you forever.

Shalom!

Your son
Jean-Wilfrid Albert

Frances finished reading the letter, exhausted. But she opened her Bible to the nineteenth chapter of Matthew and read verses twenty-seven through twenty-nine. "Then Peter said in reply, 'Look, we have left everything and followed you. What then will we have?' Jesus said to them, 'Truly I tell you, at the renewal of all things, when the Son of Man is seated on the throne of his glory, you who have followed me will also sit on twelve thrones, judging the twelve tribes of Israel. And everyone who has left houses or brothers or sisters or father or mother or children or fields, for my name's sake, will receive a hundredfold, and will inherit eternal life.'"

Two years earlier, Pere Albert "left everything" in Léogâne to follow Him to the mountains of Grande Colline.

Frances did, in essence, go to the mountains with Pere Albert, following him who followed the Lord.

She was determined to keep giving talks at churches like Sand Springs in Oklahoma and Old Stone in West Virginia so Pere Albert could build primary schools. She would fund the construction boss and add classrooms in the schools in Moreau, Bejin, Bois-neuf, and Cherident (where she would also decide on wording for a plaque). She would keep pace with the children's progress to know when to build secondary schools. She would raise money for Pere Albert's vehicle and tires and medicine.

She would keep the nurse funded.

Oh, and yes, Frances needed to remember that ladies have big fingers in the mountains.

"Let me get this straight," Frances said to Pere Albert.
"You want how many more schools?"

Frances funded a nurse in Cherident, the first step toward improving
medical care in the mountains.

Chapter 11

Apart at the Seams, Together at the Airport

The presence of each mission team is a gift of hope and love.
—Layton Evans, Fort Defiance, Virginia, 1990

On December 16, 1990, four weeks before Pere Albert wrote his lengthy letter to Frances, seventy percent of Haiti's voters cast ballots for Father Jean-Bertrand Aristide.

In February 1991 President Aristide began his term. The people expected him to bring the Haitian Army under civilian rule. They expected the army to support democracy. They expected progress.

Eight months later, President Aristide would be gone.

Frances prayed for Haiti's government, but she did not have time to worry about it. She was working harder than ever, supporting that incredible, demanding priest whose index finger reached halfway to heaven.

Pere Albert wanted a gristmill in the village of Labiche to grind corn to send to market. He billed the twenty-three-thousand-dollar project as an "opportunity." Within a month Frances raised more than half.

Then there was Pere Albert's vehicle. The last day of September 1991, Frances wrote Flo Boggs, saying, "The Land Rover has 'died.'" Frances began to raise funds for a replacement.

On October 1 the Haitian Army deposed President Aristide. His supporters rioted. The military killed hundreds. Diplomats from the United States, France, and Venezuela whisked Aristide out of the country.

General Raoul Cédras, who had led the coup, sat down in the empty presidential chair. His regime increased drug smuggling and violence. The US Coast Guard intercepted forty thousand Haitians trying to flee the country in unsafe little boats. Hundreds drowned.

When Cédras refused to negotiate Aristide's return to power, the United Nations authorized a trade embargo against Haiti. The result? Three years of crises, crippling shortages, and inflationary prices that worsened the already difficult and dangerous day-to-day lives of ordinary Haitians.

Frances's Haiti Fund paid for a postal account in Pere Albert's name at Lynx Air International in Fort Lauderdale, Florida. His American friends sent letters, checks, and packages to Lynx Air. The service flew across the Caribbean Sea to Port-au-Prince.

Even during peaceful times, getting money safely into the priest's hands was a big concern for Frances. Each month Pere Albert made the hours-long trip down the mountains of Grande Colline to pick up mail and go to the bank. He exchanged Frances's checks for Haitian gourdes to pay for his teachers, principals, nurse, laborers, medicine, materials, and tires.

Every time Pere Albert walked out of the bank in the slum suburb of Carrefour, tens of thousands of dollars hidden discreetly out of sight, he ran a risk of being followed and robbed. Each time he said a prayer.

The Lord kept him safe, month after month and year after year.

For several weeks after President Aristide was forced from the country, Lynx Air suspended mail delivery. In midfall of 1991, flights resumed. This was good news for Frances. The gristmill was funded, and she had a check for Pere Albert.

And there was a check for teachers' salaries. For this, Frances had to work a little harder, because Pere Albert had doubled his Episcopal villages from seven to fourteen. No wonder the Land Rover had died.

Pere Albert asked Frances for seven more shelter schools. Anticipating that she would say yes, he enrolled three thousand children.

Political unrest still disrupted Haiti's cities, delaying the start of the school year. Pere Albert hoped his fourteen schools would open by November first. By the grace of God, they did.

Across Haiti, food prices were high, and gas was twelve dollars a gallon.

"We need to get this embargo lifted," Frances said to Gardner. "I wouldn't feel safe traveling to Haiti right now." Gardner felt the same way.

So did Pere Albert. "I agree with you to tell people not to go into Haiti while being under the embargo. There is no way to preserve anything because there is no kerosene, no propane gas."

The embargo slowed completion of the Labiche gristmill. But Pere Albert already had a new idea: an oven in Cherident to "bake Haitian bread." He itemized for Frances the cost of the oven, its housing, building materials, the salary of the construction boss, and a diesel motor for the machine that prepared "the paste."

Frances sighed, as she always did after reading a letter from the priest. An oven? Paste? She assumed he meant dough. She sighed again. If he wanted an oven, so did she.

Pere Albert ended his long letter with a quizzical comment. "It seems that the one who is going to be the next Bishop will be one of yours."

Frances was aware that Bishop Garnier would retire within two years. She had heard that Pere Bruno, her friend in Cap-Haitien, wanted to be a candidate. He must be the one Pere Albert meant.

In mid-March Pere Bruno wrote Frances. He had been in a terrible automobile accident that killed five. Spared with minor injuries, Pere Bruno believed that God had a purpose for him as Haiti's next Episcopal bishop.

The embargo was in its seventh month. Flo wrote to her West Virginia Senator, Robert Byrd.

"I am increasingly distressed," Flo said, "by the effect of the embargo on the poorest Haitians. My friends are hungry."

Senator Byrd sent a sympathetic reply and enclosed a white paper: *Haiti: Prospects for Democracy and U.S. Policy Concerns.* The document offered no easy solution. The American government wanted President Aristide returned to power but was unsure this could be done, given Haiti's propensity for violence.

The United States Senate recognized the devastating economic impact the embargo was dealing Haiti and was exploring options. Military intervention was its last. One specialist predicted it would take twenty-five thousand American troops three years to establish control and security in Haiti.

The trade embargo continued, as did the violence.

In April 1992 Gardner developed a blood clot in one lung. To care for him, Frances stopped traveling for a few weeks. She continued fundraising through letters and phone calls.

The Church of the Good Shepherd in Lake Charles, Louisiana, wanted to fund a cinder block school in Bejin. At a cost of a thousand dollars per room, Good Shepherd sent Frances eight thousand dollars.

Pere Albert oversaw the school's construction and then went to a neighboring village with a vodou temple. Before long he had converted the entire village to Christianity. The temple came down.

Frances would say, "Pere Albert would go right up to the vodou priests, put his arm around them, and tell them, 'I just want you to know that God loves you. I just don't want you to forget that.' Pere Albert didn't hesitate to talk to anyone about the love of the Lord."

In late spring of 1992, local workers finished another shelter school, Pere Albert's fifteenth, in the newly converted village.

Katharine Church, ninety, had been the church organist at Keyser Presbyterian for fifty-three years. She listened with interest to Flo Boggs's stories of Pere Albert.

To honor her late husband Ernest, Mrs. Church decided to build a ten-room school. Frances asked Pere Albert where he would like it built. He chose a very remote location, as Frances explained to Flo.

> *He would like to build it at La Brezilienne, a village two hours beyond La Vallee. There is nothing in this village. I assume they have again extended the border of St. Matthias Parish to include this village, just as they did for La Vallee. Kind of like God's arms!!*

As Bishop Garnier expanded Pere Albert's parish again and again, Frances kept pace, raising money for his needs.

Frances also looked to Pere Albert before sending money for her original schools in Mercery, Collin, and La Colline. If Pere Albert had confidence in the current priests-in-charge, he would recommend the appropriate budgets.

Three months earlier, Pere Albert had proposed the oven in Cherident. Interest in the project increased when Frances began referring to the oven as "the bakery." Donations came in and construction began.

The priest had another idea for Cherident: a commissary. This structure, with a good lock, would house bulk quantities of rice, beans, and other staples for village women to purchase at a good price and then resell for a very modest profit. In May 1992 First Presbyterian in Shreveport, Louisiana, sent Frances eight thousand dollars for the commissary. She sent the money to Pere Albert, who stretched the donation to complete both the commissary and the bakery.

Over the years, Pere Albert did a lot of stretching. Frances would send him funds for one school, and beyond her understanding, he would construct two. Gradually, Frances and those closest to her realized that Pere Albert was a planter. His expansive vision permitted him to cut corners on construction in one village in order to extend God's reach to another.

Gardner's lung recovered. Then Frances took her turn being under the weather, which she described to Flo and Harry.

> *Can you believe that the QUEEN had to go to the hospital a few days last week? I am sure it was a reaction to medication … they gave me antibiotics … then decided to give me my last hepatitis shot when I went for a lung X-ray to rule out pneumonia. I guess I had too much "stuff" in me and my head nearly fell off … An IV and shot fixed me up and I returned home Thursday (in on Tuesday). All is well and I am going to Texarkana tomorrow night and jar them out of a million dollars!!*

She did not come home with a million dollars. But she had her health and zest for her work, though the latter was about to be tested.

Frances had long believed that the mission board of the Presbyterian Church (USA) in Louisville, Kentucky, was jealous of its ministry partner, Medical Benevolence Foundation, in suburban Houston. She called it "utter nonsense."

"Why doesn't the mission board just respect the good work that MBF does?" Frances asked Gardner. "I've tried to get those on the mission board interested in Pere Albert's schools, but they aren't."

Frances was aware that hers was the only nonmedical ministry that MBF sponsored, through an Adopt-a-Child account. She was grateful that donors could give either directly to her Haiti Fund or through MBF. Soon there would be a third option: her schools would be back in Harriet Prichard's next *Alternative Gift* catalog.

In early July 1992 a mission board leader told Frances to stop sending money directly to Pere Albert. Frances was stunned as she read a letter instructing her to send donations to the mission board in Louisville. Its staff would wire the money to an Episcopal Haitian account at a New York bank to be further wired to Bishop Garnier in Port-au-Prince. He would (somehow) connect with Pere Albert, who was hours away in the mountains with no telephone, and (somehow) get him the money. Each month.

"Ridiculous," Frances said to Gardner, waving the letter.

The mission board told Frances that the Presbyterian Church needed to honor its partnership with the Episcopal Church of Haiti. This included ensuring that the bishop knew about all funds raised for his diocese.

Separately, the mission board asked Ed Stein, MBF's new executive director, to stop being a conduit for Frances and to send to it all accrued Adopt-a-Child funds.

Frances hadn't been this angry since Pere Albert had been banished to the mountains without his Land Rover three years earlier.

Her hand shook as she telephoned MBF's office. Ed was out of the country, but he would call her soon.

Impatient, Frances wrote the mission board a fiery reply. Across two pages she gave examples of donations that had not reached their intended destination because of church bureaucracy.

Frances also itemized those who would not donate to Haiti through the Presbyterian Church: Rotarians, Kiwanis, Baptists, Methodists, and Catholics. Her list was long. Frances talked about big gifts. Small gifts. Matching gifts.

She worked herself into a literary frenzy. On page three she paused, collected herself, and took control of her pen.

> *I am not knowledgeable to understand sending money by wire to New York to be transferred to Haiti, but it would seem to me there would be a great possibility for error. The Bishop gave us permission to send scholarship money direct to Pere Albert.*

> *I request that the balance in the Adopt-a-Child account of MBF be transferred to the Haiti Fund. I have a deep interest in its use. I plan for the money to open our schools in October, giving 3,000 children the opportunity for an education and providing them with nourishing food.*

> *I realize it is impossible for me to understand modern technology when all of my contacts are made with a typewriter at my kitchen table, but I do have a vision of what can be accomplished for the children of Haiti if the Mission Board and MBF could work together.*

Go, Frances!

Ed Stein returned to Houston and promptly called.

"The mission board has been talking about this since the day I arrived," Ed said to Frances. "I had no idea I would be asked to send them the Adopt-a-Child money."

She held her breath, waiting to hear what Ed would say next.

"Of course I will send the thirty-seven thousand dollars to you."

Frances thought this was a courageous stand for Ed to take, since he had only been in his job at MBF a few weeks.

"I won't discuss this further," Frances wrote to Flo.

But Frances had trouble letting go. She wrote paragraphs more to Flo and other friends. Over time, Frances developed a better relationship with the mission board, which occasionally sponsored a project for Pere Albert's children.

For now, Frances had lost enough time to church bureaucracy. She needed more scholarships. From her disorganized address book, she selected nearly three hundred names of former donors. The response was excellent.

The trade embargo continued to cause shortages, high prices, and violence. Old Stone Presbyterian postponed its summer trip.

Frances spent the summer, as usual, working on multiple fronts. She managed her scholarship drive, traveled to make talks, and sent notes of thanks for donations, large and small. She began a new campaign for Creole books, was attentive to Gardner and the family, and stayed active in her church.

Any Episcopal priest who felt that God was calling him to replace Bishop Garnier could submit his own name. For a mid-September election, a small electoral committee narrowed the field to Pere Jean Monique Bruno, Pere Jean-Zache Duracin, and Pere Yvan François.

Years earlier Pere Albert had predicted that Pere Bruno, a man of high integrity, would be the next bishop. Then Frances learned from a friend that Pere Albert had put his *own* name in nomination, though he was not a finalist.

Frances was confused. Pere Bruno and Pere Albert were the best of friends. Pere Bruno had been the only man in the Episcopal Church to come to the mountains when Pere Albert was sent there. Frances could not imagine why Pere Albert would submit his own name instead of supporting his friend.

She began the day of the election with a prayer for Pere Bruno and then turned to her correspondence. She wrote Flo that Dr. Fred Butler from Wilmington, North Carolina, was taking a trip to Léogâne on November 20.

He asked us to go with him but Gardner didn't feel he should leave the States after the thrombosis in his lung. I am tempted to join Fred's group in Miami.

Flo was eager to return too. Her seventh trip, sponsored by Old Stone Presbyterian, was rescheduled to leave on October 12. Old Stone had led a funding drive to build a guesthouse and small clinic in Cherident. The team would check on the new buildings. Flo's husband Harry and Fran Hobbs's husband Pete were part of this team.

An envious Frances wrote Flo. "How I wish I could go!" But she had her eye on Fred Butler's trip, which was a month later.

Frances didn't hesitate to use Flo, whom she had never met, as a courier. She sent Flo checks totaling $6,500 for Pere Albert. She asked Flo to take photographs, and she couldn't help but offer useful tips.

> *Place the roll of film in a plastic bag and label it as to which village it is. Don't hesitate to take two shots of children who are particularly attractive or who might move at the time you snapped the picture.*

> *I am sure Harry wonders how people get along who don't have me to tell them what to do!! Just tell him to think of poor Gardner ... he has lived with this for 50 years ... and it hasn't been easy ... for him.*

The new school term began. All the students were excited, and Nicholas Michael was especially proud. At age fifteen, he had excelled in Cherident's primary school and was in his final year.

On October 19, Old Stone's group returned to the Shenandoah Valley, its fall foliage ablaze. The team reported that Pere Albert's new guesthouse was basic but comfortable. The clinic was cramped but functional.

Pere Albert's villages were transforming into communities of hope. Men and women wove branches and leaves for shelter schools. A few cinder block schools were finished. Happy children were everywhere.

Back in Virginia, Pete Hobbs was asked when he would return to Haiti. "It's not going to be too long," he said.

Frances was still indecisive about joining Fred Butler's group. The team would stay at Sainte Croix Hospital, but Frances wanted to go to Cherident. Though this would be her twenty-eighth trip to Haiti, she was nervous about staying alone in a guesthouse she had never seen.

Flo and Harry Boggs had been back in West Virginia ten days when Frances called from Arkansas.

"I need your advice," Frances said to Flo. "Do you think it would be all right if I went to the mountains alone?"

"Frances, it would be better if I went with you."

"But you just got back from Haiti."

"I'll go again."

Grateful, Frances coordinated schedules with Flo.

> *I will meet you at the gate. I am sure we will recognize each other. I will be wearing a blue denim skirt and a jacket with an Indian print ... kind of New Mexico or Arizona.*

After two years of letters and phone calls, the women finally met in Miami, flew across the Caribbean Sea to Haiti, were driven to Pere Albert's mountains, and became fast friends.

"For years I had seen all these pictures of Frances in that scrapbook at the hospital," Flo told me. "The Miami airport was the first time I laid eyes on her. I never took any more team trips. In Haiti she was the Queen. I teased her about it. She always got the best seat, the best bed, and the best meal.

"I did whatever the Queen wanted to do."

One year, Flo Boggs gave Frances her own tiara.

Chapter 12

This Will Boggle Your Mind

God is wonderful to use human beings to make shine His glory on this earth.
—Pere Jean-Wilfrid Albert, Cherident, Haiti, 1992

On September 16, 1992, the votes were counted. The results were so close that no one was elected to succeed Bishop Garnier. Pere Bruno and Pere Duracin had the same number of votes, Pere François fewer. Some of the Episcopal priests, mysteriously, did not vote.

Two months later Frances and Flo were in Cherident. Frances asked Pere Albert, "Why did you nominate yourself?" She was uneasy, wondering if her financial support gave Pere Albert a feeling of power. He tried to explain, but Frances thought his answer was evasive. Conversation turned elsewhere.

Though still unsettled, Frances had little time to dwell on the election. Cameras in hand, she and Flo were shuttled from village to village, down abusive roads and over remote streambeds. Word traveled quickly across the stony mountains. Eager youngsters in their brightest outfits hurried to be photographed. Smiling at the darling children, Frances took a picture of each.

Back in West Virginia, Flo wrote Pere Albert, telling him that she thought Frances was remarkable.

In Arkansas, "remarkable Frances" received a letter from Pere Bruno. Life in Cap-Haitien was difficult. The astronomical price of food had forced him to discontinue the lunch program that four hundred school children needed.

Pere Bruno wrote, "In Haiti you have to enjoy fully your day, for you never know what the next will bring." He explained to Frances that none of the three candidates for bishop had "totalized the majority."

On December 16 there was a second round of voting.

News reached Arkansas that Pere Jean-Zache Duracin had won. Pere Bruno would not be Haiti's next Episcopal bishop. Disappointed, Frances still wondered why Pere Albert had nominated himself.

On the first of February, Frances walked into the kitchen, a three-page, typed letter from Pere Albert in her hand, and a bewildered look on her face. From the piles on the table, she unearthed a piece of paper with a preprinted line at the top: A NOTE FROM FRANCES LANDERS.

She jotted a few words to Flo.

This will boggle your mind!!

Frances

Frances didn't know what else to say. She and Gardner had read Pere Albert's letter, with its grammatical conventions and typewriter errors. She had taken the letter to her church, made a copy for Flo, and taped her personal note to it. Still speechless, she read the priest's letter one more time.

Haiti January 7th 1993.

Dear Mrs. Frances Landers,

Now, it is time to share with you that experience I had during the last electoral process for a new bishop in Haiti. I have never intended to become a bishop. The task of a bishop is not easy. I would never offer myself, if I didn't receive the appeal from God.

The interesting side of that history is that I wanted to know if the one who has called me is the God I worship so that I may keep on in His way or if I am under the dominion of some force which wanted to betray me. I had in mind to abandon the priesthood if that revelation exposed me to the mockery of my brothers.

When I received a letter from the electoral committee telling me that I didn't have the number of priests to recommend me as a candidate, I said to myself that nobody was going to be elected if this is I, who have been called by God. For that, I encouraged all those who believed in my revelation to give blank votingpaper. I had in mind that the priests will be convinced to recommend me for the second synod. The electoral committee planned to organize three of these until the new bishop has been elected.

You can't imagine how the supporters of each candidate were convinced that they were going to elect their candidate during the first election. At that time, only one was right: Jean-Wilfrid Albert. I told them before that nobody was going to be elected, and that happened as I announced it. That was for me a sign that God has really called me.

Pere Albert explained to Frances that Bishop Garnier intended for the second election to be among the same three candidates. Even if the priests recommended Pere Albert, he would not be considered.

I considered that as an obstacle set up before me. I have addressed God in a prayer beseeching Him to enable the bishop to change his mind if this is Him who has called me. Everyone knows that Bishop Garnier is not someone who changes his mind easily.

But Bishop Garnier *did* change his mind and explained to Pere Albert that his supporters should write a letter of recommendation.

When I told that to the priests on whom I counted to recommend me, I fell on their resistance. They didn't believe in what I told them. They said that the bishop was playing tricks on me. I have convinced them to go to his office personally. Some of them have been there and could find out that the bishop has kept his word. But they were very few to be able to help me reaching my goal.

One week after, I saw in a dream a big obstacle set up on my way. I thought, that obstruction concerned the second synod and I was supposed to wait for the last one. I was still believing that the second one was going to take place as the first one. I said to myself that I am not going to encourage anybody to recommend me, because of that obstacle I saw before me.

In a last meeting with some of the priests, they made a decision to recommend me seriously after the second synod, if nobody has been elected. At the surprise of all of us, ten days before that second synod, bishop Garnier has ordained four new deacon and engaged an old priest that he knows were in favor of father Zache his favorite one. That is in that circumstances that Father Zache has been elected at the second synod.

I can tell also that I have misunderstood the meaning of that obstacle I saw in my way. I thought it was for the second synod. I couldn't understand it was definitive, because of the call I received from Him.

God doesn't want to force anybody to do His will. He wants to use His Love to convince His lamb to obey Him. That is really great! In all that, I was seeking God, I can tell you that I find out a new size of Him. During that electoral process, He never abandon me and visited me many times to support me.

I am glad that the priests were not able to support me. I know that the work we are doing in the mountains, is better than a bishop's job. Now, I have peace in my conscience for having done what I could as a human being to do God's Will.

Jean-Wilfrid Albert was pressed by both sides: on one, I faced the priests' resistance and on the other, I faced the bishop who wanted to impose father Zache. God really called me, but men were in my way.

I can tell you that I have received a letter from the new elected bishop. He is not going to transfer me because he knows the importance of the work I am doing there.

SHALOM!

Your son.
Jean-Wilfrid Albert

With her own mind boggled, Frances waited for Flo's reaction.

"I had to read it a second and third time," Flo replied. "You can see by his letter how important it is to him that you understand."

Frances agreed that many of Pere Albert's sentences were not clear. But the big picture was. The priest believed God had called him to become the next bishop. He felt thwarted by his colleagues and Bishop Garnier. He was appeased by the vital importance of his mountain mission to bring families to Christ and education to the children.

The more Frances thought about Pere Albert's convictions, the better she understood. God *did* want schools, more schools, in the mountains. He had chosen Pere Albert as his instrument.

God had chosen *her* too.

Frances smiled, gave thanks, and reached for her pen to write more notes.

Pere Albert was fond of holding Bible studies in a cornfield.

Chapter 13

Haiti Happenings

We celebrated our fifty-first wedding anniversary Sunday, and all of
our children gave us scholarships, which was a perfect gift.
—Frances Landers, El Dorado, Arkansas, 1993

The Caribbean island of Hispaniola is a small spot on the world map. Haiti's history of suffering has always been vastly disproportional to its size.

In 1993 Haiti's government barely functioned in the cities. Port-au-Prince, home to almost two million people, had one fire station. Few traffic lights worked at any given time.

The government was virtually invisible in the countryside and on the coasts. If a health clinic or school existed, foreign nonprofit organizations provided it. Electricity was beyond sparse. Roads were not maintained. People in the isolated southwestern coastal village of Jérémie, for example, watched their only road deteriorate year after year.

For Jérémie's farmers, who brought animals and produce to the markets in Port-au-Prince, the worsening road was not their only problem. The ongoing fuel embargo made the trip by tap-tap or truck too expensive.

Ferry services, a cheaper form of transportation, sprang up. Travel over water became common.

The government spent no more time overseeing ferry travel than it did repairing roads. Boats were dreadfully overcrowded. A US Coast Guard official called the ferryboat *Neptune* a disaster waiting to happen.

While victims of mass Haitian drownings usually died while trying to flee their country, the tragedy on February 16, 1993, was different. The overloaded *Neptune* was making its routine voyage of two hundred nautical miles from Jérémie to Port-au-Prince.

That Tuesday, as the *Neptune* sailed the coastline just past Sainte Croix Hospital, skies turned dark. The boat caught a small local storm. There was no moon that night and no radio contact. Winds picked up. The triple-decked *Neptune*, its one hundred sixty feet bulging with passengers and livestock, listed in rough seas.

Then it capsized.

No one paid any attention when the ferryboat did not dock.

The *Neptune* had neither life jackets nor lifeboats. The disaster was compared, unfavorably, to the *Titanic*. Seven hundred to seventeen hundred passengers—no one knew for sure—drowned. Three hundred survived, clinging to whatever would float, including carcasses of dead animals, until currents brought them ashore.

On Thursday dead bodies began washing up by the dozens on beaches. Attention turned to the irresponsibility of Haiti's government in providing ordinary services for its citizens.

Dr. Richard and Dr. Judith Brown, current medical directors of Sainte Croix Hospital, received sixty of the three hundred who were rescued. They suffered exposure, sunburn, and dehydration. The hospital staff and missionaries Tom and Nory Clayton worked all night to get nourishment into the victims. The exhausted Haitians did not care that the hospital had insufficient linens; they were happy to be alive.

By Friday all sixty Haitians were out of danger. The Browns and Claytons were grateful that no one had died at Sainte Croix Hospital.

In a national day of mourning, Haitians grieved. The government dodged accountability. Deposed President Aristide phoned in his sympathy from somewhere. Pro- and anti-Aristide supporters clashed in violence. The embargo continued. Memories of the *Neptune* disaster began to fade.

Nineteen ninety-three looked to be another year of challenges. It would be a year of many happenings too.

Early in the year, Frances "preached" (she always used quotation marks) at her church.

"During our early visits," Frances said in her sermon, "we heard the expression, 'Over the mountains, more mountains,' signifying the hopelessness of Haiti. No matter how hard Haitians struggled to climb one mountain, there was always another mountain facing them.

"On our recent visit, it occurred to me that this is no longer a valid statement. As we traveled over a mountain to the south, we arrived at the village of La Brezilienne. A school was under construction to give new hope to the children.

"As we traveled over the mountain in another direction, we came to Labiche where a gristmill has been installed. The women no longer walk six hours with corn on their heads to catch public transportation to Port-au-Prince to have their corn ground.

"We traveled over the next mountain to Cherident and saw a commissary and bakery. In Bejin there was a handicraft class where young people were making items to sell.

"But the most beautiful sight was the children walking all over the mountains in clean school uniforms, singing, 'Come and go with me to my Father's house where there is joy, joy, joy.' The children in Haiti are singing because you have shared."

By letter, Frances relayed all of this to Flo and then explained,

At that point everyone is supposed to wipe their eyes, get out their checkbooks, and start writing!!

Pere Albert was counting on a lot of American checkbooks.

In early March, to communicate his bold vision for St. Matthias Parish, he typed a two-page chart with sixteen rows and thirteen columns. He titled it, "Projects we would like to realize in each village."

Down the paper's left side, Pere Albert listed his sixteen villages. Across the top, he itemized thirteen projects, including "concrete block school" and "feeding program."

He filled each square of his matrix with a yes if the village already had the project, or a no if the village did not.

Only three villages had school buildings. Pere Albert wanted thirteen shelter schools replaced with ones of concrete block. Ten schools needed noontime meals of rice and beans.

Pere Albert wanted eight more clinics, two more corn mills, and six commissaries. He wanted a "loan project" and "goat project" in each village. He was satisfied that Cherident had the lone "oven project" (the bakery, as Frances named it). But *nos* abounded under the headings of "agriculture" (to teach farmers how to improve their crop yield) and "good water system program" (to capture rainwater).

Finally, Pere Albert wanted one more handicraft class.

He pulled the second page from the typewriter carriage, corrected a couple of errors by hand, and underlined his highest priorities. He addressed an envelope to Frances, used stamps she'd brought on her last visit, and handed the letter to the next person headed to the post office in Port-au-Prince.

Three weeks later, Frances opened the envelope and studied the chart for an hour. She sighed.

She had just raised two hundred thousand dollars for scholarships to pay the salaries of eighty-five teachers and principals, and meals in six schools.

Thirty-six hundred students were now enrolled, including one hundred fifty in Cherident's new seven-year secondary school. Frances smiled as she visualized the older students, whom she had watched grow up year to year. No longer wearing cute yellow-and-white-checked uniforms, the youth looked grown up in uniforms of two shades of blue.

Frances could hardly fathom making a dent in any of Pere Albert's "projects." But she'd try. Time to ramp up her fundraising. And her prayer.

Prayer works.

Pete and Fran Hobbs and Harry and Flo Boggs became ardent fundraisers for Frances's Haiti Fund, speaking to groups across the Shenandoah Valley.

In Sand Springs, Oklahoma, First Presbyterian gave eight thousand dollars for an eight-room concrete block school in Barreau. When Pere Albert needed two additional rooms, the church sent two thousand dollars more.

In Lake Charles, Louisiana, Frances spoke to the Church of the Good Shepherd. Its mission committee voted to fund a school and clinic in Bejin. When Pere Albert asked for four thousand dollars more than his original request, the committee phoned Frances.

"Why does Pere Albert always need more money?"

Frances said, "Just go and see for yourselves. If you think you are being used, withdraw your support."

With a dose of skepticism, Good Shepherd sent three members to check out Bejin. Frances told Flo,

> *Well, they thought it was the greatest thing they had ever seen. They came right home and confronted a wealthy friend and told him they wanted $4,000.00. He gave it!!!*

Billy Blake, a generous donor, was on the trip. His daughter told Frances that he was so touched by the experience that he couldn't talk about it without tearing up.

Pere Albert accepted an invitation to come to Good Shepherd after Easter. Frances was asked too, but she decided Good Shepherd's worshippers needed the priest all to themselves. She went to Houston instead. There Dr. Richard Brown of Sainte Croix Hospital was speaking at an MBF conference.

Dr. Brown had asked to meet Frances. She didn't know why, unless, as she told Flo, "he wants to see a seventy-six-year-old woman who runs all over the country raising money ... and would like some of the income."

She *did* have a knack for fundraising. In eastern Texas, a church in Corsicana funded a school in La Vallee. Frances visited a church in Longview, came home with two thousand dollars, and received another two thousand in the mail. A swing over to Bastrop in northeast Louisiana netted four thousand.

One morning Frances opened her mail to find thirty-four thousand dollars from Harriet Prichard's Alternative Gift Market. In June she flew to California and thanked Harriet in person. She brought home some nice donations from Apple Valley Presbyterian.

Of course, another letter came from Pere Albert. He needed four thousand dollars more for the school at Barreau. Haiti's Episcopal Church could buy no more land, so the school would be built in the mountainside, two stories, increasing the cost of concrete.

Frances had already tapped the church in Sand Springs as much as her conscience would allow. She took four thousand dollars out of "money on hand" and prayed for new donors.

The summer of 1993, Pastor Rob Sherrard led the annual Windy Cove trip to Sainte Croix Hospital, with a day trip to Pere Albert's mountains. Randy and Melinda Edwards from Raleigh Court Presbyterian in Roanoke, Virginia, were on this team. They were astonished when Pastor Rob predicted that soon they would lead their own team. Rob was right. Raleigh Court, including member Rob Crittenden, became strong and lasting supporters of Frances's work.

John Reed of Tinkling Spring Presbyterian in Fishersville, Virginia, was also on that Windy Cove trip. He was instrumental in kindling his church's ongoing passion for the mission work in Grande Colline.

When John came home, he called Frances, whom he had never met.

"Pere Albert is on the march for the Lord," John said.

Frances shared John's remark with a man in Camden, Arkansas, prompting him to send her five thousand dollars, and within weeks, twenty-five thousand more.

Individuals, churches, and organizations—in Apple Valley, Bastrop, Camden, Corsicana, El Dorado, Fishersville, Keyser, Houston, Lake Charles, Longview, Millboro, Roanoke, Sand Springs, and many more American cities—were increasingly, and happily, changing kids' lives in rural Haiti.

Child by child, village by village, story by story—punctuated by photographs, sparkling eyes, a smile, and a lilting voice—Frances had a style that melted resistance, opened checkbooks, and gained followers.

If she leveraged her time, Frances knew she could do even more. Mary Jo Oliver, Frances's long-time church friend, suggested a newsletter.

During their regular Saturday morning "breakfast out," Frances told Gardner, "I have to do it. It's time for me to reach out to people more frequently. Mary Jo will help me."

Other friends volunteered to computerize Frances's mailing list, manage layout and printing, attach labels, and sort and mail each issue. The church offered to pay postage. Volume 1, Number 1 of *Haiti Happenings* arrived in mailboxes in September 1993. Frances wrote her first regular column.

> *What would I do without friends? I have depended on you for years to reach out to the children of Haiti, giving them the message, "We care."*
>
> *Please share this newsletter with someone who does not know about the Haiti Fund and explain that 100% of gifts will be used for the purpose given. When people realize they can send a child to school and provide a daily nutritious meal for 16 cents a day, no one will want to be left out. This is the greatest bargain in the world today!!!!*

"After hearing the very first Landers report on their mission trip to Haiti," Mary Jo wrote in a small column, "I began to long for a way to become involved in this wonderful project. Earlier this year, the Lord Jesus gave me an idea that has grown into the first edition of *Haiti Happenings*."

Frances included a hand-drawn map of Pere Albert's mountain parish: seventeen villages with five thousand schoolchildren.

"Just look at how much your gifts give," one headline ran. Four dollars for a Bible, six dollars for shoes, and seven for a school uniform. Thirty dollars fed a child. A scholarship was fifty-five. Nine hundred sixty paid for a lay evangelist. One thousand dollars built a classroom, two thousand provided benches and desks, and ten thousand created a ten-room school.

With a printed donation form and included envelope, readers could easily choose a few appealing options, write a check, and find a stamp. Soon many envelopes found their way to Frances at 1801 West Block Street.

She chose not to overwhelm her supporters with *all* of the needs on Pere Albert's chart of thirteen columns. No need to bring up commissaries, clinics, corn mills, goats, or a handicraft class. Not just yet.

The people of El Dorado came alongside Frances's ministry in thoughtful ways. A noted artist, Maria Villegas, drew sketches of Pere Albert's schools and the gristmill and granted Frances permission to freely use them. Another friend funded pen-and-ink drawings of Haitian scenes. The new artwork appeared in the second issue of *Haiti Happenings*, which reached Frances's supporters at the beginning of December—the season of Advent, the season of generous giving.

Frances's column was upbeat. Mary Jo's column had grown in parallel with her increasing volunteer hours. In Pere Albert's own column, he itemized needs and requests.

Another donation form. Another envelope.

Issue-to-issue, year-to-year, Frances's messages in *Haiti Happenings* were simple, consistent, and true.

"Your generosity brings God's people from darkness to light."

"Education is the hope of Haiti."

The Landerses' mailbox overflowed.

Mission School - La Vallee, Haiti

Frances appreciated the generous gift of Maria Villegas's artwork.

Pere Albert oversaw construction of the schools. Here, in LeBeau.

When Frances showed this photo to her church's mission
committee, she was given funds for new tires.

Chapter 14

Two Steps Forward

I will "preach" in Mt. Pleasant, Texas, the last Sunday of the month.
I haven't been there in a long time,
so I hope they can find their checkbooks.
—Frances Landers, El Dorado, Arkansas, 1995

In November 1993 Pere Bruno heard arguing beneath his second-floor office window that overlooked the Atlantic Ocean. An older woman rolled on the ground, trying to break free from the restraining grasp of two young men whose voices were firm.

Prompted by the Holy Spirit, Pere Bruno went downstairs.

"The youngsters were trying to restrain their mother from committing suicide by jumping into the ocean," Pere Bruno told his American supporters. "I had to use all my pastoral skills to convince her to come to the school yard, where we sat down and I ministered to her."

This was one case among hundreds, Pere Bruno explained. People who could not keep up with the desperate situation of the country wanted to take their lives. The embargo by the United Nations had not yet brought President Aristide back, but it had caused enormous suffering.

Frances prayed that perhaps the next few years would be marked more by progress than violence. Perhaps St. Matthias Parish could take a lasting step forward. Perhaps two.

The pastor of Keyser Presbyterian, Flo Boggs's church, asked Frances to "fill the pulpit" on February 27, 1994. Seven years earlier, Pere Albert had preached where Frances would stand. Ten years prior, Windy Cove had sent its first mission team to Haiti.

It was time for a reunion.

Pastor Rob Sherrard sent an engaging invitation to all who had been on Windy Cove-sponsored trips from 1984 to 1993.

"We have a special reason for a Haiti reunion," Rob wrote. "Frances Landers is coming to speak at Keyser Presbyterian. Not only have our team members been eager to meet Mrs. Landers, but she is extremely interested in meeting you folks who have been involved in the work in Haiti."

Turnout was splendid: sixty-eight people from twenty-four churches. Weather was perfect. There was no snow, as Pere Albert had experienced in 1987, though a few days later thirteen inches fell.

The special guest was a hit. Pastor Rob told his congregation, "Frances Landers is my kind of woman."

Fran Hobbs finally met Frances and called her "a delight," adding that Windy Cove had "many enthusiastic responses to her Saturday afternoon talk."

On Sunday morning Flo introduced Frances to the Keyser congregation.

"Her office is her kitchen table," Flo said. "Her office equipment is a good pen and a Walmart typewriter. She has two main pillars of support. One is an understanding husband who eats his lunch standing up because of that table. The other is faith in a God who moves people to respond to the needs of those Jesus called 'the least of these.'"

Keyser's congregation warmly responded to Frances's sermon, "How Big is Your World?" She returned to El Dorado with $2,825 and a lot of new friends.

At the reunion Frances met John Reed, the spirited man from Tinkling Spring Presbyterian. On his first trip to Pere Albert's mountains a year earlier, John had suggested building a vocational school in Cherident to give young adults employable skills.

"How soon?" Pere Albert had asked.

Easter week, 1994, John brought to Pere Albert ten thousand dollars that he had raised for the vocational school.

That Sunday in Cherident's St. Matthias Episcopal Church, young Girbson Bijou led the procession down the small aisle. Girbson, whom Pere Albert identified as a gifted musician, played a beat-up trumpet that John Reed had donated on his first trip.

John returned to the United States, bearing witness to Pere Albert's powerful presence. Cherident and twenty-two other villages hosted Easter services. Ten thousand men, women, and children—who five years earlier had been surrounded by vodou—celebrated the resurrection of Jesus Christ.

"Thanks to those who support our lay evangelists," Frances wrote in May's *Haiti Happenings*. She knew Pere Albert had relied on his worship assistants in his many churches on that blessed Easter Sunday.

The first few months of 1994, Frances traveled to five states. She told stories of the children in the mountains and showed their pictures. One boy had a polka-dot handkerchief tucked in the pocket of his yellow and white shirt. A smiling girl held her black hair in place with a yellow barrette. Kindergarteners, each with a hand on the next child's shoulder, formed a solitary line as they walked to the outdoor kitchen.

"Many mothers go without food to save money for fabric for school uniforms," Frances told her audiences. "These children are in school because people like you gave fifty-five-dollar scholarships."

Frances clicked another image onto the screen. A good-looking young man in a blue uniform smiled broadly. "This is Michael. He was twelve when Pere Albert came to Cherident and enrolled him in third grade. Now Michael is in his first year of high school. He is sixteen, with great potential."

Another photograph. A cinder-block school with a concrete roof—no frills, no windows, no electricity. Just hundreds of smiling children in yellow and white, pouring from their classrooms at the end of the day.

"This school building exists because a church donated a thousand dollars a room. Our priest has the concrete block made right in the villages."

Slides, narration, questions, donations.

In Fort Smith, Arkansas, First Presbyterian adopted a village, as Louisiana's Good Shepherd had done. Frances was gleeful for this large gift.

She celebrated small donations too. In Deerfield Beach, Florida, children of Community Presbyterian gave two Haitian children scholarships, uniforms, shoes, and Christmas gifts. Their fundraiser? The youngsters picked tomatoes and sold them to the congregation, earning $160.

It took two years for Frances to complete the twenty-nine-thousand-dollar "opportunity" to buy a vehicle for Pere Albert. *Haiti Happenings* featured his photo, the priest standing by a heavy-duty, four-wheel-drive, six-cylinder, diesel Toyota pickup truck.

"Before the dealer in Port-au-Prince could get a truck," Frances wrote, "the embargo was enforced. It has not been lifted, but by some unknown miracle, the dealer received two Toyota trucks in February."

Few needs were as pressing for Pere Albert as accessible water. Women spent as many as seven hours each day fetching water for drinking and cooking. Not *clean* water. *Any* water, scooped out of dirty streambeds into hollow gourds, plastic bottles, or buckets.

Water weighs eight pounds a gallon. Common across the mountains was the sight of a peasant woman coming back up a rocky path with a five-gallon, forty-pound bucket on her head.

When a natural spring was discovered two miles from the village of Duny, Frances raised money for plastic pipe. In Bejin, Pete Hobbs, John

Hallis, and others helped Pere Albert install a hydraulic pump near a small waterfall to divert water to a reservoir.

Pere Albert asked Frances to add reservoirs to her menu of giving options. Twelve thousand dollars each. He wanted seventeen.

In mid-1994 fuel climbed to thirty-three dollars a gallon. Lynx Air stopped delivering mail, and Frances was cut off from corresponding with Pere Albert. She relied on periodic conversations with Pere Bruno, who was reachable by telephone.

From his Cap-Haitien home, Pere Bruno watched US Navy ships enforce the embargo. Surveillance helicopters trailed the coastline. An invasion of Haiti felt imminent.

It was.

For months the United Nations had tried to end Haiti's corrupt political crisis by restoring President Aristide to power. All of the initiatives had failed. Repression mounted. The United Nations authorized the United States to lead a multinational force to uproot the Haitian Army.

In mid-September, twenty thousand troops peacefully invaded Haiti. The project was called Operation Uphold Democracy. United States President Bill Clinton sent a negotiating team, led by former President Jimmy Carter, to persuade military leaders to step down.

On September 19, 1994, Army General Cédras agreed.

Pere Bruno wrote to Flo. "This is very painful for many Haitians which feel they are not free any longer."

But the effort was effective. In October President Aristide returned to Haiti. His faithful followers danced in the streets.

Aristide had many challenges. Had Haiti's only problem been poverty, rebuilding its ravaged economy might have been conceivable. But crime and corruption remained, and Haiti's government-owned businesses were poorly operated. The three-year embargo left Haiti's roads, bridges, ports, sanitation facilities, water, education, and health care in shambles.

President Aristide's country had few bright spots.

One was the Episcopal mountain parish of St. Matthias.

The third week in October, over seven thousand eager children in crisp uniforms ran, laughing and singing, across streambeds and grasslands, rocky fields and hills. They crowded into twenty-four schools. Twenty-four principals and 167 teachers greeted their pupils. The children lined up quietly. School bells rang.

The 1994–1995 school year had begun.

Frances couldn't be much help to President Aristide, but she'd give her all for Pere Albert's kids.

Pere Albert missed his American friends and was grateful when the violence subsided in the cities. In mid-November 1994 he wrote to Flo: "Haiti is ready now to receive the team and we will be pleased to welcome you."

Wait. Not quite yet. The next day, rain began. It pummeled southern Haiti for three nights. Within twenty-four hours, Port-au-Prince received nine inches. Thirteen inches deluged Jacmel in twelve hours.

Hurricane Gordon was only a tropical storm during much of its twelve-day rampage across the southern Atlantic and the Caribbean. Hispaniola bore less of its brunt than did Cuba and the southeastern United States. But these particulars didn't matter to the million and a half Haitians who suffered days of downpours, destruction, and death.

Millions of tons of mud and gravel slid down barren hillsides. The landslides wiped out anything and anyone in the way. Overflowing streambeds swept away people and livestock. Three feet of churning water flooded Léogâne. Three rivers turned into one, but not before the bridges were destroyed. When floodwaters receded from Sainte Croix Hospital, mud was two feet deep.

Hurricane Gordon destroyed eleven thousand humble homes. Ninety thousand people had no shelter. Damage was an estimated fifty million dollars.

The human toll climbed. In Haitian disasters, casualty figures are always inexact. A conservative estimate was eleven hundred dead. American soldiers risked their lives plucking drowning Haitians from floodwater currents racing more than forty miles an hour. Had the US Army not been serving as peacekeepers during Aristide's return, the toll would have been higher.

Under Haiti's tropical sun, Pere Albert's concrete block schools dried out. Shelter schools, their palm leaves and cornstalks shredded, were reconstructed. Determined Haitians scrubbed mud from their clothes and patched their washed-out roads. Eventually, bridges were more or less repaired. Hurricane Gordon became another statistic in the chronicle of Haiti's fragile development. Life for the average Haitian stumbled on.

Harriet Prichard, in her 1994–1995 *Alternative Gift Market* catalog, offered supporters twenty-three global projects. Two were Pere Albert's. Donors could help Frances's Haiti Fund buy school lunches. Or they could purchase goats, donkeys, and mules for village families.

Frances was ecstatic to turn the need for livestock over to Harriet. A woman from North Carolina had just written a page-long letter asking many specific questions about baby goats and nanny goats. Though Frances got a big kick out of the letter, all the minute details of this or any topic were a little much for her. She tried very hard to juggle the big items and let the little ones go.

Harriet's catalog write-up included an anecdote from Pere Albert: "When a goat is delivered to a family's hut, the children jump up and down, clapping their hands and screaming as if a convertible sports car had just been driven to their door."

The catalog text explained that purchased animals would be delivered to Pere Albert's seventeen mountain villages and that he would decide which families should receive them.

As if Pere Albert didn't have enough to do.

In early 1995 Pete and Fran Hobbs raised money to buy Pere Albert a ten-ton dump truck. It saw a lot of use as the priest continued his relentless push to convert villagers from vodou to Christianity, expand his churches, and give Frances the "opportunity" to build more schools.

In Cherident the dump truck helped with the construction of John Reed's dream: a sixteen-room, two-story vocational school. During lunch breaks, students from the secondary school down to first grade carried rocks to support the building's foundation.

Pere Albert met them at the work site.

"This school is for you. So it is good for you to help build it."

As Pere Albert oversaw construction of the vocational school, the Virginia communities around John Reed's church, Tinkling Spring Presbyterian, united in a "Tools for Schools in Haiti" campaign. In three days, a twenty-ton container was filled to the brim with tools, lighting, a generator, stackable chairs, and classroom supplies. Shipping the container to Port-au-Prince and then up to the mountains was, itself, a minor miracle.

Harriet Prichard, on her second visit with Pere Albert, shared good news. His animal project had brought in sixty thousand dollars.

Frances told Fran and Pete Hobbs, "I wish I could get that amount, but people give for animals quicker than for education. I am not complaining. Harriet raised thirty thousand dollars for our school lunches."

The total, ninety thousand dollars, was the most money that the Alternative Gift Market had ever received for two related projects.

Pere Albert was giddy over his "raising animal project." In a letter to Frances, he spelled out the distribution plan for a thousand baby chicks, fifteen hundred goats and sheep, sixty female donkeys, ten male horses, food, medicine, and a janitor's salary for the chickens.

And rules. Pere Albert's "raising animal project" had so many rules.

Each woman pledged to sell the firstborn animal and give the money to Pere Albert to build a commissary. She would give the second animal to another woman to expand the program. When the third animal was born, the woman could sell the "ancient one" and keep the "new one."

Pere Albert had a rule for when an animal died from disease. He had a different rule for one that died from negligence. Other rules spelled out who could own reproductive female animals and who could own the males.

All of this, Pere Albert concluded, was so that "gradually all those poor ladies may find some improvement in their life."

Frances had never seen him pour so much energy into a project. Maybe she was, just a little, jealous of all those animals.

On her trips to see Pere Albert's schools, Harriet Prichard was especially bothered by Haiti's barren hillsides. The primary reason so many people had died during Hurricane Gordon was the flooding caused by the lack of trees.

In 1995 Harriet had an idea, a life-changing one that would soon introduce Frances to a remarkable man from California: Scott Sabin.

Harriet was aware of Scott's work. He was executive director of Plant with Purpose (originally named Floresta) based in San Diego. Scott's nonprofit was dedicated to healing the land and its people.

In 1984 Plant with Purpose started working in impoverished rural communities in the Dominican Republic and then expanded to Mexico. Scott Sabin's organization taught villagers to plant trees and improve farming and irrigation techniques. The ministry empowered men and women, through Christ-centered cooperatives, to best use their land, trees, seed, water, rocks, and each other.

Small loans were part of Plant with Purpose's arsenal against poverty. A few hundred dollars started a small, sustainable business and increased the borrower's standard of living and self-esteem.

Remembering her first impression of a near treeless Haiti, Harriet encouraged Scott to visit Pere Albert's mountain parish.

"Just go and see," Harriet told Scott, reminiscent of Pere Albert's words to Frances and Gardner nearly nine years earlier.

"I was in the Dominican Republic, reviewing our work," Scott told me. "I said to my DR director, 'We are on the same island as Haiti. It sounds like a fun trip. Let's just drive over there.'"

Scott and his director, Eldon Garcia, drove for hours under blazing sun, over rocky roads, through streams, past dilapidated houses and small cemeteries and markets that seemed to sell only mangos, looking for Cherident. The men had never seen mountains so barren, rugged, and overpopulated. The brown hillsides were steep and sparsely covered with sickly corn plants.

"We got lost and showed up two days late," Scott said. "But it was worth it. We spent fifteen hours with Pere Albert."

The priest drove Scott and Eldon to many of his villages, showing them the schools and churches. Happy, hungry, bright-eyed children greeted them wherever they went.

The priest encouraged Scott to expand his agricultural ministry into Grande Colline. For fifteen hours he encouraged Scott.

"We have land. We have water. But we are starving," Pere Albert said as the men sat at a table, a dim oil lamp flickering on their faces. Scott replied that perhaps by 1997, Plant with Purpose would be ready to begin work in Haiti.

Pere Albert leaned forward. "I do not think we can wait that long."

It was never easy to say no to Pere Albert.

Though not wanting to overstretch his nonprofit, Scott was cautiously intrigued. He wondered what would be the minimum that Plant with Purpose could do for Pere Albert.

"Maybe we can teach the farmers how to graft fruit trees," he told the priest. "That would be enough."

Pere Albert pointed out to Scott, not too subtly, that John Reed's vocational school was being built in Cherident.

Scott took the hint. He suggested, "What if we sponsor an agronomy class? We can pay the salary of a qualified teacher."

Maybe that would be enough.

To Pere Albert, no, that would not be enough. But it was a start.

Soon Frances's phone rang with a long-distance call from San Diego. It was Scott Sabin. He had heard about Frances from Pere Albert and Harriet.

Scott had seen, firsthand, how the Lord had called Frances to bring hope to St. Matthias Parish by educating the children. It appeared to Scott that the Lord had called him to work there too, to teach the parents how to care for their land.

Pere Albert's new truck. Plant with Purpose. New concrete-block schools. The promise of a vocational school. More school lunches. Even all of Pere Albert's animals.

Frances was encouraged. As 1995 came to a close, she knew that the work in Haiti had taken one lasting step—maybe even two—forward.

Guest speaker Frances Landers listened to her introduction at
a Presbyterian gathering in Harrisonburg, Virginia.

Frances shared her inspiring story hundreds of times.
Here, in Romney, West Virginia.

Shopping at a market, Frances modeled her new look for Flo Boggs.

Frances relaxed over breakfast at Port-au-Prince's Hotel Montana before flying home after a tiring but rewarding visit to the mountains.

Chapter 15

One Step Back

*Over the years, some of our team members had difficulty enjoying the good
parts of Haiti while knowing the terrible poverty elsewhere in the country.*
—*Windy Cove Presbyterian Church, Millboro, Virginia, 2011*

For the 1995–1996 school year, Haiti's government raised salaries of
public school teachers by more than one hundred percent. Pere Albert
wrote Frances. He knew she couldn't match that large of an increase, but
perhaps she could add twenty percent more to his monthly budject (as he
spelled it).

By the way, he mentioned, he had added two primary schools and now
had four secondary schools. One more thing. The vocational school needed
ten teachers, one principal, and one secretary. Frances wrote Flo.

> *I assume I should raise my monthly check to $14,000,
> but I have no idea where the money is coming from.
> I will turn that over to God!!*

Pere Albert sensed that Frances needed a pep talk. "I am not afraid of
the future concerning our school budject. According to my experience with
the Lord, it is good to depend upon Him and if our mission in the mountains
pleases Him then we will have enough to keep running all that we have
realized for His Glory."

Frances appreciated the encouragement. Mission work in Haiti was hard.
And it was not for everyone. A dentist just back from Cherident called her.
"I don't like Pere Albert," the dentist said. "He was always late, he made me
ride in the back of the truck, and the patients didn't thank me for pulling
their teeth."

Frances reasoned that the dentist likely would not return.

127

President Aristide's term ended in February 1996. The effects of the embargo remained. Food prices were high. Illegal guns were readily available. Banks had little faith in the future and granted few loans.

René Préval succeeded Aristide, the first back-to-back democratically elected presidents in Haiti's history. While turmoil decreased, the average Haitian's life was, on balance, the same.

But Pere Albert's life soon changed. He sent Frances a heart-rending letter. She read it, and she shivered.

> This is to tell you now that I have had an awful wreck last week. The Toyota truck had a breakdown and the driver went to the garage to fix it. By this time, the driver was going shopping and left a janitor in the truck. When the technician finished, he gave the key to that janitor for the driver. After some minutes, the janitor who didn't know how to drive started the truck and by that, broke the legs of two men and a woman, killed a little girl coming from school and broke two cars plus our truck.

Frances had to put the letter down. She was heartsick.

The Toyota truck that took two years to fund? The truck that miraculously showed up during the embargo? In the wrong hands, killing a little girl? Coming home from school?

Frances thought of the lovely little girls across St. Matthias Parish.

She wiped away tears and then continued to read.

> The Haitian state insurance declines to take any responsibility of that wreck. They said that the author of that "accident" (wreck) didn't have license. I am obliged now to take a lawyer so that I may not spend too much money. I have just received today the US $1000 from Cosby Church. I am going to send a thank you note to the church.
>
> I can tell you that I am going to use that money to pay the lawyer. Now, I have a bad need of about US $3000 to help the families afflicted, to organize funeral, to take care of theirs in hospital and repair all the vehicles damaged. I need to do that for seeking peace. I wonder if it is possible for you to send letters out to churches you know will respond.

I am not going to lose hope nor discouraged. I feel ready to work for Jesus even in Hell.

Poor Pere Albert. Frances knew he felt terrible. All of this on his shoulders, as if he had been behind the wheel.

She forwarded copies of the letter to his closest American friends and mailed the letter to churches that routinely donated to the Haiti Fund. And she tapped into the sympathies of her personal friends, including Blanche Carper of Asheville, North Carolina.

Blanche and her husband Day gave Pere Albert $89.90, the cost of two tickets to an elaborate house and garden festival close to their home. It was a luxury they would gladly forego.

Within a week, Frances sent three thousand dollars to Haiti. When more donations arrived, she set them aside in a new vehicle fund. Pere Albert helped fundraise too. He typed a letter to twenty-seven American churches. After explaining the accident, the priest bottom-lined his request: thirty-six thousand dollars for a new vehicle.

Pere Albert instructed donors to "mail what you have collected to Mrs. Landers." He typed her address as 1801 West Black Street (instead of Block), but she received generous responses almost immediately.

Frances went back on the road, racking up miles and raising money. Up to the Shenandoah Valley for five talks in one weekend. Down to Mississippi to speak at a church. Three trips to Little Rock, one to see her granddaughter Allison receive her master's diploma. A week later, a trip to California to help Harriet Prichard celebrate Alternative Gifts International's tenth anniversary.

Scott Sabin attended, driving north from San Diego to Pasadena, delighted to finally meet Frances. Plant with Purpose would be in the next *Alternative Gift Market* catalog, giving Scott a boost for his new work in St. Matthias Parish, which included teaching a two-year agronomy class in the vocational school.

Allison Landers wanted to go to Haiti with her grandmother. Frances asked Flo to come along. How could Flo say no to the Queen?

On Sunday morning the three women attended a service on the side of a mountain near the village of Moreau. The church was built of bamboo poles with a roof of palm leaves.

During the service, Pere Albert asked Allison to come to the little altar made of concrete block. He told his congregation that the trip was Allison's graduation gift, and he asked the young people to come forward to help bless her. Pere Albert prayed for Allison's future as a child of God.

It was a poignant, tearful moment for Grandmother.

As usual, Pere Albert shared his vision and needs with Frances. When she left Cherident, he wrote them down. Five pages. Topping his list were salary increases for his two hundred teachers, raising his requested monthly budget from fourteen thousand dollars to twenty-one. "I know that is going to be very hard for you, this is why we have to invest some money in projects which can generate funds."

Pere Albert proposed building six income-producing commissaries over three years to hold soap, kerosene, milk, spices, matches, ten drums of kitchen oil, and two hundred bags each of flour, sugar, and rice.

Following up on a conversation between him and Frances about "that library we need," the priest listed sixty-six textbook titles.

The letter, which continued with many more "opportunities," was in the mail when Frances developed abdominal cramps.

Had she not been careful about what she had eaten?

When she returned from Haiti, Frances often landed in the hospital with respiratory problems that included pneumonia. The dust of Haiti damaged her lungs and weakened her heart. But she had never been sick from the food. Frances checked with Allison and Flo. Both were fine.

After taking antibiotics for three days, Frances's stomach was still acting up. She wrote to Flo.

> *I'm waiting for the gastroenterologist (I had to "look" to spell) to give me an appointment.*

On Thursday, July 11, Frances was scheduled to speak to local Rotarians. She went to the specialist instead. By the time Pere Albert's letter reached her Arkansas mailbox, she was unable to give it any attention. Her test results were back. At seventy-nine, Frances Landers had colon cancer.

A colonoscopy uncovered a large, ulcerated polyp. Frances's doctor told her that it probably had not spread outside her colon. Since it was so big, however, it no doubt had malignant cells.

Monday, July 15, Gardner drove Frances to a hotel near Little Rock's hospital. Tuesday's pre-op procedures went smoothly. Frances, due at the admitting office at 5:30 Wednesday morning, took her last antibiotic the night before. She later related details in a letter to several friends.

> *About 30 minutes after taking the pills I became deathly ill. I made it to the bathroom and called for Gardner. He says I passed out and he couldn't find a pulse. After being revived with cold towels, Gardner was able to get me to the bed. He called Jim and the surgeon. Jim called an ambulance.*

When the ambulance arrived, I was incoherent and could not move from the bed to the gurney, so they rolled me in the bed sheet and lifted me so I could be strapped on. I had an IV immediately.

Frances woke up at 5:30, exhausted. She knew she would never be able to undergo surgery. At 6:00 her surgeon, Dr. Cliff Parnell, came to her bed. He had been a high school classmate of Jim Landers, a longtime family friend, and one of the boys whom Gardner, Frances, and their sons took on ski weekends.

"She always loved us ... regardless," Dr. Parnell told his nurse, remembering the boys' antics. Now he prayed for Frances. The few words she remembered were, "In Jesus Christ, the healer of all of life."

In about an hour, I could feel life coming back into me. I was so anxious to go on with the surgery that each time I would feel this surge of strength, I would say to the nurse, "I'm better."

Frances was in surgery an hour later, on schedule.

I will never forget how at peace I was. They removed the polyp and part of the colon. Of course, I was on all kinds of "tubes," which wasn't pleasant for the family to see, but I had no pain.

Back home, Frances rested. Pere Albert's long letter remained unread. Two weeks after Frances's surgery, he wrote again.

I have received a letter from Blanche Carper telling that you have to have a major surgery. We keep praying for you. I believe that God will help you to get over that difficulty so that you may do His work with a good health. When God wants His work to be done, He preserves all those He uses as His instruments to achieve His purpose. I can tell you that the God I worship, you worship, will help you get rid of that worry so that you may continue to work for Him.

Pere Albert knew Frances needed to focus on her health. But a third of his piece of paper was still blank. He couldn't help himself. Once again he asked about increasing the budget, suggesting Frances send three thousand dollars more each month if six thousand was out of reach. He asked if she had made progress funding the textbook library and then ended, "I believe that God will enable you to be able to come in February. Maybe at that time we may have a good transportation."

The priest sincerely wanted to see Frances in seven months. He was also reminding her about the thirty-six thousand dollars for a new vehicle.

Frances's chemotherapy began August 13. Daily she tried to gain strength. To boost her spirits, she chose a long pair of clip earrings each day, so visitors would not think she looked sick.

She typed notes when she could and relied on others when she could not. Pastor Rob Sherrard was a generous helper, contacting churches for donations to Pere Albert's vehicle fund. Pastor Rob wrote, "Reliable transportation is essential to Father Albert's ministry. His presence at the outposts of his parish represents the real hope of the gospel for these mountain people."

By September Pastor Rob received ten thousand dollars. Frances, trying not to fret about falling behind in her work, wrote to Flo.

> *We will mail out a letter for scholarships. I know I won't have enough for a full year. I probably told you that I received $25,000 from Alternative Gift Markets, but their money will go to Plant with Purpose next year. This will be great for St. Matthias Parish, but will still not provide scholarships. I will think about it when I am stronger.*

> *Just know that I have never been depressed one minute about this. I have so many laughs stored in my memory of our trips to Haiti, all I have to do is close my eyes and "go to the mountains."*

Phone calls, cards, flowers, and prayers flowed into 1801 West Block Street. Frances's good friend Mary Spencer visited. After complimenting Frances on her earrings, Mary gave her a nightshirt. Its artwork, by the popular artist Mary Englebreit, was of a young girl, crown on her head, holding a flowing sheet of paper. "The QUEEN has SPOKEN," read a sign.

Frances had such a laugh. "I was always the Queen in Haiti," she told Flo. "Just think how you will have to treat me on our next trip, now that I have had an operation."

She shielded her family from her emotional highs and lows. "It hasn't been easy for them," Frances said to Flo. "Not only did my sons face the possibility that I might not have good news, but they had to support Gardner."

Frances did open up to Flo and her other close friends: Blanche Carper, Edie Covert, Mary Jo Oliver, and Mary Spencer. In a September letter to these women, she admitted:

> *Now, your "FRIEND" who was NOT going to get sick from the chemo did fine until the 5th treatment. After that I fell apart. I put on the longest earrings I had and still couldn't cope. I became so dehydrated that I had to go to the hospital for four hours of IV, but was checked by my internist who said that I was going to be fine.*

Perhaps. But Frances doubted her ability to continue the work. She wrote Pere Albert. "I probably need to say this is the time to give it up. This is the last year that I can be responsible for your school budget."

Pere Albert asked his thousands of parishioners to pray.

During chemotherapy, Frances wrote as many notes as she could. She increased Pere Albert's monthly funding. She helped Mary Jo with *Haiti Happenings*. She talked of resuming her travels, riding with daughter-in-law Lynn to Second Presbyterian in Little Rock. To Sand Springs, Oklahoma, relying on her son Jim's private pilot. To Lyon College in Batesville, Arkansas, getting there somehow.

"If God wants me to do these things, I will have the strength," she told Gardner. Frances and her whole family continued to receive wonderful care and support from Dr. Cliff Parnell. His skills and dedication to Frances were instrumental in her recovery.

One day she realized that she had energy to tackle Pere Albert's long letter full of special projects. Six commissaries? The idea intrigued her. Some months earlier, John Trimble of her church had given a sizable donation for a reforestation effort. Frances sent it to Pere Albert. One commissary, she reasoned, could house seeds and plants.

The textbook library? Frances knew a woman who also battled colon cancer. Perhaps she might give half of the needed amount.

The fall issue of *Haiti Happenings* talked about commissaries (five thousand dollars each, not stocked), a central library (fifty-one hundred dollars), and the new vehicle (twenty-five thousand dollars still needed).

Frances didn't act like someone ready to give up her work.

By November the vehicle was funded. Frances mailed a check for forty thousand dollars to Reverend Tom Litteer, who had moved from Sand Springs, Oklahoma, to Sparta, New Jersey. Tom was headed to Haiti.

Pere Albert picked up the American pastor at the Port-au-Prince airport. Tom gave the priest a hug and then the check. Pere Albert stood in the parking lot, laughing and praising God. That week he purchased an Isuzu Trooper, the same make and model that had served him well for eight years.

Though Frances hoped her chemotherapy would end after three months, it took eight. She remained confident, telling Pastor Rob Sherrard, "I take my treatments in a room with many others, so I use this opportunity to interest them in our Haiti project. My blessings during this time have been abundant."

Her third series of chemo concluded mid-January, right before Raleigh Court Presbyterian sent her ten thousand dollars for a school at La Revoir. This was a blessing for the many children who could not cross a river to attend Frances's nearest school in Bainet.

Frances copied Raleigh Court's letter for Flo, and she added a note at the top: "This check did me more good than chemo. I go tomorrow to see if I need more—probably not. I feel great."

Her final treatment was March 5, 1997. Her eightieth birthday.

Frances asked if she could go to Haiti—soon. Her oncologist nodded, knowing the trip would be far better for her than more chemotherapy.

On a springtime Sunday in Cherident in 1997, Frances walked toward St. Matthias Church. A young man asked, "Are you Mrs. Landers?"

She assured him that she was.

"We have been praying for you," he said.

"Yes, I know. I'm here. Thank you."

Her cancer in remission, Frances felt better than she had in years.

A decade after the ordeal, Frances summarized her chemotherapy. "You're weak, you lose weight, and you feel sick. But there was never a time when I did not think I would get well. I don't believe that it is all mental, but I do think it helps to have something beyond yourself to think about."

Back in Cherident, Frances imagined the opportunities that
the new vocational school would give young people.

Chapter 16

More of Everything

My oncologist gave me high doses of vitamins and suggested I stay active.
My children had a big laugh about this.
—*Frances Landers, El Dorado, Arkansas, 1997*

Back on the speaker circuit, twenty pounds lighter and feeling wonderful, Frances went to Bastrop, Louisiana, to speak at First Presbyterian. Standing in the church parlor, she looked up to see the pastor, Thomas Reinowski, staring at her.

Frances soon forgot about that moment. A week after she returned to El Dorado, a letter arrived from Bastrop. With a check for $1,300 was a note of apology from Pastor Reinowski. He had been caught off guard, he explained, expecting to see Frances's eyes dulled from her months of chemotherapy. He had anticipated that her spirit perhaps would be diminished.

After reading the pastor's well wishes, Frances smiled. No, she was not ready to stop working for Pere Albert.

She opened another envelope. Reverend Tom Litteer's church in Sparta, New Jersey, agreed to fund benches for Raleigh Court's school at La Revoir.

A third letter brought a request from Harriet Prichard for project ideas for her next catalog. With trepidation, Frances wrote Pere Albert. His last letter had exhausted her with all that discussion about teachers' salaries and commissaries and library books. But Frances knew Harriet valued impactful projects for her Alternative Gift Markets. The more ideas, the better.

Be careful what you wish for. The adage crossed Frances's mind, and for good reason. Soon five handwritten pages arrived from the mountains.

Topping Pere Albert's long list was a "fish pond project."

Pere Albert wrote a full page about ponds for breeding fish. "Fish like tilapia is not expensive to raise," he said. To start, he would be content with one hundred ponds. Seventy thousand dollars.

Another page detailed a "corn silo project" at twenty thousand dollars that would allow farmers to store their harvest for a better price.

A revolving loan fund would cost fifty thousand.

He requested more commissaries like the one in Cherident. "We can start them one after one," Pere Albert wrote, suggesting fifty thousand dollars as a good goal.

The priest elaborated on the textbooks, which he called "the bank of books project." He now wanted five libraries. Twenty-five thousand dollars.

Pere Albert told Frances to talk to Harriet about all of the proposed projects. But "here are some others," he said, offering additional ideas—seventeen of them. Lay evangelists, benches, pigs, sewing machines, tools, seeds, chickens, Bibles, hymnals, a Bible college, shoes, roof repair, and more.

Word got around about Pere Albert's ideas. It wasn't long before Frances heard from retired missionary Harvey Musser.

"I understand Pere Albert sent you requests for a million dollars."

Frances wasn't about to raise a million dollars, but a line in Pere Albert's letter gave her pretty nearly a million laughs. At the end of his fifth page of "opportunities," the priest wrote: "I believe that God will make you enough strong to come to Haiti at least once a year until 90 years old. Nothing is impossible to God. I remember that Sara give birth to a child at that age."

After she copied the long letter for Flo, Frances added a note.

You will get lots of laughs—Please, God, no babies!!

For her 1997–1998 *Alternative Gift Market* catalog, Harriet Prichard chose the commissaries, raising money for five community stores across the mountains. Over two thousand women pledged to become members of the cooperatives. They would purchase bags of rice or flour and resell them for a small profit to generate family income.

Harriet's description in the catalog explained that there would be "no middleman," since Pere Albert would drive his truck to Port-au-Prince and purchase large quantities of the staples at wholesale prices.

Frances chuckled as she read the write-up. Pere Albert, one of God's greatest spokesmen of all time, would have loved being called a middleman.

At age eighty, Frances wondered if she could keep up with all that swirled around her. Lots went well, but not everything panned out.

She flew to Texas to film a commercial about the Haiti Fund, sponsored by a well-meaning man. She did her best, though she wrote friends that she needed Tammy Faye Baker's eyelashes.

The commercial, she later commented, "was a complete washout, and my eyelashes had nothing to do with it."

Then Frances thought Lyon College might be interested in supporting Cherident's vocational school. She made an appointment to speak with the president. Jim Landers's pilot flew the two hundred miles to Batesville, Arkansas, only for Frances to learn that the president was not available.

Whenever Frances's spirits were a little low, Gardner gave her a hug and told her it was God's way of keeping her humble.

A North Carolina woman also helped Frances keep perspective. Each month, every month, she wrote a check for six dollars for a pair of shoes so another child could go to school.

Harvey and Doris Ann Musser sent Frances false eyelashes. She was ready for her next television offer.

Pere Albert's letter of May 15, 1997, cheered Frances even more than the eyelashes. As much as the priest frustrated Frances with his endless requests, she valued his spiritual wisdom.

> *I find out that you feel discouraged after your visit at Lyon College. I can tell you that according to me, it was a successful visit: we have to sow the seed before the harvest. From the Psalm 126:5-6 we read: "Those who sow in tears shall reap with joyful shouting. He who goes to and fro weeping carrying his bag of seed, shall indeed come again with a shout of joy, bringing his sheaves with him."*

Pere Albert was sure Lyon College would eventually get involved with Haiti. His letter ended, "We keep on praying for you and we believe that the Lord will make you very happy in your old days."

Frances was feeling older every day. "They are working Grandmother too hard!" she wrote to Flo on August 5. Two days earlier she'd been on the phone with a group from Westminster Presbyterian in Westlake Village, California.

> *It was the Mission Committee and Pastor. They asked me to talk, amplified so the entire room could hear. I did that and they asked questions... then the pastor closed with prayer. The entire time was about 20 minutes... it was a first for me.*

A few weeks earlier, the pastor, Reverend Dick Thompson, had been in conversation with three others. Two, Ben and Sara Small, attended his church. The third was Sara's aunt. Her name? Harriet Prichard.

"Just go and see," Harriet said to Ben and Dick.

Those familiar words.

Frances's enthusiasm radiated through the southern California speakerphone. The committee voted to send Dick and Ben to Haiti, just to see.

To support twenty-eight schools, Frances needed in excess of twenty thousand dollars a month, plus seven thousand for the vocational school. John Reed was regularly in Cherident, overseeing the progress of its first classes in auto mechanics, art, and agronomy. On one trip, in response to a question from his church about the safety of traveling to Haiti, John brought his young daughter Molly.

"I thought that was a good way to prove my confidence in Pere Albert's ministry," John told me, adding that Molly had a terrific time.

On October 29, 1997, Frances mailed a letter to supporters, its tone and appearance so personal that recipients thought it was written just to them.

"I am so full of good news that I hardly know where to start!" her letter began. Raleigh Court had finished paying for its school in La Revoir, and over twenty-one thousand dollars more had reached the Landerses' mailbox for scholarships.

Frances had returned from "preaching" at First Presbyterian in Romney, West Virginia, with seven thousand dollars. Then she took a trip farther north to Reverend Tom Litteer's church, First Presbyterian, in Sparta, New Jersey, and came home with thirty-five hundred dollars.

Over and over, she told supporters, "I tell myself every day that this is God's project, not yours or mine."

Tony Steiner of Sparta's First Presbyterian agreed. "Frances was just wonderful," he told me. "She was an example of what the Lord can do, once you put everything in God's hands. I loved her spirit and admired her endless drive from her typewriter in the kitchen."

One fall morning Frances received a call from Pastor Thomas Evans of First Presbyterian in Magnolia, Arkansas. A member of Magnolia's Rotary Club, he asked her to speak in October. Knowing time was tight at Rotary meetings, Frances said yes, *if* she could have a full twenty minutes to talk and show her slides. Pastor Evans agreed.

But a previous speaker overran his time. Seven minutes were left for Frances. She told her story, without the slides, in four minutes.

On November 5, a contrite W. P. Florence Jr. sent a long, heartfelt letter to Frances, asking forgiveness for having encroached on her time. He enclosed a personal check for two hundred dollars.

Frances sent a copy of his letter to Flo, adding commentary in the margins:

They gave me 7 minutes - I made a 4-minute talk without slides - So they were out 3 minutes before one o'clock. I was furious!! I had come 45 min. early so I could be ready - but I stayed cool and collected.

More than cool and collected, Frances was downright classy in her reply to Mr. Florence.

"God works in mysterious ways ..." If I had shown my slides I think those attending would have told me that they enjoyed them, but I doubt if they would have whipped out their checkbooks to make a contribution. Since not being able to do the program planned, I have received several gracious letters and generous checks from your Rotarians.

Your letter was a bonus. Your gift will support four children for a year and provide them with a nourishing meal. For most of these children, the meal they have at school is the only food they have each day.

I accept your apology. I have spoken at many service clubs and I know that members can't stay for a program that runs over the time.

Just know that NOT seeing the slides has probably helped more children than SEEING the slides. One hundred percent of all gifts go direct to Haiti to give a child the opportunity for a new life.

She made a copy of this letter for Flo too, adding,

Don't they know they can't treat the Queen like this?

To ensure that Pere Albert's Christmas boxes reached him on time, Frances shipped them in mid-November. Shopping for the priest was never difficult. He could use anything practical. This year's assortment included medicine, T-shirts, paper towels, toilet tissue, blankets, towels, candles, shampoo, paper plates and cups, plastic dinnerware, and baby wipes.

The latter item was familiar to mission teams. Baby wipes—Wet Ones®—were on every packing list. Even when bottled hand sanitizer came along, many travelers still slipped a package of Wet Ones into their luggage.

"Use the Wet Ones!" Pere Albert would call out, waggling his index finger each time a visitor was handed an empty plate, glass, fork, or knife. He wanted no one to return home ill with a bacterial disease.

"Use the Wet Ones!" Pere Albert knew they would help.

He was right.

He was right about something else. Frances *was* invited back to Lyon College in Batesville. At a Thanksgiving chapel gathering in 1997, the eighty-year-old woman from Arkansas gave the main message, "The Choice Is Ours."

She asked that her honorarium check be made out to the Haiti Fund, and she thanked Lyon College officials, who said students would prayerfully consider how to become involved in Pere Albert's mountains.

Pere Albert *was* right. The seeds at Lyon College had been sown. Soon there would be a harvest.

This was the work. Seeds and prayers and harvest. Churches going up and vodou temples coming down. More lives for Christ. More schools and vocational classes, teachers and textbooks. More generous supporters. More commissaries. More children's smiles. More lives changed.

More hope.

Pere Albert introduced Frances to the congregation of
Cherident's St. Matthias Episcopal Church.

The children of St. Matthias Parish knew that education was a gift from God.

The road through Cherident.

Chapter 17

Cherident: A Wide
Spot in the Road

*At eighty-one years of age, Frances Landers is spry
and full of the vigor of one possessed with a sense of purpose.*
—Christopher Spencer, El Dorado News-Times, 1998

"I feel close to God up here," Frances said when she was in Haiti's mountains. Cherident, the parish seat of St. Matthias, was her second home. In February 1998 Frances made her thirty-fourth trip to Haiti in twenty-one years.

For the first time, a newspaper reporter accompanied her.

In his article for El Dorado's daily paper on February 23, Christopher Spencer summed up Frances's commitment to Haiti: "Three weeks ago, Frances Landers left home to come home."

It was often difficult to listen to news stories about Haiti. The images? Sometimes it was impossible not to look away. Frances couldn't *stay* away.

Deplaning in Port-au-Prince, Frances and her companions jostled their way through customs and out into the sultry sunshine. They connected with their driver and began, in a creaking vehicle with shot suspension, the intolerably slow journey out of the slums of the capital city. They headed southwest past Léogâne and then farther up into the beautiful, barren mountains of Grande Colline to Cherident.

Once in the countryside, Frances rolled down her window.

On crystalline days like this, heaven seemed somehow closer than in the United States. The sky was a richer blue. The clouds, suspended over the mountaintops, were a whiter white. The air grew hot, but it was always clear.

The hillsides were denuded, the fields full of more rocks than crops.

Frances watched a tethered chestnut horse, a brown cow, and a few dingy goats. Each dreadfully thin animal looked for something to eat.

Ramshackle huts and little listing houses were scattered up the hills on both sides of the dirt road. Red-crowned roosters strutted without purpose. Frances smiled. Roosters awakened her, always, an hour before daybreak.

Funny, she thought. *The roosters make me feel at home.*

Dusk came early in Cherident. In mid-afternoon the sun was low and the shadows long.

Resolute Haitian women returned from a market that was miles away, baskets atop their heads. The men finished working the tired land, slung machetes over their shoulders, and headed up the road.

Children and teens, hundreds of them, had just finished school. They carried no backpacks or schoolbooks, just smiles. A cluster of young children in clean, crisp uniforms of yellow and white waved at the vehicle and hurried to catch up. They sprinted over the rocky terrain and easily outpaced the exhausted car as it picked its way along every inch.

When the children recognized the woman in the front seat, they called out to her. "Ma Ma! Ma Ma!" It was almost a chant, one of reverence and gratitude. They waved and ran alongside the car and began to sing.

Mrs. Landers was the reason that they were in school.

Cherident had no intersections—just a single, narrow, rutted road and a few simple buildings on each side. The village of Cherident was, in fact, little more than a wide spot in the road.

It was wider—much wider, Frances reflected—than it had been nine years earlier, before Pere Albert had come. The church had been there then, been there in fact for seventy-five years. But now the church had new paint, new life, and overflowing joy. There was a lovely kindergarten, an energetic primary school, and a secondary school of two stories. There was a large vocational school with empty rooms for additional classes. There was an outdoor kitchen, though rudimentary, an infrequently used clinic, the bakery, a commissary, and the guesthouse.

Ah, the guesthouse. In a few more minutes, Frances would glance left and right for spiders and then set her little suitcase on a narrow cot. She would wonder if one of the toilets would work. She'd anticipate tomorrow morning's feeble, cold shower.

Anything but fancy, the guesthouse was nevertheless proof that many people cared for the future of those who lived in the mountains.

As the driver neared Cherident, creeping across jagged rocks wedged into the deeply gouged road, Frances's smile grew involuntarily wider.

St. Matthias Episcopal Church greeted visitors roadside. It was a white stone structure with a sloping, corrugated tin roof and an arched double door that faced the road. The wooden door, twice the height of Pere Albert, was opened in welcome. Two smaller arched doors bookended the larger one.

All were refreshed from time to time with a new coat of lively green paint. Above the door at the peak of the roof, the thick, chiseled concrete cross was painted vibrant green as well.

Behind the church was the outdoor kitchen, if one could call it that, where each school day mothers cooked beans or rice in a black kettle over a charcoal fire. The deforested mountainsides of southern Haiti could scarcely tolerate chopping another tree, but its fuel fed the children.

The guesthouse was up a little hill off a dirt driveway, tucked behind the church and the kitchen. A single story of cinderblock, it had a wooden door and a concrete front porch. The guesthouse's central room was long and narrow, large enough for a rectangular wooden table that seated sixteen. Matching dormitory rooms flanked each side of the big room. Narrow wood-frame cots held thin mattresses. There were no pillows.

A small, barely functioning bathroom was in each dorm room. The showers were pipes through the wall with small spigots. A storage tank—a cistern—was on the roof to supply water, cold and not clean. Sometimes the toilets flushed. Young Haitians routinely hauled buckets to the roof, hoping more water pressure would be of help.

At the back of the guesthouse, an indoor kitchen was little more than a counter and sink to prepare food and stack dirty dishes. Two small bedrooms housed the young women who took care of visitors.

The best feature of the guesthouse was its front porch, a gathering place on quiet, dark evenings, where Creole and French and English voices intermixed long into the night. The Americans carried high-backed dining room chairs, painted pale blue, to the porch, and vied for the single rocking chair. In later years, new chairs and rockers were added, richly stained and with woven seats.

Luc—some called him Papa Luc—was Cherident's carpenter. He built the chairs and cots, grateful for the Americans who commissioned them. Luc was a good carpenter, and the furniture was pleasant for him to make. Sadly, he spent too much time building wooden coffins, often tiny ones.

Heaven seemed closer too on soft, gentle nights. In the earlier years, no cell phones rang. A feeble, generator-powered light barely bit into the pitch-black of the night. The stars, millions of them, sparkled for hours. A flash of lightning was a teasing question mark about the chance for late-night rain. A breeze drifted by. Fireflies danced down low. The roosters were fast asleep.

Frances was right. God felt nearby.

There were rain showers in Cherident, and thunderstorms. Hurricanes too. But most mission teams avoided the storm season and never saw the full range of weather that Haitians endured.

Yes, he was there, waiting for Frances. Pere Albert was in his customary spot, sitting in an old metal school chair with an attached writing surface.

"His outdoor office," the Americans called this chair that was too small for his large and lanky frame. At the edge of the dusty road, across from the church and next to the commissary, the priest greeted his people as they walked by. He praised or admonished them, solved their disputes, heard their concerns, and offered prayer.

This day he sat in his school chair to wait for his friend from Arkansas.

The vehicle rattled to a stop. Frances laughed and waved. She climbed out of the tired car, loosened her stiff neck, returned Pere Albert's big bear hug, and retrieved her overnight bag.

She and her companions came up the front porch and stepped into the guesthouse. The golden sunlight of late afternoon streamed through the windows that had neither glass nor screens. The table was set for dinner, the plates mismatched and the glasses upside down to keep them clean.

The young women—Rose, Denise, Gracieuse, and Viergela—had modestly decorated the pale-yellow dining room walls with welcome signs, plastic pompoms, and a few balloons.

A green lizard scurried over Frances's foot. Outside, Pere Albert called her name.

Frances smiled. She was back home.

She never unpacked her travel bag. The dormitory room had no dresser, hooks, or spare chair. Since this trip's team was small, suitcases were left on vacant beds, zipped up so spiders or crickets could not make themselves at home.

Frances did take out her candle and matches before dusk. On each trip, she brought a stout candle large enough in diameter to be freestanding. Since the guesthouse walls and floor were concrete, she kept the flame burning all night.

Dinner was jovial. Pere Albert schooled the young women to prepare the food carefully so the Americans would not get sick. Sometimes the priest ate with them. Often he invited others, leaders in the village or a visiting doctor. Always the food was ample.

"It is time to eat. Come. Now."

No matter what his American friends were doing, Pere Albert scooped them up at precise times for their three meals a day. Platters appeared on the table as if by magic, although the young women had worked for hours to prepare them. Some meals made sense; some did not. Spaghetti for breakfast was common. Or hot dogs.

At dinner that evening there were fifteen platters: tomatoes and lettuce and onions, fried plantains, a delicious spicy coleslaw called pikliz, mangos and pineapple, bread, beans and rice, and more. The meat on one platter might have been chicken, but it could have been goat.

Many Americans stuck to the vegetables. Sitting at the dinner table one evening, Pere Albert suddenly said, "Scott, did you try that mashed vegetable?"

"Pere Albert, yes, I ate that mashed vegetable," Scott replied.

"Scott, eat some more."

Scott Sabin had returned to Cherident in May 1997 to hire Jean-Marie Desilus as the director of Haiti's Plant with Purpose. Dezo, as he was known, was a handsome and intelligent man who had thrived in Frances's schools. He was a mathematics teacher in Cherident's secondary school when Scott met him. Pere Albert recommended Dezo highly. Scott would call him "one of the most talented administrators I ever met."

Pere Albert gave Plant with Purpose an office on the upper floor of the vocational school. Scott asked Dezo to teach the agronomy class two days a week and to set up farmer cooperatives the other three.

Dezo hired and groomed Guy Paraison as his agronomist and, later, credit manager. When Dezo was elected to Haiti's Congress in 2000—a tribute to the quality of Frances's schools—Guy succeeded him as director. When Dezo's term ended, he returned to Plant with Purpose to work for Guy.

Still today, Plant with Purpose is vastly successful, teaching villagers about seeds and seedlings, crop rotation, irrigation and trees, loans, and Christian discipleship.

Yet in 1997, all of this was still to come for the skeptical farmers that Scott and Dezo gathered in a field of nonproductive corn stubble. Through an interpreter, Scott talked of the long-term benefits of planting new trees, working together to remove rocks from fields, and helping each other farm.

"Cooperation" was not a word widely used in the vocabulary of Haiti, where day-to-day survival framed the culture. Pere Albert was trying to change this, but progress was slow. Scott met with resistance.

A farmer standing in the back frowned, crossed his arms, and raised his voice. "I cannot wait three or four years," he said in insistent Creole. "My family is hungry now."

Dezo and Scott had their work cut out for them.

The 1997–1998 school year gave Frances a new challenge. Though schools were open ten months, the Haitian government passed a regulation requiring twelve months' salaries for principals and teachers.

Frances adjusted Pere Albert's budget and told donors, "This is only fair, as their salaries are so small. We keep our kitchens open during the vacation months to assure that children have sufficient nutrition."

This was true in many of Pere Albert's villages; kitchens did remain open all year. But in other communities, difficult logistics or high costs precluded noontime meals, even during the school year. Frances was concerned about the children in these villages and began to look for partnerships with organizations that specialized in food programs.

In 1997 Reverend Dick Thompson and Ben Small of Westminster Presbyterian in southern California took Harriet Prichard's advice to "just go and see." The two men traveled to Cherident and met Pere Albert. Dick knew his church would return to Haiti's mountains many times.

In the spring of 1999, Ben and teammate Don Miller helped young Haitian men install a pump to improve water flow to the guesthouse. They fixed a broken generator. Dick Thompson led Sunday worship.

In 2000 Ben and Don taught bright Haitian students to install a solar collection panel on the roof of the vocational school. Ben had designed the system, and the Westminster team had carried an odd assortment of things (including fluorescent lights) through airport customs and up the mountains.

"We didn't think we'd ever solve all of the problems we faced," Don said. But just hours before the team headed down the mountains to the Port-au-Prince airport, the lights flickered and stayed on. Several rooms of the vocational school were lit, including the Plant with Purpose office and a classroom where students could study after dark.

Pere Albert kept a close watch on the solar installation. Since the vocational school was close to the road, shiny new solar panels would be a temptation for someone passing by. Pere Albert had barked out instructions for the Haitian students to build a tamperproof frame for the panels.

It didn't matter. Almost as soon as the team returned to California, here came the news. Someone had stolen the solar panels. Spirits sagged.

Back in Cherident, Pere Albert stood in front of his parishioners. He told them forcefully that he wanted the solar panels back.

It took a while, but they were returned. Eager Haitian youths could not wait for the next time Ben and Don came from California to help reinstall the panels. When they did, the lights came back on.

On the 1999 trip, I had my camera. Pere Albert, of course, noticed.

"Martha. You are going to three schools. The driver is ready. Now. You will take pictures of each child. Write down their names and their ages. This is for Frances Landers."

Pere Albert thrust into my hands a plastic bag filled with rolls of film.

One seldom knew precisely what task the tall priest was assigning, or for what purpose. Only in hindsight could most mission workers, even Frances, piece together what this visionary man had in mind all along.

I knew very little about Frances's work, though I was aware that she was responsible for the smiles of the children who followed us everywhere. Perhaps I was supposed to document an accurate roster of the three schools. I snapped photo after photo as quickly as I could.

When I figured out that Frances needed appealing photographs for fundraising, and that other mission teams had donated the film, I paid attention to lighting and composition as I captured the charming faces of the young children.

I sought out the secondary school students too, like twenty-one-year-old Michael, who was about to graduate. Michael was handsome and seemed wise, as though education had unlocked the secrets of life.

On May 7, 1999, Frances wrote her first letter to me.

Martha, the pictures you sent are the best I have ever had. They arrived 30 minutes ago and I have quickly gone through them. They brought tears.

Yes, Frances had the gift of making each of us feel indispensible to her mission.

The vocational school, championed by John Reed and Tinkling Spring Presbyterian, was in its second year. It had blossomed. Dezo's two-year agronomy class was going well. Auto mechanics and art instruction were also successes. Pere Albert asked Frances to fund a seamstress class. Since solar power did not yet reach into that classroom, she rounded up money for pedal sewing machines, along with tables and chairs. Soon classes in computer instruction and other practical subjects were added in the school.

Kerosene for Pere Albert's small generator was stored in the commissary. The generator was like a gold nugget in Cherident, valuable and fiercely guarded. Pere Albert's highest priority for its use was to help the young people "make loud music."

Pere Albert was convinced that if the youth formed choirs and praise bands, they would stay in the villages rather than move to the too-often grisly cities, especially Port-au-Prince. For years the priest's American friends supplied soundboards, amplifiers, microphones, guitars, portable organs, drums, and all sorts of woodwind, string, and brass instruments.

In the El Dorado church office one day, Frances nearly tripped over a donated trombone. Pere Albert requested musical gear so often that she scarcely gave it a second thought.

The trombone was one of many little projects Frances delegated to Mary Jo Oliver. "You might want to have the instrument checked out before you send it to Haiti," she helpfully jotted in a note.

It is a testament to Mary Jo that she continued to volunteer.

When darkness fell at five o'clock, there was scant light in Cherident. A solar-powered glow from the vocational school. A generator-powered glow in a room of young musicians. An occasional candle or flashlight. Fireflies.

But there was electricity of another kind—a buzz of anticipation—in the village. Each time more kids were enrolled in school, or a visiting doctor worked in the clinic, or a trombone arrived, the parents in the community believed it might, just might, be possible for their children to step beyond poverty.

Frances had not stayed in Cherident's guesthouse many times before she concluded that God spent a disproportionate amount of His time caring for this wide spot in the road.

Pere Albert enjoyed three generations of the Landers family—
Frances, Jason, and Mike—on the guesthouse porch.

Chapter 18

Village Vignettes

*We traveled the "road" to Daneau. Several times we had to descend
from the Trooper and push it through the rocky road.
The final leg of the journey was completed on foot.*
—*Ginny Mattox, Marietta, Georgia, 2000*

Pere Albert's villages had many things in common. Poverty and rocks. Not
enough food and unclean water. Insufficient healthcare. Little homes that
leaked and were shared with bugs or rats. Worship spaces, no matter how
humble. Schools. Generosity. Tenacious joy. Hope.

The villages of St. Matthias parish were also diverse in topography, size,
and accessibility.

Bras de Gauche, "left arm," was one of Pere Albert's most remote
communities. He came to this congregation four Sundays a year, often
coinciding with Windy Cove's annual visit to the mountains.

In July 1996 Pastor Rob Sherrard's team rode with Pere Albert from
Cherident to Bras de Gauche. Forty miles, five hours each way, was a good
estimate, though car trouble (a near certainly) added time.

Since Pere Albert's Toyota had been wrecked by the janitor in the horrible
accident four months earlier, the worn-out, eight-year-old Isuzu Trooper was
the only vehicle in operation. Before the Trooper was to the top of the second
mountain, Pere Albert had to tinker with the engine.

The problem sounded serious, but the team made the trip with no
mechanical breakdown. Just past the town of Bainet, Pere Albert had to
ford the river. He told the Americans to "pick up everything" on the floor
of the car.

Pastor Rob wrote, "We thought he was joking. He wasn't! When we
reached the other side, Pere Albert casually reached back and opened the

door to let the water out. The swollen river had been up past the floorboard to about six inches below the hood."

For three hours more, Pere Albert drove on heavily rutted roads across mountain ridges with splendid views. As the Trooper approached each jagged rock, he had to weigh a tradeoff: should the rock go under the axle or under the worn tire tread?

After descending down twisted curves, the road became nothing but river rock. The priest forded the river several more times, and the group arrived at Bras de Gauche. It was half past noon.

The thatched-roof church overflowed as two hundred people sang and waited. The villagers had no income, little education, and few possessions except faith, rocks, and time. They were dressed in their one nice outfit, crisp and clean. The children were as patient as the adults in waiting for their priest to arrive.

A new cinder-block church and school were complete except for the roofs. Pere Albert shut off the Trooper and removed from the trunk his robe and stole. He directed Rob's team to seats of honor at the front of the church and then began three hours of worship.

Following an afternoon meal, the Trooper started out for Cherident.

Pastor Rob wrote, "Just after dark we had a flat tire. In removing the lugs, we found that one was smaller than the others. Of course, the lug wrench did not fit. Pere Albert walked to a friend's house for help. Finally, with a sledgehammer and chisel, we removed the lug and put on the spare tire. What a view of the night sky from the top of that mountain. The interruption only enhanced our trip." The cheerful Pastor Rob told his congregation, "It is a long trip, but one you don't want to miss."

In July 1998 another Windy Cove team visited Bras de Gauche. The truck broke down in Bainet. Again the faithful Episcopalians sang until Pere Albert arrived. Again after worship, women served lunch to the Americans. Again Pere Albert called out, "Use the Wet Ones!"

Pastor Rob declared the thirteen hours "a glorious day."

In April 1999 our Westminster Presbyterian team experienced the arduous drive to Bras de Gauche. The road was often just a streambed, the flat tire inevitable. Singing floated out of the church when we finally rumbled to a stop. The service was unforgettably rich, the Haitians unendingly gracious.

After worship and a meal (and the Wet Ones), our silent prayer filled Pere Albert's vehicle as he drove back across the river rock with no spare tire. We let out a collective sigh of relief as the priest got us safely back on smoother roads and, eventually, into Bainet for tire repair.

Coming back to Cherident, the night was pitch-black. The headlights caught a glimpse of one person, then another, two and three more, walking at the side of the road. Each time when I turned around and looked out the back window, the people had been swallowed up into darkness.

After an exhausting fourteen-hour day of travel, we walked into the guesthouse, prepared to head to bed. On the dining table were thirteen platters of food. The young women hovered nearby to tend to any needs that we, half asleep, might still have.

The day after the long Sunday to Bras de Gauche, the 1998 Windy Cove team was back in Pere Albert's Isuzu Trooper. Hours later the group stopped in Daneau, a little village up a winding and inhospitable road at the top of a mountain. West Virginia's Romney Presbyterian planned to raise thirteen thousand dollars for a school there. Tom Stump of Romney rode in the back of the Trooper, eager to see the site of the future school.

Tom returned to West Virginia and wrote Frances, telling her that a drink of coconut milk, fresh from a tree at the site, had sealed the covenant. Romney would build the school. Frances was grateful for the generous gift that would bring hope to the children in Daneau.

On July 17, 1998, Frances reached the two-year mark since her diagnosis of cancer. Her body scan was clear. That summer Dennis Falasco succeeded Charles Brown as pastor of Frances's church. Pastor Dennis was eager to learn more about Frances's work.

"Would it be possible to accompany you on your next trip?"

Frances said, "Certainly. Who do you want to take?"

Pastor Dennis asked Mary Jo Oliver, Frances's faithful volunteer, to take her first trip. Also from El Dorado were Mike and Sydney Murphy. Mary Jo invited her daughter, Sylvia Brady, from Little Rock. Frances's Mississippi friend Ruth Standefer was delighted to round out the team.

Pere Albert drove the group over terrible roads to visit a possible site for a new school. Standing on the remote hillside, Sylvia told Pere Albert that she thought she could drive his vehicle.

"We got back in the SUV," Mary Jo told me. "Pere Albert had Sylvia get in the driver's seat. He folded himself up in the tiny luggage compartment, all the while with that deep, signature laugh that was uniquely his."

Sylvia drove a short distance before Pere Albert took over. Still laughing, he told her, "You are the only white woman who has ever driven on this road."

Sunday morning the team walked from the guesthouse to St. Matthias Episcopal Church to hear Pere Albert preach. The service, his first of the day, lasted several hours. He invited his friends to go with him to the second church.

"It is a long drive up into the mountains. Then we will walk for two hours," Pere Albert said. The Americans dutifully climbed in the vehicle.

Partway on foot, the group found the path too steep. "Turn around," the priest said. "Go back down. Wait for me at the vehicle."

Pere Albert climbed on and disappeared. The early afternoon air was humid and still. To cool off, Mary Jo reached under her skirt to step out of her half-slip. A little voice out of nowhere said, "Ooh-la-la."

A young Haitian lad, about four, was peeking through some brush. It took a long time for Mary Jo and her companions to stop laughing and then decide which way to go to find the vehicle. One cornfield looked promising to Dennis. He went on ahead but did not return. Again out of nowhere, a few young men appeared and directed the Americans the right way.

"They watched us carefully," Mary Jo told me, "and moved close if they thought we would lose our footing. One went to find Dennis. Back at the vehicle, which was parked in the hot sun, other Haitians came to us. These people brought chairs and set them in the shade. At the time we did not realize the significance of this gesture of hospitality. Chairs are prized possessions for Haitians, who have almost nothing. By sharing their valuable chairs, they showed us great honor."

Despite the English-to-Creole language barrier, the Americans discovered that the Haitians were Christian. Voices in two languages sang "Amazing Grace" and other hymns for more than an hour.

While Pere Albert praised the Lord at the top of a mountain, the Americans and their new friends worshipped not far from a cornfield.

"Early in May, I was privileged to take six people to Haiti," Frances wrote. Her *Haiti Happenings* article summarized the trip and then explained that Pere Albert needed a second heavy-duty car.

"As more people visit St. Matthias Parish, lives will be changed both in Haiti and in our own churches. It is imperative that we have safe transportation from Port-au-Prince to the mountains. An extra vehicle will free Pere Albert to send his driver to pick up supplies while he goes in the opposite direction to check construction progress of schools and churches."

Soon Frances received a third of the needed thirty thousand dollars.

In April 1999 political unrest paralyzed Port-au-Prince for days. After a month's delay, Frances went on a long-awaited trip with her son Mike, daughter-in-law Susan, grandson Jason, and Flo Boggs.

The Landers family and Flo delighted in having dinner with Pere Albert the first evening in Cherident, though Mike first had to chase a chicken out of the dining room. Jason quipped that the guesthouse reminded him of a "rundown Boy Scout camp."

Pere Albert wasted no time assigning a task for Mike, Susan, and Jason. They left early the next morning with their competent and handsome young driver, Jean-Robert, to find a suitable village for the next new school.

An hour later they arrived at the village of LeBeau. A school, funded by First Presbyterian of Sparta, New Jersey, was under construction.

Jean-Robert pressed on farther into the mountains. He turned onto a road barely wider than a footpath that led into steep and dense terrain. Creeping along ridges and rocks, the vehicle reached the crest of the mountain.

Mike, Susan, and Jason were astounded at the view from the mountaintop. Fields of corn surrounded small, thatched-roof shanties on neighboring hills. Banana, lime, and mango trees spilled down the valleys.

Nearby, an open-air structure of bamboo poles and banana leaves provided scant protection for an assortment of crude wooden benches and a chalkboard with yesterday's lessons.

This was the village of Lamothe.

In the background, the Landers family heard the rhythmic clanging of hoes and machetes as a line of farm laborers toiled in the sun. Suddenly dozens of curious children appeared. Jean-Robert told them that the Americans had come to see where a school building would be constructed.

The children were ecstatic.

"We were overcome by the remoteness and beauty of the area," Mike said, "and we agreed that Lamothe would be a great location for the new school. New life and hope for these beautiful people."

Yes, the villages of St. Matthias were diverse. At the top of a mountain or base of a riverbed. Accessible by car or only on foot. A few with light from a noisy generator, but most isolated in the pitch-black night.

But in each village there was hope. Ten years earlier, Pere Albert had had seven churches and schools, and fewer than one hundred Christians. Now eight thousand adults in thirty-one churches had attended confirmation classes, been baptized, and proclaimed their faith in Jesus Christ. Thousands of precious children, hungry to learn, were receiving the gift of education.

On a few white index cards, Frances wrote a story about a young girl. Espérance (Creole for Hope) could have lived in any of Pere Albert's villages.

Frances smiled at her audience. Her eyes sparkled. Her gray-blonde hair framed her happy face. She began.

"As the sun rises over the rugged mountains of south Haiti, children peek out of their huts with a feeling of excitement."

Frances stretched out the next words. "This ... is a school day."

She paused and smiled again.

"Espérance, who lives in a small hut with her parents and brothers and sisters, rolls off her banana-bark hut and slips into her uniform and shoes. Her older sisters have gone to the mountain stream, an hour's walk from their hut, to get the day's supply of water. They may be late for school, but they will join Espérance later.

"Before Espérance departs for school, her mother combs her hair and ties two yellow bows that she wears each day. They are very special because they match her school uniform.

"During her walk through the sugar cane field, she meets friends who share her excitement. Madame Joseph, their teacher, is so pretty and kind. Going to school is fun. When more children join them, they begin to sing their favorite song: "Come and go with me to my Father's house, where there is joy, joy, joy!"

Frances stopped to make eye contact with those in front of her. She let the image of the singing children settle among them.

"Soon the group arrives at the school building adjacent to their mission church where her family worships each Sunday. Before they were invited to the church, her parents went to the vodou temple to worship. Sometimes Espérance was scared of the vodou priest as he claimed to cast out evil spirits and gave them bitter potions to drink.

"Now," Frances said, "they worship in the church where the priest tells them about God's love for all people, including each member of her family. He tells them it is very special to be a child of God."

Frances described a school yard full of children and teachers waiting for the morning bell to ring. "At the tone, all line up outside of their classrooms and become very quiet. A prayer is said and a hymn is sung. Thus starts the day. The benches that the children file into are very rustic. Some are boards resting on concrete blocks. But all the children listen intently.

"At the chalkboard, Madame Joseph starts with the math lesson. Later that morning, each child will have the opportunity to take that precious piece of chalk and work his or her math lesson for the day."

Perhaps Frances thought of Millie Payne, the skinny little Oklahoma girl who helped a first-year teacher survive mathematics.

With palms open, Frances stretched out her hands. "Why does Espérance have a school to attend in the remote mountains of south Haiti? Because she is supported by a scholarship of fifty-five dollars per year. Many churches and individuals have joined together to bring hope to these for whom life is a continuous struggle."

Over the years Frances varied this story, keeping it fresh with a different child's name, a different teacher. When Frances told the story to current Haiti Fund donors, she tailored the ending to thank her audience for their specific gifts. When she finished, Frances set down her index cards, showed a few more slides, added a few remarks, and addressed questions.

She smiled that smile.

Inevitably, Frances's audience smiled back, unsure whether to be more amazed at her energy or her conviction of the power of education.

Donations increased, and Frances's mountain of gifts, to be shared among Pere Albert's villages, rose taller.

Chapter 19

Haiti Education Foundation

I recently returned from the Haiti mission in Cherident.
Thank you for allowing me to grow spiritually through your Foundation.
—Judy Barrick, Keyser, West Virginia, 2000

In 1998, during a fundraising trip to Texas, Frances and her daughter-in-law Lynn spent a few delightful hours with Lynn's cousin, Evelyn Howell, and her husband Paul. The Howells were members of Houston's St. John the Divine Episcopal Church.

Paul and Evelyn, intrigued with Frances's Haiti ministry, decided to "just go and see." Frances threatened Pere Albert "within an inch of his life" if the Howells' visit was not wonderful.

It was. The Houston couple returned from Pere Albert's Episcopal parish to their own, bursting with ideas. Evelyn told Frances that she and Paul believed the guesthouse should be enlarged.

And Evelyn wasn't complaining, but the bathrooms were very dirty, and the toilets did not always work. Could this be fixed?

Frances smiled. She contacted the next group scheduled to go to Cherident and asked if they could take a plumber to work on the bathrooms.

Then she wrote Evelyn and Paul.

> *You will laugh ... My friend Flo always says ... "I will clean the bathrooms!!" Sure enough ... she brings rubber gloves and cleaning supplies each time we go.*

Frances hoped that Evelyn and Paul appreciated the humor. Of course the guesthouse bathrooms were dirty and the toilets didn't always work.

In early January 1999, Pere Bruno sent Frances a surprising letter. He had moved from Cap-Haitien to Santo Domingo in the Dominican Republic to pastor a church with a Spanish- and English-speaking congregation.

"I am by myself," Pere Bruno wrote. His wife and five daughters would join him when the school year ended. Pere Bruno missed his parishioners in northern Haiti, but he had bowed to church politics, the details unclear to Frances.

Pere Bruno's faith would help him adjust to his new cultural setting. "I bless the Lord for this opportunity to continue to serve Him. I know He has a plan for me. I do not know it yet."

Frances respected Pere Bruno's soul searching. She had been doing her own. Her El Dorado church had given the Haiti Fund tremendous support and a nonprofit roof for nearly eighteen years. But Frances sensed that her work needed to be an independent nonprofit organization.

With the help of her son Mike, Frances applied for 501(c)(3) status. On January 15, 1999, her ministry was renamed Haiti Education Foundation, Inc., and was nicknamed HEF. Its charter board of directors was small: Frances, Mike, and Mary Jo Oliver.

Frances told her Haiti Fund faithful, "Well, I finally did it. The IRS documents scare me to death, but I had to do it to assure the future of the schools."

Scholarships remained Frances's primary need. "If someone gives fifty-five dollars a year," Frances reiterated, "fifty-five dollars goes to Haiti. This has been, really, the secret of our success." It was a simple message delivered with authenticity and joy to supporters from Oregon to Florida, from New York to California.

Her message reached Kentucky too. Pastor Ed Hurley of The Presbyterian Church in Bowling Green called Frances, offering to build a school. She was elated. Years earlier, Ed had been in Frances's Sunday school class in El Dorado.

In March Frances brought her energy to Johnson City, Tennessee. She later said to Evelyn Howell, "I was told I was the first female to bring a sermon from the pulpit. I may be the last, but they have had one!"

Evelyn and Paul were eager to share HEF's ministry with their own church. The Howells' enthusiasm led their pastor, Father Larry Hall, to invite Pere Albert and Frances to St. John the Divine in early May.

A flurry of lists, e-mails, invitations, and press releases preceded the weekend, which promised to be very nearly as big as Texas. Frances and Pere Albert were warmly received. St. John the Divine and other Houston churches joined Frances's growing network.

And just in time. Again Pere Albert expanded his parish and asked Frances for three new schools—and more. A shoe factory? Why not?

Footwear was not mandatory for children to attend school, but parents' pride demanded it. Many mountain families could not afford shoes from the cities. Sometimes a peasant farmer dug through a pile of clothing at a roadside market and found two mismatched shoes—for five children. Often one pair of shoes was shared among siblings.

Pere Albert told Frances, "Parents who cannot afford to buy shoes will get a pair of plastic sandals which will last for two to three months and cost U.S. one dollar. When we have the funds, we will try to pick up all kids who are wearing plastic sandals to give them a new pair of shoes. The parents will be asked to give U.S. one dollar."

This was, in Pere Albert's eyes, a stopgap solution. He believed a little factory was the answer, providing both shoes and jobs. But his shoe factory remained a dream.

The priest also asked Frances to ship a little rice to Haiti. "I don't believe I can get into the export business," she wrote Paul and Evelyn. "But I never thought I would be in the school business, either."

A little fish farm, a little shoe factory, a little rice: every idea was prefaced by the qualifier "little." This man of vision believed that faith, education, and a few other "little" things would change his people's lives.

For Mother's Day, 1999, Frances received a fax machine. Coincidentally, Harry Boggs bought one for Flo. He tested it, sending a fax to Frances. "I programmed your number as 01 so Flo can communicate rapidly. She won't have to go the post office at midnight anymore."

"So we both have a fax," Frances faxed back. "How fun! I'm glad I am Number 01." Still the Queen.

Frances's fax machine saw daily use, but she was not comfortable with such technologies. "I don't 'do' e-mail, so I don't understand it," she admitted to friends. And referring to Suzanne Werkema, a generous woman who created HEF's website, Frances said, "I have no idea what she is talking about. All I do is thank her and write a check for any expense involved."

Suzanne, who had learned of Frances's ministry from Harriet Prichard, created haitifoundation.org. Terms like HTML sounded like a foreign language to eighty-two-year-old Frances, but she was very pleased with the website that Suzanne faithfully maintained.

It wasn't long before Frances received a donation from a woman in Oregon who had discovered HEF through the Internet. Frances was thrilled.

She was not thrilled with Pere Albert. He was proud, justifiably, of his teenaged musical groups who wrote and performed spiritual songs using the musical gear that Tinkling Spring Presbyterian and other churches regularly supplied. Cherident's first ensemble, Espérans, included nine female voices, rich and harmonized. The young men made the most of donated instruments. A second group, equally talented, soon formed.

But what *was* Pere Albert thinking?

Since American visitors loved listening to the youths' music in Haiti, it made total sense to Pere Albert that they should tour the United States. During his stay in Houston, he had met a friend of former President George H. W. Bush, prompting a question to Paul and Evelyn Howell: "Would it be possible that George Bush may help us get American visas for the group of 26 teenagers? I know it is not easy to realize that."

Pere Albert's vision grew. He wanted to send one hundred teens to Houston. Frances, dumbfounded, faxed Flo and Harry in West Virginia.

> Can you believe that crazy Pere Albert wrote my Houston friends and asked if they knew ex-President Bush - and if *he* could get visas for 100 teenagers to come to the States. And - if they would pay transportation - furnish musical instruments - food and lodging for 10 days. They, the Houston people, figured that would cost $100,000.
>
> I could beat him with a baseball bat.

Two days later Frances faxed Evelyn and Paul, saying that she had "not yet recovered from Pere Albert's stupidity."

> Pere Albert is honest and thousands of children have a better life because of him, but it is *so* difficult to understand his Haitian mind.

Frances calmed down long enough to thank a Houston woman who gave HEF thirty thousand dollars. But when Mary Jo Oliver came home from vacation, Frances began again. They started to laugh about the whole situation, and Frances almost forgot she was mad.

She sent a final outburst to Evelyn and Paul.

> He needs to know it was a stupid mistake and he *almost* lost an 82-year-old fundraiser.
>
> Such an outrageous request. Those children (most of them) have never been out of those mountains. They have never *seen* an *airplane* or a *bathroom* - or

water out of a spigot. Just coming to Miami would be a horror trip for them.

In July Frances and Flo spent several days in Cherident. Frances brought Pere Albert a check for a new vehicle. She also requested that he apologize to the Houston church for his "outrageous request." A month later Pere Albert obliged, sending a letter to St. John the Divine. "I am really sorry for asking you for what you can't afford. Don't feel embarrassed with that. Teeth are used to bite tongue but that doesn't prevent them from staying in the same room together."

It was Pere Albert's form of an apology.

Frances received an encouraging letter from Pere Bruno, now in his seventh month of ministry in the Dominican Republic.

"One member of my Church told me that my presence in the community has changed whole attitudes towards Haitians. Praise the Lord I at least accomplished something."

God did have a plan for Pere Bruno's life. Frances was pleased that he had been open to discovering it.

In midsummer George Brandon and Daniel Hileman of West Virginia's Romney Presbyterian made a trip to Grande Colline. Pere Albert pressed the men to increase their church's support of the village of Daneau.

"I returned overwhelmed with a sense of God's call to be even more committed to the work in the mountains," George told Frances. He wanted to ship a container of lumber to Pere Albert for school benches. Build cisterns to capture rainwater. Purchase a large generator to treat and purify water. Send professional musicians to teach the teens. Bring medicine to the clinic. Look into fishponds.

George Brandon was Pere Albert's kind of guy.

"Most of all, we need to make sure that the people of the parish want to see any of these things happen," George said.

Frances respected his comment. Since the needs in Pere Albert's villages were many, it was easy for well-meaning Americans to "decide" what the Haitians needed, irrespective of culture or practicality.

Scholarships, Frances reminded herself, was *her* priority. "Other people can worry about water and health care and electrifying Cherident," she said to Gardner. "As you know, I have no way of knowing who is capable of what. I just listen. But I do think this George Brandon is serious."

Just then, Harriet Prichard called with good news. She had selected Frances's schools for her next catalog. But this wasn't all that excited Frances.

"We need to gather the people who are involved in Pere Albert's ministry," Harriet had suggested. "Would you host a weekend conference in El Dorado? Perhaps next March?"

Within two hours, Frances sent a letter to "Those Who Love Haiti," proposing dates and asking for help and prayer.

Scott Sabin of San Diego-based Plant with Purpose replied almost immediately. He would "love to participate in a GATHERING!"

Frances smiled. Somebody else valued capital letters.

Over the next months, Frances and Mary Jo spent hours planning the HUG (Haiti United Gathering) conference, winnowing down an agenda that could have spanned scholarships, school construction, vocational training, clean water, health care, the guesthouse, generators for electricity, transportation, endowments, and more.

Though Frances was pleased with Haiti Education Foundation's success and growth, her kitchen table ministry had inevitably become more complex. She and Mike and Mary Jo decided to expand HEF's board of directors to provide more perspective and leadership.

On March 13, 2000, ten days before HUG, four El Dorado supporters— Betty Ballard, Pastor Dennis Falasco, Margaret Marsh, and Mike Murphy— were elected to the HEF board.

An advisory board was set up too. From Arkansas: Jim Matheney (El Dorado) and Don Johnson (Little Rock); from Texas: Bill O'Neal (Longview) and Evelyn Howell (Houston); and from the Shenandoah Valley: Flo Boggs (Keyser) and Rob Crittenden (Roanoke).

When Flo received the minutes of the board meeting, she faxed a reply to Queen Frances.

"What an honor to serve on the advisory board. I gratefully accept (especially since I've already been elected)."

Frances appreciated the varied personalities of her volunteer leaders. She told Paul and Evelyn, for example, that Rob Crittenden was "a delightful young man who helps me regularly. He owns a winery and is always so upbeat, I believe he must sample his product regularly."

HUG drew ninety people from eleven states. Pere Albert flew in, delighted to see many Americans who knew him but not each other. Texans and Californians met Virginians and West Virginians. Those from Arkansas met others from Louisiana and New Jersey. Frances gave guests a tour of her office—the kitchen table and files stacked in all of the chairs.

Her catered catfish dinner was elegant.

Frances and Pere Albert were heartened by the conference. John Reed reaffirmed his commitment to the vocational school. Rob Crittenden signaled an interest in health care. Those from Houston—David Grizzle, Bob Stinson, Fannie Tapper, and Paul and Evelyn Howell—returned home eager to convince St. John the Divine to enlarge Cherident's guesthouse.

Shortly after HUG, George Brandon's West Virginia church loaded a forty-foot container bound for Cherident. It held lumber for three hundred benches and a school bell for the village of Daneau, a handcrafted pulpit, tires, six diesel generators, welding supplies for the vocational school, and four hundred steel posts to support concrete school roofs. A man donated his lifetime collection of one hundred and two ball caps. Flo slipped in size thirteen shoes for Pere Albert.

John Reed went back to Haiti for a singularly wonderful purpose. He brought his fiancée, Anne. Pere Albert married the couple, who honeymooned in Cherident's guesthouse. John and Anne remained dedicated to Pere Albert's mountain ministry, taking three or four young people each year for a six-day, life-changing visit.

Ten days after the HUG conference, Frances landed in the hospital with pneumonia. She recovered enough to attend her granddaughter Andrea's wedding but avoided mentioning this to her doctor, who would have said no.

In mid-2000 Bishop Duracin acknowledged that Pere Albert's workload—thirty-two churches and as many schools—was unduly heavy. He appointed Pere Irnel Duveaux to share the work in St. Matthias Parish. Pere Irnel brought his wife and young child to Cherident.

The bishop did not, however, provide housing for Pere Irnel. Pere Albert felt obliged to give up the rector's house, as decrepit as it was. He moved his few belongings to a lower-level classroom in the vocational school, perhaps ten feet square. The room had neither kitchen nor bathroom. It housed a small bed, a smaller dresser, and an even smaller desk, as well as scattered papers, a few books, letters from friends, and his well-worn Bible.

Again Pere Albert asked Frances to increase the school budget for the upcoming year. Thirty-five thousand dollars a month funded 288 teachers, assistants, and principals; school lunches; the vocational school; lay evangelists; and a part-time doctor and nurse.

Frances knew that Pere Albert used every penny wisely.

Speaking of pennies, Pere Albert still felt that schooling should not be totally free. He asked parents to pay, if they could, fifty or sixty cents a month—in Haitian currency, a large handful of gourdes. If subsistence farmers could not afford to pay—and many could not, especially during times of drought or hurricanes—their children remained in school.

Across the United States, interest in Haiti Education Foundation continued to grow. Evelyn and Paul Howell believed that supporters should receive a monthly update on HEF's successes and needs. They encouraged Frances to publish a monthly newsletter in addition to the twice-annual *Haiti Happenings*.

Frances did her best. In August 2000 she published the first *Hope for Haiti*, spotlighting Clear Lake Presbyterian's first trip. This Houston team told of "eye-opening experiences we will remember for the rest of our lives."

Hope for Haiti was well received. But Frances was overloaded with correspondence and phone calls, travel and talks, juggling Pere Albert's needs, coordinating volunteers, keeping track of donations and expenses, caring for family and friends, and attending to her health and Gardner's. *Hope for Haiti* was not sustainable beyond a handful of issues.

The Clear Lake travelers *did* have a marvelous trip. They were impressed with the classes in the vocational school and enjoyed visiting several of Frances's schools.

In Cherident's primary school, a Haitian girl reached out shyly to touch the arm of an American girl about her same age, curious to know what a light-skinned person felt like.

Hearing from previous teams how much Pere Albert valued music in his parish, the Texans had brought more equipment. Young Haitian men borrowed Pere Albert's generator. A new soundboard and speakers were up and running within a day.

That evening the ten Americans walked down the path from the guesthouse to the St. Matthias sanctuary. A concert featured singers, a keyboard, electric guitars, a drum machine, and lots of brass. Girbson Bijou, the young musical genius, played several instruments equally well.

Girbson's resilient trumpet was now held together with duct tape.

For two hours, rich Caribbean music floated out of the church and into the darkness.

Chapter 20

Rocky Roads and Rocking Chairs

I found life in Haiti for the people to be very hard.
Everything has to be done by hand and very primitively.
—*Jennie Mathias, Romney, West Virginia 2000*

In Cherident the front porch of the guesthouse was the perfect place to dream big, especially after a long day, an evening meal, and some music. Over the years, dedicated Haiti Education Foundation supporters spent countless hours on the porch. Under stars and fireflies, Americans talked with their Haitian friends of challenges and potential.

Rocking chair talk.

Hundreds of Americans would identify with this phrase. So many needs, so much potential for the people whose priest routinely told his friends from the United States, "I think that you can do more."

The Clear Lake team had sat on the front porch, discussing endlessly the lack of accessible and clean water across Pere Albert's parish.

American doctors and nurses, after an exhausting day in the ill-equipped clinic, would collapse on the porch, wishing for better medical facilities. Ann Brockenbrough, a nurse from Virginia, sent Frances pages of suggestions. Phil Langsdon, a doctor from Tennessee, envisioned a large hospital to replace the clinic.

One spring night in 2000, Ben Small took his turn in the lone rocking chair. Ben was a talented construction contractor, a guy of action. He believed his southern California team should do more.

But what?

Ben rocked furiously, frustrated by the inadequacies that surrounded him. This was Bob Sears's first visit to Cherident. Later he commented that he thought Ben just might cut two grooves in the porch's cement floor.

Fannie Tapper also spent time in the rocking chair on that trip, concerned that HEF's budget did not include college tuition, even for a few deserving students. She decided that once back in Houston, she would call Frances Landers and ask, "After high school, what is next?"

The question haunted many mission teams who watched the children, year to year. The little ones generally sported sparkling eyes and wide grins. Teenaged eyes too often lacked luster. Though they had received a good basic education, college was out of reach, and jobs were few.

In July 2000 George Brandon's team from West Virginia was certain that ninety days was enough time for the shipping container to reach Port-au-Prince and clear customs. The group's agenda centered on seeing the container—with its lumber, school bell, pulpit, generators, welding supplies, baseball caps, and Pere Albert's shoes—safely up the mountains.

But the shipment was still locked up at the port.

George sat in Cherident's rocking chair, listening for a tap-tap to rumble up the road. He just knew someone would rap a rock on the steel side of a colorful truck and, when the tap-tap stopped, climb down to tell George that his container was through customs. No one came.

Back in Arkansas, Frances prayed daily for the large shipment and for George's team. She told a friend, "I am not sure I would want to spend ten days with a bored George Brandon with no container to work on."

The team revised its agenda and cleaned and repainted both the clinic and the guesthouse, the latter in an appealing shade of light yellow.

How did George do without his shipping container? Frances learned that his disappointment did not hamper his enjoyment of the trip.

In mid-August Frances opened her mail to learn that Virginia's Massanutten Presbyterian pledged eighteen thousand dollars for a school at Moreau. Just then, her phone rang. It was Pere Albert, using a prepaid phone card and a satellite telephone that worked sporadically.

Frances put the letter down and gave her full attention to Pere Albert. Often, because of his accent and the phone connection, he was hard to understand.

This message, however, was clear. Pere Albert asked Frances to relay a message to George. Bishop Duracin had signed the documents to release the shipping container from customs. A driver with a large truck and extra men for security had been hired. In spots, villagers had widened the narrow road by hand.

The large container had arrived safely in Cherident.

Frances was as delighted to deliver the news to George as she was with Massanutten's eighteen thousand dollars. George, pleased, was already spearheading the shipment of another container.

"George will do great things for the Haitians," Frances told Paul and Evelyn Howell, "but they will never meet his time schedule."

Such was the reality of "Haiti time."

Later in August, Evelyn Howell and Fannie Tapper went to Cherident with Bob Stinson, an architect, and Rick Maykopet, a contractor. This was a fact-finding trip for St. John the Divine. Its mission committee believed that funding the guesthouse expansion and a school building in Lamothe was just a start. The Texans also wanted to build an apartment for Pere Albert and Pere Irnel, and separate housing for the guesthouse staff.

The St. John team brought measuring tapes, sketchpads, cameras, calculators, and, at Pere Albert's request, a six-month supply of medicine for a stomach ailment that had become chronic.

Bob Stinson drew sketches of a two-story guesthouse, its staircase on the outside. In the bathrooms, tile and mirrors. In the showers, small electric heaters. On doors and windows, screens. These were luxuries for the average Haitian. For American mission teams, they provided the comforts of home.

Paul Howell, battling leukemia, was not able make the trip. Pere Albert knew that Paul would be concerned about Evelyn's safety, and he called Frances with an update.

"Everybody is fine, very busy, and doing God's will."

Frances relayed the good news to Paul, telling him, "They will have lots to report to us." The team did. Evelyn wanted to send Frances the construction drawings for the guesthouse. Frances was interested but firm.

One thing I would like everyone to know is that plans for the guesthouse or other projects do NOT have to be approved by me. They need to be approved by Pere Albert, and he DOES talk everything over with the Bishop. I do well to DO what I DO.

Nonetheless, Frances received the Houston team's fourteen-page trip report, full of plans, lists, priorities, questions, and observations. Health care. Housing. Furnishings. Electricity. Water. Vehicles. College.

Without a doubt, Frances reflected, her original focus-on-the-schools ministry was now part of a larger, more complicated and interrelated endeavor. Across the United States, people wanted to involve Frances in their efforts.

Frances did not want that responsibility.

But she could not wait for her *own* turn to sit in a rocking chair on that porch, surrounded by a few of her beautiful Haitian children.

In 1998 Frances's teammates included (clockwise) Mike Murphy, Sylvia Brady, Sydney Murphy, Ruth Standefer, Mary Jo Oliver, and (behind the camera) Pastor Dennis Falasco.

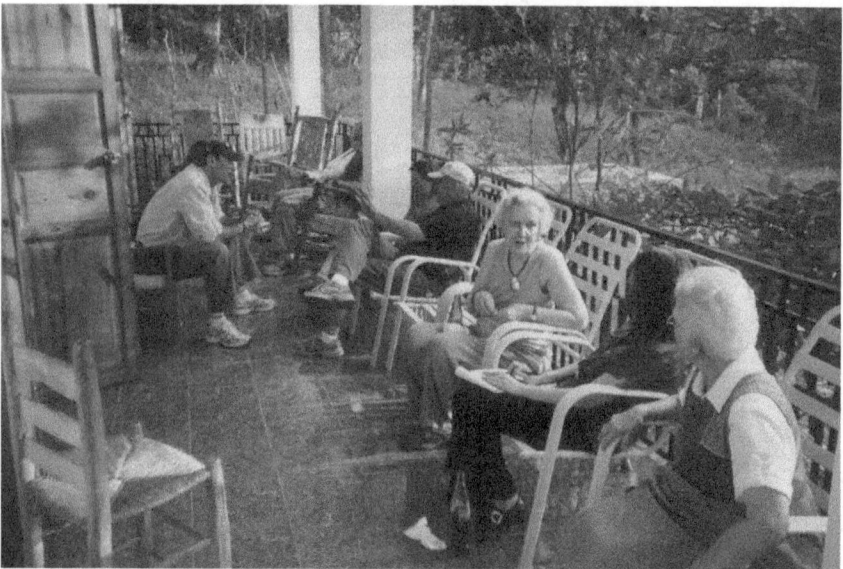

Frances chatted with teammates
on the porch of the remodeled guesthouse.

Chapter 21

Under Construction

During 2002 several construction projects were completed. The guesthouse
at Cherident is enlarged and is now a two-story structure.
—Frances Landers, El Dorado, Arkansas, 2003

One thing was clear. Pere Albert's vision for St. Matthias Parish extended far
beyond churches and schools. He dreamed of unprecedented economic and
community development in his remote, impoverished villages. Cherident, his
parish seat, was the logical starting point.

Tinkling Spring Presbyterian had rallied around the creation of the
vocational school. St. John the Divine Episcopal and Romney Presbyterian
were the two other churches most eager to champion building projects for
Pere Albert. In January 2001 Houston's Fannie Tapper, Bob Stinson, and
Charles McCord paired up with West Virginia's George Brandon and Daniel
Hileman.

Off to the mountains they went.

Pere Albert was eager to ramp up construction. "I want you to form
a committee to keep our construction work going," the priest told Bob
Stinson. Pere Albert wanted Harry Theodore, an engineer and principal of
the vocational school, to be his general contractor.

Cherident's guesthouse expansion was Pere Albert's highest priority,
followed by a rock crusher and concrete mixer to improve the quality of
cinder blocks. Pere Albert envisioned a concrete plant to supply building
materials across Grande Colline. He was open to the idea of clergy housing
for himself and Pere Irnel, and he supported a bottled water plant. The clinic
needed work, but that could wait.

Noting that local Haitians had somehow built the parish's schools by
hand, the Texans added a front-end loader to the list.

Before returning to Romney, George and Daniel tracked down the first shipping container's items. All were either in use or safely stored for later. The two men confirmed that their second container—filled with hand tools, enough steel and paint for thirty lockable doors, and massive quantities of wooden beams, plywood, and lumber—was en route to Cherident.

Back in Houston, Bob Stinson wrote to tell Pere Albert that yes, he would chair a Capital Improvements Committee. The team would raise funds, coordinate Cherident's building projects through telephone meetings, and periodically go to Haiti to sync up with the priest.

Bob asked Frances to join the committee. She was impressed with Bob, but she said, "This is not my area of expertise, nor do I have time." She suggested that he ask Don Johnson, an accountant and attorney who gave HEF hands-on financial help and solid tax advice. Don, from Little Rock, was the brother of Frances's daughter-in-law, Susan.

The Capital Improvements Committee included a number of other key Haiti supporters from four states. Frances thought the roster sounded excellent, especially since she was not on it.

Evelyn Howell's chief role was keeping Frances in the loop as conference calls mounted up.

Complications mounted as well. Even for committee members who had been to the mountains, it was hard to reconcile the cultural differences between Haiti and the United States. Grande Colline was an extraordinarily remote region, with few conveniences and virtually no technology. Challenges were not only daily but also unpredictable.

Pere Albert, with so many responsibilities in his spread-out parish, was not accessible by telephone as often as the committee wanted. On occasion he used funds for what he felt to be a more urgent need than that which the donor had designated. Sometimes he wanted to start a new project before an earlier one was finished.

Those from St. John the Divine had an added concern. Two years earlier, the church had given money for the school in Lamothe. Because the road into the village was treacherous and frequently washed out, no progress could be reported to the Houston congregation.

In Grande Colline, *everything* took time, time, and more time.

Frances understood. And she sympathized. She had long ago realized that she could not micromanage Pere Albert's decisions or actions. The expanse between Frances's Arkansas kitchen table and Pere Albert's roadside metal school desk was far larger than mere miles.

Over the years Frances had also learned that to increase communications and decrease confusion, there was no substitute to paying Pere Albert a visit. She was right. A trip to Cherident assured Houston's Charles McCord that Harry Theodore's abilities and integrity as a general contractor were top-notch. Another trip to evaluate Pere Albert's recordkeeping confirmed to first-time traveler David Grizzle that the priest was remarkably detailed.

Funds for the construction projects were raised. At a successful Houston art exhibit, Fannie Tapper sold beautiful photographs of Haiti. A family at St. John the Divine offered to fund the priests' apartment. First Presbyterian in Sparta, New Jersey, contributed heartily toward a front-end loader.

Progress was made. Bob Stinson finalized the guesthouse blueprints. George Brandon connected with a water expert, Wil Howie of Living Waters for the World, to spec out a bottled water plant. George's church shipped a third container.

Amidst a swirl of e-mails, faxes, and phone calls, Evelyn Howell cared for her husband Paul. Aware that his leukemia was winning the fight, Frances sent a newsy fax to him and Evelyn every afternoon to provide a distraction. Frances was grateful for Paul's dedication to Haiti, including his significant contribution to the guesthouse renovation.

Evelyn too was dedicated. In August 2001 she and Frances had a long phone conversation. Then Frances updated Mary Jo Oliver.

> *Evelyn's BIG subject was the "front-end loader" and would I ask the Shreveport church for $40,000 to get one. As you know, I can't get upset with Evelyn about ANYTHING. We ended the conversation with my telling her I would PRAY about it. I could not sleep. FINALLY, it came to me that I should put the ball back in their court.*

Frances sent a fax to Houston.

> *Dear Paul and Evelyn,*
>
> *I had the most BRILLIANT thought. Would it be possible for St. John's and St. Martin's to join their youth to raise money to purchase a "front-end loader" or whatever the "THING" is called ... but we are going to name it "FAITH". Would there be one of these "THINGS" in Houston? Someone could take a picture of the youth sitting on it and "driving" it. Could someone put big letters on it ... "FAITH" in English and French?*
>
> *Now, all we need is for 500 persons in each church to give $40.00. Is my math right? I woke up at midnight*

> *and figured it again ... if 1,000 persons gave $40.00*
> *we would have the $40,000 we need for the "THING".*

Within two hours, Evelyn replied. She loved Frances's proposal and told her that if God wanted a big yellow machine named "Faith" in the mountains, it would, indeed, soon be "chuggin' along."

Frances, always trying to focus on schools and scholarships, was relieved. She felt she had driven the front-end loader herself from El Dorado to Houston.

Though Pere Albert's Houston supporters chose to raise funds for the front-end loader in another way, Frances's idea about the youth groups was characteristic of her exuberance and creativity.

Paul Howell passed away the first of September. Ten days later, September 11, 2001, Frances began her day preparing a deposit of twelve thousand dollars given to HEF in Paul's memory. Then tragedy struck. Frances and Gardner, like people around the globe, mourned the victims of the terrorist attacks on America's east coast.

When Pere Bruno heard the sad news, he e-mailed Frances from Santo Domingo. "We will be with you in your fight against the Devil."

In 2002 a rock crusher and concrete mixer began improving the quality of cinder blocks. The two-story guesthouse was completed. It was lovely, and it was appreciated by dozens of future mission teams.

In November Bishop Duracin made a decision that eliminated the need for a new priests' apartment in Cherident. The bishop split St. Matthias roughly in half and named Pere Irnel priest-in-charge of a new parish, Ascension. St. John the Divine offered to build Pere Irnel a home in Bainet, Ascension's new parish seat.

Pere Albert remained in his monk-like room in Cherident's vocational school. Pere Irnel sent Frances a reassuring e-mail, promising his continued association with Haiti Education Foundation.

"Fourteen years before, St. Matthias was not so big with all these churches, schools and etc ... The division of St. Matthias Parish in two parishes is the result of father Albert's spiritual, material works with your prayers and supports. So it is our task in Haiti to keep alive what you have spent maybe twenty years to construct. I must let you know that I never think, one day I will break relationship with HEF to be connected to a separate paralleled organization. As a young priest, I stand on father Albert's shoulders to see further. Be certain that father Albert and I will continue to work together because God calls us for that."

Pere Irnel remained faithful to the educational mission of Pere Albert and Frances. Each month Frances continued to wire to Pere Albert funds for all of the schools. He transferred, every month, the appropriate amount to Pere Irnel's account.

In April 2003 Father Larry Hall in Houston wrote Bishop Duracin, telling him to expect a Caterpillar 924F 1996 model front-end loading machine sometime in May. Many months came and went with no front-end loader. Such was life in Haiti.

Seven months later, Pere Albert found the machine collecting dust in customs and had it shipped to Cherident. The first week of December, he climbed in the driver's seat to check out the controls.

Finally, Harry Theodore's workers were able to widen the road to Lamothe and begin building the school funded by St. John the Divine.

Two and a half years had passed since Frances conceived of high schoolers in Texas teaming up to fund "Faith." But the front-end loader was, as Evelyn Howell had said, now "chuggin' along in the mountains."

Frances knew that building projects rarely went as quickly or smoothly as donors wanted. Disappointments were inevitable. And there were aspects of Pere Albert's ministry that she could never explain.

"I wish I had all the answers," Frances told friends. "I don't. I have stopped asking. As long as God gives me the strength to work, I am going to try to send what it takes each month to pay the teachers, the lay evangelists, and the doctor. I have learned to just trust Pere Albert."

Frances also trusted the Lord. "I really am able to turn all of this over to God. He has been in control from the beginning, including my mistakes."

The early years in Sainte Croix Hospital's guesthouse. From left, Dr. David McNeeley, Dr. Jim Landers, Pere Jean-Wilfrid Albert, Frances Landers, Dr. Gardner Landers, Myra Johnson, Dr. Bill Landers, Lynn Landers, and Heather Payne.

Frances and Gardner at home in El Dorado, Arkansas.

Chapter 22

Fundraising for All Ages

Thanks so much to Frances and the Foundation
for allowing me to be a part of this!
—*Scott Little, Romney, West Virginia, 2001*

Frances inherently trusted many others beyond God and Pere Albert. How else could she have so effectively led her complex ministry?

She had incredible volunteers. Margaret Marsh, Betty Ballard, and Mary Jo Oliver were invaluable, recording donations and keeping Haiti Education Foundation's books straight. Don Johnson made sure that HEF's tax accounting was flawless and worked with Douglas Jackson at Merrill Lynch to manage HEF's investment account. From Pennsylvania, Suzanne Werkema maintained the website.

"All of this challenges my brain," Frances said to Gardner. His support for his wife could not have been stronger. Frances also relied on her sons and daughters-in-law for advice, encouragement, and companionable transportation to dozens of speaking engagements across many states. Her loving family and good friends were her sounding boards.

Mostly, Frances was pragmatic. She told Evelyn Howell:

> We will not be listed in the Alternative Gift catalog next year ... or the next. Harriet seems to think we should be self sustaining. Perhaps we would be if we had invested a large percent of our income in a professional fundraiser, but that was not what I feel God called me to do. Harriet's benevolent program has millions, but about 23% is used for salaries and expenses. Of course, that is GOOD, but I never envisioned such for us. I simply wanted an avenue where 100% of the gift would reach the one in need.

Over the years, a number of donors gave gifts of stock to Haiti Education Foundation. Occasionally, people left bequests in their wills. Periodically, Frances and Mary Jo applied to foundations for grant money. Many churches were generous. First Presbyterian in Shreveport, Louisiana, for example, awarded HEF an annual grant for a building project or vehicle. First Presbyterian in Fort Smith, Arkansas, funded vehicles and schools.

Years earlier, St. John the Divine in Houston had produced an excellent videotape of Frances and Pere Albert. Frances sent copies to many interested people. If she could not accept a speaking engagement, the video (later converted to a DVD) often substituted for her personal appearance.

On the film, Frances and Pere Albert offered moving summaries of their ministry of education in the mountains. Frances concluded her remarks by asking viewers to reflect on a question: "What is my gift?"

"Sometimes we forget," Frances said, smiling.

Support for Haiti Education Foundation grew after the *Arkansas Democrat-Gazette* ran a two-page article about Frances in late 2001.

"One never knows who will be touched," she said to Mary Jo.

In December 2001, between year-end gifts from faithful supporters and donations inspired by publicity, Frances received record-high monthly contributions: one hundred eleven thousand dollars.

The generosity flowed into 2002. Dr. Ivory Kinslow, a local ophthalmologist, surprised Frances with an offer to lead a drive for scholarships. Ivory had never been involved in such a project. Frances feared that the young Scottish doctor, whom she called "super-smart and darling," didn't "understand the pitfalls."

As Ivory planned the fundraiser, Frances put the details on another event. For their sixtieth wedding anniversary, she and Gardner invited First Presbyterian's congregation to a Sunday brunch. One hundred fifty church members, including Ivory, and the entire Landers family attended.

Ivory Kinslow encountered no pitfalls. Her enthusiasm was contagious. She paired El Dorado's First Presbyterian with First Presbyterian of Sparta, New Jersey. Adults and youth groups raised over sixty thousand dollars for nearly eleven hundred scholarships.

Frances was elated. A few years earlier, Pastor Dennis Falasco had moved from El Dorado to a church in Idaho. After Dennis departed, it had become harder for Haiti Education Foundation to generate sustained interest within Frances's church. Ivory's scholarship drive was a big boost.

When Pastor Daniel Loomis came to First Presbyterian, he strongly supported Frances's work, prompting her to add him to HEF's board of directors.

A month after the anniversary brunch, Frances turned eighty-five. Gardner was eighty-eight. The couple gave thanks for their active lives. Both had cataract surgery. Gardner had a knee problem that took him temporarily off the golf course. Frances took heart medication. She attended a book club, as she told Flo Boggs, "just to get out with friends and get away from writing letters that I love too much." Frances had close friends, including Dottie Medlin, who did not attend First Presbyterian and thus provided her fresh perspectives.

Both Gardner and Frances still drove, though they avoided busy highways. They surrounded themselves with two and then three generations of family. They attended weddings and baptisms and spent ample time with their grandchildren and great-grandchildren. All in all, though Frances was always busy with Haiti, she led a remarkably balanced life.

In mid-May 2002 Frances spoke to the local Rotary Club. At the meeting she accepted Rotary's Paul Harris Award. A thousand dollars was sent to Rotary International in Frances's name.

Frances was brilliant in delivering her message in a way that impacted a particular audience. She asked the Rotarians to leave sixteen cents by their plates to feed and educate a child for one day. This began a tradition. The El Dorado Rotary Club continues to send regular contributions to Haiti Education Foundation.

After a church dinner in Mt. Pleasant, Texas, a man at Frances's table got out his checkbook and gave her two thousand dollars. She stood up to thank the gentleman, whom she did not know.

He said, "I want a hug!"

For several days Frances wondered aloud whether the man enjoyed his hug as much as she enjoyed his two thousand dollars.

"I think you can understand why the mail is so interesting for me," Frances wrote to Evelyn. "I received a letter from a donor in Hawaii. I have not heard from her for almost a year. She said, 'I have not forgotten you' and enclosed a check for one hundred dollars."

Upon receiving another surprise check in the mail, Frances said, "I spoke there years ago. I guess God tapped them on the shoulder."

From California, Ben Small called Frances and invited her to come to Westlake Village. Ben and Reverend Dick Thompson had met her at El Dorado's HUG conference two years earlier. As part of her California trip, Frances would speak at the two worship services of Westminster Presbyterian.

Sunday morning, June 2, 2002, my husband Don and I picked Frances up at a nearby hotel. Gracious, energetic, dedicated—all that we had learned about her by reputation, letter, and telephone—was confirmed in person.

Frances would speak toward the beginning of each service. She asked her typical questions.

"Where shall I sit? When do I speak? For how long?"

"We have given you four minutes," Dick Thompson said.

"Four minutes?" Frances was amused and a bit surprised. She turned to me as I sat to her left in a front-row pew.

"Why, I will have to think about how I want to condense my message."

She took a prayer request card and pencil from the pew rack and made some notes. Then she relaxed to enjoy the familiar Presbyterian order of worship. Soon Dick introduced her.

Frances walked to the microphone on the chancel. Blending the comfort of a favorite grandmother with the eloquence of a polished speaker, she explained her ministry, beginning with her first school in Mercery.

"Hope comes from education," she concluded, adding that she believed teaching Haiti's young would eventually change the country.

Amid applause, Frances walked back to the pew and set her note card on the cushion. A special offering was collected for HEF.

After the second service we left the pew to greet people in the courtyard. Frances didn't notice that I'd picked up the prayer card with her hastily penciled notes. I was curious.

Thirty-eight words were spread evenly down the card. At the top, Frances had drawn a circle around the words "saw a need." Then she'd written, "How did you get into this," under which she'd added "Pere Albert." She underscored "Why education?" and "Mercery School - 400," referring to its enrollment.

In the middle of the prayer card, in large letters, Frances had written, "Future." She'd underlined the word three times, a reminder to transition her story from Mercery to Grande Colline. Underlined once was "went to the mtns." Next was "turning on the light," underscored twice.

A verse from the New Testament book of Galatians had been preprinted in red on the prayer card: "Bear one another's burdens, and in this way you will fulfill the law of Christ."

Frances took time to read the verse before writing her closing note: "You can change a life for $55 – do you know, a little number."

In four minutes, Frances touched the hearts of many Californians.

The next morning, Don and I took Frances to Los Angeles International Airport for her return to Arkansas. We had a delightful conversation during the fifty-minute drive.

As Don neared LAX, Frances said, "Please let me out at the curb."

"We are happy to come in with you, Frances," I said.

"Martha, I am eighty-five. If I let everyone do things for me, I will not stay sharp. I need to read the signs and find my way. You have done so much for me on this trip. But I need to go into the airport alone."

We parked at the curb and took her little suitcase out of the trunk. Frances hugged us and thanked us again. She turned and disappeared into the throng of people at one of the nation's busiest airports.

A week later I telephoned Frances with good news. The special offering from the two services totaled eight thousand dollars.

"Why, that's a thousand dollars a minute," she said. "Not bad."

In July Frances agreed to accompany two young executives of Motorola, Inc., to Port-au-Prince. The company's cell phone business was doing well in Haiti, and Motorola wanted to help a school close to the airport. Frances and the Motorola managers visited the village of Thomazeau.

Frances provided modest support for the Episcopal school there, since this village was where Pere Albert had been born. But she had never visited.

The village was extremely poor, the weather stifling. Frances came home and told Gardner, "I was so hot I thought I was going to die."

Within weeks Frances received a sizable grant from Motorola for the Thomazeau school. Frances could not wait to tell Pere Albert, whom she knew would react with childlike glee.

Though Frances spent hours visiting Haiti's elementary schools, it was rare to find her in an American one. One spring day, unsure of what to expect, she spoke to third- and fourth-graders in New Braunfels, Texas.

The three hundred sixty children were attentive and asked great questions. They were also energetic fundraisers. A week before Frances arrived, teachers had given a dollar to each child.

"They were to take their dollars, invest them, and bring the results to a market they had at school," Frances told Pete and Fran Hobbs. The children sold bird feeders, fresh flowers, cookies and brownies, bookmarks, treasure boxes, and more. Fifty-cent manicures brought in twenty-four dollars.

Frances received a check for nearly two thousand dollars. Through their ingenuity, the children had increased their one-dollar gifts fivefold.

The creativity of children delighted and humbled Frances.

Sunday school classes in Romney, West Virginia, were challenged to raise a mile of pennies—$844.70—for Haiti. The children's pennies totaled a thousand dollars instead.

In Staunton, Virginia, children packed school bags for young boys and girls in Cherident. El Dorado's kids raised two thousand dollars in a skate-a-thon at the local rink.

Frances launched a "Got Milk?" campaign after Pere Albert explained that in many villages children left for school at four in the morning. They arrived three hours later, hungry, tired, and unable to focus. The priest found that when children had milk at the start of the day, their learning improved. Children in many American churches began turning nickels into glasses of milk.

At First Presbyterian's vacation Bible school in Sparta, boys and girls threw their coins in Golden Giving Creek. The pony express (a child on a stick horse) collected each day's donations. The children raised fifteen hundred dollars. A girl with a birthday that week asked guests to bring monetary gifts, adding another four hundred dollars for Haiti's children.

Krista Lovell from Nashville, Tennessee, created a board game about Grande Colline. Winding paths led from little huts to schoolrooms. Some paths were full of blessings—a glass of milk or pair of shoes. Others were fraught with challenges—a lost book or a missing goat.

Across the United States, children learned much about the lives of boys and girls their age who lived in Haiti.

Frances Landers and Pere Albert changed the lives of these children in Morreau, and tens of thousands of others across Grande Colline.

Chapter 23

Seeds and Harvest

Once you have tasted the adventure of life while walking in God's will,
you never want to return to that other existence.
—Chris McRae, Fort Smith, Arkansas, 2002

Grande Colline had all the makings of a great board game. Its territory was rugged and difficult to maneuver. Its people were poor but gracious. Their lives were uncertain, challenges endless, opportunities large and interrelated.

Health care, clean water, and higher education: these rocking chair topics regularly found their way to a specific mailbox, telephone, fax machine, or inbox in El Dorado, Arkansas.

One morning Frances's mail included a letter signed by seven graduates from her secondary schools. They wanted to go on to college. Their farming parents could not provide. Could Frances help?

The Haitian government required students to take a year of preparatory classes called Terminal II in Port-au-Prince before beginning university course work. The seven students asked for seventeen hundred dollars each for tuition, books, and lodging, adding that Pere Albert had given them permission to write to Frances.

She recognized the first name. She had watched Jean-Pierre Jackson and his five younger siblings grow up in Cherident. She knew Jackson's six friends too, having been a part of their lives for years.

Shortly after Frances read Jackson's letter, her telephone rang. It was Fannie Tapper from Houston. "Frances, your schools have ignited the minds of thousands of young people. After secondary school, what is next?"

"I do what I can, Fannie. Someone else will have to look after college. If you want to begin a higher education program, you have my blessing."

Fannie, like other Americans, developed friendships with many of the high school students in Cherident, including Jackson. Once home, travelers received letters and e-mails from the Haitian youths. Always, they lifted the Americans up in prayer. Always, they thanked God for their blessings. Often, they sought financial help for their education.

Viergela Louis, a perky teen with a desire to get ahead, corresponded with many of us. Fannie took a special interest in Viergela and partnered with other American women to fund her Terminal II classes. Fannie continued to pay for Viergela's university coursework.

Soon other individuals and churches supported college students. Evelyn Howell, for example, sponsored Marie-Ange Nicolas for nursing school, and Californians Ralph and Anne Wuerker funded a young woman named Agathna.

John and Anne Reed sent musician Girbson Bijou to college. He would go on to work for Habitat for Humanity in Port-au-Prince, returning to Cherident each weekend to teach music in a little school that was named Frances Landers Ecole de Musique. Girbson refused compensation for leading his superb orchestra, simply wanting to give back to the community that changed his life.

Frances was grateful that Fannie Tapper and others were committed to higher education. She helped Fannie administer donations and send acknowledgments. Pere Albert was diligent about dispensing funds to the students and monitoring their progress.

As the higher education effort expanded, complexities crept in. Scholarship donations fell short. Haitian parents who had pledged partial support of their son or daughter were not able to come through.

Fannie, perceiving a lack of accountability in secular colleges, focused on students who would attend Port-au-Prince's Episcopal University. She sent the money she raised directly to Bishop Duracin.

At Pere Albert's request, Frances put more of her own energy into the college program. But she had difficulty juggling the individual needs of the older students with the collective needs of nearly twelve thousand younger ones. When Ann Smith of Fort Smith's First Presbyterian called about college scholarships, Frances asked her to contact Fannie Tapper.

Fannie, who worked closely with the president of Haiti's Episcopal University, was delighted to explain the detailed academic reporting that Ann's church would receive. Would First Presbyterian like to sponsor a future teacher or a preacher? A young man or young woman?

Frances gave Fannie's exuberance high praise. By 2003 dozens of young people were in Port-au-Prince's universities, studying education, business, theology, and more.

Pere Albert told *Haiti Happenings*' readers, "It is really a privilege for a teenager from a poor family to be able to go to university in Port-au-Prince. That is a precious gift from God."

Nicholas Michael, twenty-six, was in his fourth year of agronomy studies. He looked forward to working for Plant with Purpose in Cherident.

"That is what we would like to realize in our education program," Pere Albert said. "Educate the kids until they are able to come back to work for the improvement of their villages."

The seeds of learning that these students had sown during their many years in Haiti Education Foundation's schools were reaping a harvest.

At age eighty-five, there were still times when Frances wanted to revisit her own college days.

> *I wish I had majored in "FILING" in college. Every chair is FULL.*

Just how much did Frances need to improve her organizational skills?

> *Mary Jo,*
>
> *When I told you that I did not have the large posters to send to Fort Smith, why didn't you say, "Yes, you have those posters. You have so much stuff on top of other stuff that you don't know what you have!!"*
>
> *You didn't have the nerve to tell me that, but you thought it and you were RIGHT. I DO HAVE THOSE POSTERS!!!*
>
> *I am going to blame Mary. I named her "chairman of filing." When I asked if we had those posters, she said, "NO". Well, SHE put them UNDER my bubble mailers. When I got ready to mail "stuff" today, there were the posters. I will bring them to you on Monday.*

After a few more paragraphs, Frances added a postscript:

> *If you want me to resign, I will - after I bring you the posters -*

Frances had been cancer free for six years. But approaching eighty-six, despite the assistance of Mary Jo and others, Frances needed more help. When a generous friend offered to fund an executive director for Haiti Education Foundation, Frances thought of Mary Jo's daughter, Susan Oliver Turbeville.

She kept the idea to herself. Susan helped out at her parents' business, and Frances did not want to get in the way.

As Frances prayed for the right answer, Mary Jo asked her a question. "How about Susan?"

Laughing, Frances confessed that she'd had the same thought. Mary Jo called Susan, who was on an outing with her children, and asked her to think about this. Susan knew she had been given a rare opportunity and immediately said yes.

"I was keenly aware when Frances got involved with Haiti, and all that she was doing there," Susan told me. "While I was away in college, Mother became very involved with Frances's work. I graduated, moved back to El Dorado, got married, and started a family."

Frances was a terrific mentor, and Susan an excellent protégé. Like Frances, Susan had deep faith and an engaging personality. She took responsibility for *Haiti Happenings*, HEF's brochure, the mailing list, website, trip coordination, and many other tasks. Mary Jo happily focused her volunteer activity on HEF's financials. Frances wrote to Evelyn Howell:

> *Susan is working so hard … twenty-four hours a day, which I knew would be her schedule.*

For *Haiti Happenings'* readers, Frances added,

> *Let me assure I am not retiring, but things will get accomplished that I have not had the time to complete.*

Since Susan's salary was paid by a private donation, Frances continued to promote the fact that Haiti Education Foundation deducted nothing for administrative overhead. HEF did have expenses, of course, including printing and postage, Pere Albert's phone cards, and his Lynx Air account. These were paid from the interest generated by HEF's investments.

Mary Jo and Susan set aside a time of prayer each Monday morning, asking God to bless and grant strength to HEF's ministry.

Though mother and daughter were integral to HEF's success, neither tried to wrestle pen and notepaper from Frances. Personal correspondence continued to delight her, and she kept at it, in abundance.

For five years Frances had treated heart arrhythmia with medication, but her condition had gotten more difficult to control. On September 23, with her customary optimism, Frances sent a little note card to Flo and Harry Boggs.

I am stretched out on a bed at the Heart Hospital in Little Rock. What a life!! Tomorrow I will have my cardioversion (what I have been calling a "shock"). Gardner is home, doing fine. He calls me to ask what to "punch" on the microwave.

Frances fared well. After a short rest she returned to the speaking circuit and helped Gardner celebrate his ninetieth birthday. She was fitted with a pacemaker and then hearing aids. She scheduled another trip to Haiti after the first of the year.

Technology was slow to arrive in the region of Grande Colline. Getting Internet access to the mountains was a challenge. Pere Albert wrestled for years with the two Internet providers in Haiti, who always seemed to need one thousand dollars more to bring e-mail capability to Cherident. Instead the priest used Port-au-Prince-based e-mail accounts of young adults like Viergela or Ancy Fils-Aime to reach his friends in the United States.

Ancy was one of Pere Albert's drivers. The priest, with an eye for integrity and potential, chose as his drivers the most responsible young men in his parish. Drivers transported American teams to and from the airport. They chaperoned the visitors, picked up mail and supplies, and took sick villagers to Sainte Croix Hospital in Léogâne.

All of the drivers furthered their education beyond high school. Ancy, who became Pere Albert's trusted assistant, spoke little English until American friends provided him with lessons.

As Pere Albert's health began to fail, Ancy drove to the bank in Carrefour, exchanged Frances's checks for Haitian gourdes, and drove back into the mountains. Like Pere Albert, Ancy prayed for his safety each time he handled so much cash. He gave the proper amount to each priest, who distributed it to each principal, who paid the teaching staff.

Year to year, more of the priests, principals, teachers, assistants, drivers, and agronomists who worked in the mountains of Grande Colline received their undergraduate education there in Frances's schools.

It was a growing harvest.

The vocational school was reaping harvest too. Jean-Robert, one of Pere Albert's drivers, was a top student in Dezo's agronomy class. After Jean-Robert graduated from the two-year program, Pere Albert hired him as Cherident's grammar school principal.

Harry Theodore, the vocational school principal who had managed Cherident's construction projects, also taught electricity. Art, tailoring and dressmaking, carpentry, computer instruction, welding, and auto mechanics rounded out the school's courses. Over four hundred young men and women, each of whom contributed about a dollar to attend, were learning marketable skills.

First Presbyterian of Sand Springs, Oklahoma, sent Frances the monthly funds to operate the vocational school. John Reed was delighted that this church sustained what his church, Tinkling Spring, had begun.

One summer, travelers returned from Cherident with news that surprised Frances. She shared it with friends.

> *I did NOT KNOW they had put my name on the vocational school building. I can't believe they did that. I can't believe that Pere Albert let them. I don't believe it will be there long.*

The lettering above the second story was large and neatly painted in several colors: "Frances Landers Tech, Ecole Secondaire & Professionnelle."

Frances thought that John Reed, not she, deserved the recognition. But she smiled, thinking of her own high school's valedictorian, Mildred Andrews, and its salutatorian, Frances Landers herself. In Collinsville, Oklahoma, and in Cherident, Haiti, each had been honored for her contribution to education through the naming of a school.

Led by Guy and Dezo, Plant with Purpose continued to extend the impact of farmers' cooperatives, tree planting, microcredit loans, and more.

But who would create the equivalent success in health care?

Pere Albert wanted two small clinics in remote areas of Grande Colline. Frances questioned the request.

"We must first get the one clinic we have in repair," she said, referring to the building in Cherident and knowing that "we" did not mean "Frances."

At one time Frances had funded a nurse. Gardner regularly shipped medicine. A donor from Virginia paid for a Haitian doctor, Claude Bellanger, to come up from Bainet and treat patients on weekends. This was a start. But Pere Albert recognized that others, not Dr. and Mrs. Landers, needed to tackle the health-care problem.

A few times a year, American teams hosted medical or dental clinics in Cherident. Always the small roadside rooms were dusty and needed to be cleaned before patients could be seen. A crowd of sick villagers waited.

Four nurse practitioners from Houston's MD Anderson Hospital saw six hundred patients in four days. The nurses could identify, without asking, the children who had scholarships. The boys and girls who were in school and received a daily meal were healthier, bright, and active.

The nurses ran out of medicine. Remaining villagers went back home to wait until Dr. Bellanger or the next American group returned.

In March 2002 First Presbyterian of Fort Smith sent a team of ten to Cherident. Chris McRae, who had grown up in El Dorado and knew Frances well, led the group. A four-day clinic was the trip's focus.

Late the third day, as the tired doctors and nurses wrapped up, a woman brought her granddaughter—in labor—to the clinic porch. Neither Dr. Steve Edmondson nor Dr. J. P. Bell had delivered a baby in years. They looked at each other without speaking.

"I will deliver the child," J. P. finally said. Nurse Gayle Sherrill and Gretchen Jacks placed a mat on the concrete floor of a back room, and made the mother as comfortable as possible. An hour later, the nurses heard a baby cry.

From the back room, J. P. exclaimed, "It's a boy!"

After a one-hour rest, the mother held her new son close, and with her grandmother began a thirty-minute walk back to their little hut.

The following February, twelve people from the Fort Smith area returned to Cherident. Steve Edmondson and his wife Ann led this trip.

In addition to holding a vacation Bible school, the group hosted another clinic. After cleaning the rooms and organizing the pharmacy, Charlotte Flanders and Gretchen, back a second time, registered patients. Gayle, another repeat traveler, assisted J. P. and Steve. Nurses Candy Bell, Jaquie Core, and Carol Hall also helped the doctors and managed the pharmacy.

Of the eight hundred patients treated, the most common ailments were high blood pressure, headaches, intestinal problems, anemia, and wounds. This trip there were no babies to deliver.

Weeklong clinics like these were important seeds, valuable little sprouts, and tender shoots. But thus far, improved health care had no sustaining harvest.

Chris McRae, Dudley Flanders, the Clear Lake team, George Brandon, and Wil Howie all shared deep concern about the lack of accessible, clean water in the mountains. Even though the clinic saw more traffic, how could a villager's health be improved without clean water?

These conversations across Arkansas, Texas, West Virginia, and Tennessee increased. The bottled water plant that Living Waters for the World had attempted was fraught with shortcomings. Wil Howie planted a new seed: a plan for a water-purification system.

Pere Albert, drawing on his abundant faith, knew it was just a matter of time before Cherident would have clean water and a clinic that regularly opened its doors.

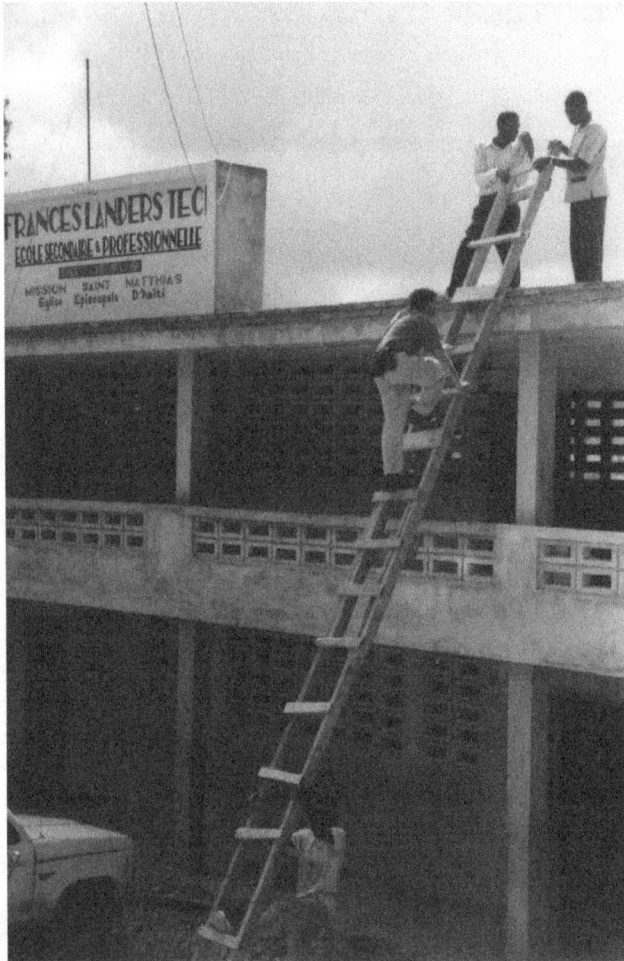

Californian Bob Sears scaled a somewhat precarious ladder to check the solar installation on the roof of Frances Landers Tech.

Chapter 24

Ten Percent, Give or Take

There is hope for the hopeless where education is provided.
Yes, much more is needed.
But with time and money on God's side, much more can be accomplished.
—*Jo McCall, El Dorado, Arkansas, 2004*

President Aristide, back in office since 2001, had an uneasy relationship with Haiti's seven and a half million citizens. Though he built a hundred public schools and fought drug trafficking and corruption, his presidency saw scant economic gain.

In January 2004 predictions of impending unrest in Port-au-Prince caused two American teams to cancel trips to Pere Albert's mountains. Frances, nearly eighty-seven, chose to keep her plans. Gardner supported her decision, prompting her to say, "You don't think like a ninety-year-old."

"We had a great trip," Frances wrote to Tom Litteer in New Jersey upon her return. Her executive director, Susan Turbeville, finally had the chance to meet the Haitian people she'd come to love.

Mary Jo Oliver and Lynn Landers shepherded two other first-time visitors. Jo McCall had been Frances's strong supporter for years. Laura Landers, Mike and Susan's daughter-in-law, had wanted to go to Haiti ever since her husband Jason had shared stories about the trip he took with his parents in 1999.

In Cherident Pere Albert led a worship service in honor of Frances. Hundreds of Haitian adults and children attended. Pere Albert thanked God for Frances and asked His blessing on her health. Choirs sang to her, and the children gathered around her. Frances, deeply moved, could barely speak.

The six women left Haiti on February 3. The next day violence broke out in Port-au-Prince. Frances wrote Flo.

I know we have all been disgusted with what we see on television, but when we see the children in school we get a different picture. Mothers have saved from the sale of produce to buy uniforms and shoes. Children have walked miles for the opportunity to LEARN and then they give thanks to GOD for their MANY BLESSINGS. We are humbled by their example.

For the 2003–2004 school year, Haiti Education Foundation funded primary and secondary schools in forty villages. Frances Landers Tech began another prosperous term.

Even Frances, who had grown her ministry school by school, could scarcely grasp the full picture. In these Episcopal villages scattered across rugged mountainsides and streambeds, over twelve thousand students sat close together on rustic benches, without fidgeting, to learn.

Augustin Grakieuse, a first-grade teacher in Cherident, walked an hour each morning to her job. She taught her pupils to read, write their *ABCs*, add, and subtract. To reinforce what they learned, the children sang songs. Thanks to Frances's latest program, they had a daily glass of milk.

Each month Madame Grakieuse earned one hundred dollars.

Ocean Drive Presbyterian in North Myrtle Beach, South Carolina, answered Frances's request for two schools in the coastal town of Jacmel, now part of Ascension Parish. Construction was underway.

First Presbyterian in Gainesville, Georgia, funded the replacement of Pillard's shelter school. The peasant families were in awe of the completed two-story school.

Thanks to the front-end loader, which Frances continued to call "Faith," construction was coming along on the school in Lamothe.

These rural mountain villages seemed a world way from the dangers in Port-au-Prince.

That was how Pere Albert wanted it.

In February a gang member was killed in the city. The man's brother blamed the assassination on President Aristide. The event was all that rival political parties needed to spark a revolt. Rebels spread violence from Cap-Haitien in the north to Port-au-Prince in the south. Fifty people died. On February 28, 2004, American officials, helped by Canada and France, escorted Aristide and his family onto a jet bound for Jamaica. Aristide told the media that the United States kidnapped him.

He went on to South Africa where he stayed for seven years.

Violence in Port-au-Prince lasted for months, keeping American teams away from Haiti and causing concern for the university students in Port-au-Prince. The young people were challenged to keep focused on their coursework.

When the Episcopal University finally wrapped up its term, Viergela Louis's grades were among the top in her class.

"We live in a world where there is more violence than love," Pere Albert wrote in April's *Haiti Happenings*. "If you would like to lead a happy life, you will have to make the decision to live in unity with Jesus."

Pere Albert and Pere Irnel regularly reminded their own parishioners to have faith. In May a hurricane brought flooding to Grande Colline, destroyed two schools, killed livestock, and ruined crops.

Frances sent Pere Albert three thousand dollars. He met with one hundred families and gave them each thirty dollars. The parents were torn between using the money for animals or seed.

Pere Albert told his villagers, "Choose one and leave the other in God's hands. I do not have any more money for you."

The priest had not realized that Frances had launched a funding drive for hurricane relief. Soon he received a second check for three thousand dollars.

He praised the Lord and met with the families again.

"God has been with you. Now you can complete the other choice."

Pere Albert told Frances, "You can't imagine how those people were happy when they were aware of that gift which had been sent for them."

In El Dorado, after practicing law for thirty-two years, Mike Landers was elected to the state position of circuit judge. Frances often relied on her son's sound judgment and diplomacy. He was the first with whom she talked about a growing concern.

It was a long-standing practice of the Episcopal Church of Haiti to deduct for administrative expenses ten percent of donations for schools.

"I will not be a part of this," Frances had told Pere Albert back in 1981. Bishop Garnier, and later Bishop Duracin, valued Frances's fundraising. Both allowed her to send money directly to Pere Albert. Knowing of the backlash from many American donors, especially non-Episcopalians, the bishops did not press Frances for their ten percent.

For twenty-three years Frances had told donors that every penny went to the ministry. As a result, HEF funded more than half of the Episcopal schools in Haiti, including ten of the twelve secondary schools.

In May 2004 Frances received an e-mail from Pere Albert, sent from Ancy's e-mail account. The priest talked about "the ten percent."

He had finally learned how to spell "budget."

"I would like you to know that the bishop wants us to give him ten per cent from our monthly budget. In his last meeting with the clergy, he stressed on that. You and I, we must study a strategy to prevent the bishop from taking the bread which is given to the kids to fill his pocket which is already full of that."

Ten percent of Pere Albert's monthly income, which approached forty thousand dollars, would have been sizable.

Pere Albert told Bishop Duracin that the only way to give the diocese ten percent was to close some of the schools. The bishop replied that he was not interested in closing schools, but he asked Pere Albert for a list.

Pere Albert wrote, "I am waiting for the response. I can tell you really that I have not in mind to close any school but I would like him to find out that such a decision will not be good for the diocese. We have to be careful so that we may continue to serve the little lamb of God in the mountains. We have to give the less money we can to the bishop."

Frances told Flo:

> *I take my usual stand, "I am not going to worry about it." But I think about it 24 hours a day. I would not hesitate to say, NO ... close our work in Haiti. Maybe I would not mean it, but I could SAY IT.*

Pere Albert and Frances stood firm. They did not give ten percent to the bishop and did not close any schools. Before long, the issue was eclipsed by more pressing ones.

In June 2004 a fifteen-country United Nations peacekeeping force stepped onto Haitian soil. The United States contributed a thousand Marines. Tenuous calm replaced most of the violence, but again Haitians resented the intrusion of foreign military.

Frances began a fundraising drive called Reaching Higher to increase the number of college scholarships. She promoted the program—two thousand dollars in tuition for each student—in the next *Haiti Happenings*.

She enjoyed adding to Fannie Tapper's higher education successes, but at the heart of her ministry were the younger children and the giving spirit of the Americans who supported them.

For twenty-two years John Calvin Presbyterian, a small church in Shreveport, Louisiana, funded fifty-five-dollar scholarships. Every year this congregation of about seventy tried to increase by one the scholarships they supported. Pastor Arthur Vance reminded his flock that this year, 2004, $1,815 was needed for thirty-three scholarships.

The amount seemed unattainable, the pastor wrote to Frances, until each member was challenged to save fifty cents a week "from their luxuries." The church exceeded its goal by three hundred dollars.

"We rejoice at the work being done in Haiti," Pastor Art told Frances. But she knew that *she* was the one who rejoiced.

As 2004 wound down, Gardner and Frances had several minor health concerns. In August Gardner had a small TIA, a mini-stroke, but it caused him little noticeable change. Frances's goal was to get her husband back on the golf course as quickly as she could.

Later that month, Frances fell in the kitchen. She tore ligaments in one leg but suffered no broken bones. Her only indignity was wearing a blue protective boot to her talks.

Three weeks later, severe difficulty in breathing led to the discovery that a blood clot from her injured leg had broken loose and lodged in her lung. With rest, she recovered.

During these weeks Mike Landers, Ann Smith, Gretchen Jacks, Mary Jo Oliver, and Susan Turbeville handled Frances's speaking engagements. When she resumed travel, Mike, Susan Landers, or Lynn Landers drove. Son Jim also offered his business jet for his mother's comfort.

More and more, Frances was grateful for her loving family, friends, and supporters.

On Thanksgiving morning, two weeks after Gardner turned ninety-one, he and his bride of sixty-two years were up early.

"Can you believe that this 'old couple' got up and went out for breakfast at six in the morning?" Frances wrote to Flo and Harry. "That is our favorite thing to do."

The rest of Thanksgiving Day, Frances and Gardner enjoyed family and talked about the ability to send each month at least forty thousand dollars to the mountains.

"It truly is God's miracle," Frances said to her husband, glancing at a recent letter she'd received from Pere Albert.

> *I have received your nice letter and the birthday gift you have forwarded for your son in Haiti. As you know, there are many people whose names have been inscribed in the heavenly book. These people*

have already started to live the eternal life from this earth. Please keep living with God. You will be pleased by His presence.

Frances did not know how she could be more thankful on this late-November day that twenty-five years earlier God had introduced her to the complicated, demanding, and wonderful Pere Albert.

Chapter 25

The Rest of the Way to Heaven

"Well done, good and faithful servant. Come and enjoy your Master's happiness."
We can all imagine God greeting Pere Albert with just those words.
—*Ann Smith, Fort Smith, Arkansas, 2005*

Pere Jean-Wilfrid Albert
October 29, 1948–July 6, 2005

Christmas 2004 was near. As Pere Albert had done each year since 1979, he asked Frances if donors could send something to help the poorest of the poor. She had always responded, but only now did she fully understand.

"I did not realize this was a term commonly used in Haiti," Frances wrote on New Year's Day. "'The poorest of the poor' are those who are always hungry." Frances thanked her supporters for the three thousand dollars she had wired to Pere Albert.

His congregations shared the gift but not for themselves. Churches sent teams to the most remote areas, seeking out the least fortunate. They distributed food and told illiterate peasants the Christmas story.

"This is true evangelism," Frances said. "Your gifts for scholarships are also true evangelism. Education helps a child take the giant step out of poverty."

Frances was unaware that Pere Albert had not participated in the poorest of the poor ministry. He wasn't even in Haiti. Ancy Fils-Aime and Pere Irnel spread the money among the villages that Pere Albert would have chosen.

Frequent travelers, like George Brandon, would mention that Pere Albert was in poor health. But Frances had no idea how ill he was. While in New Jersey visiting his brother Josef, Pere Albert said he did not feel well.

A routine examination uncovered pancreatic cancer. On December 21, the beloved priest was admitted to Long Island Jewish Medical Center.

On January 6, 2005, unaware of Pere Albert's situation, Frances wired over fifty-seven thousand dollars. Thirty-five thousand was the monthly budget for teachers' salaries and the feeding program. One thousand dollars would buy milk. Another thousand would buy tires. Sixty-five hundred was allocated for college scholarships. The remaining fourteen thousand dollars was half of a grant from First Presbyterian, Shreveport, to replace the hurricane-destroyed school in La Vallee.

The next day, Pere Albert called Frances. His tone was very serious. Frances had trouble understanding him, but she could tell he was sharing bad news. She sent a fax to Evelyn Howell.

> *I am not sure I understood exactly what he said. I think he told me he had been diagnosed with cancer. I did understand him to say that he didn't know how long he had to live.*

Pere Albert learned from Ancy of Frances's monthly wire transfer. On January 10, the priest sent her a letter from Josef's e-mail. He thanked Frances for the money and confirmed how it would be spent. Then he wrote:

> *I got cancer in my pancreas. I do not know how many days I will spend on this earth before going to the Father. If I go this year, Ancy will e-mail a letter to you so that you may know how to keep working for the glory of the Lord. I believe that if I go, God will enable you and our friends in U.S.A. to continue our mission in the mountain. If any problem with the Bishop, get in touch with father Irnel, Harry and Ancy to have their advice. While I am still on this earth, I will continue my mission until the Lord calls me to join Him.*
>
> *I know that you love me. I love you too. I can tell you that, I am not afraid. I am happy because I know I will go to the Father.*

News spread.

"So sad to know that he's been there through Christmas," Suzanne Thompson said. "Dick will contact him today."

Suzanne's husband, Reverend Dick Thompson, reached his good friend. Pere Albert was in good spirits, the telephone by his hospital bed. He worried more about his people than his medical condition.

Bob Sears also called Pere Albert from southern California.

"We are coming to Haiti in April. We want to talk about health care. You need to be there!"

From Dallas, Roger Quillin, pastor of Northridge Presbyterian, called. Pere Albert picked up the phone on the first ring. Roger told Frances, "He sounded wonderful. But of course he's not."

Jim Luther called from Houston and reported that Pere Albert "seemed his usual self."

On January 14, Reverend Tom Litteer drove from New Jersey to the New York hospital. Pere Albert's doctor told Tom that since the cancer had spread, there would be no surgery. An oncologist would meet with Pere Albert to discuss treatment. Tom left his business card and assured the doctor that funds would be raised to pay for chemotherapy.

Fran Hobbs, by phone from Virginia, caught Pere Albert just before he was discharged from the hospital. She told Frances, "He was laughing."

Back at Josef's, Pere Albert called Frances. "I am supposed to take chemotherapy. Thomas Litteer took the engagement to support that. I can tell you that I am afraid, because such a load will be too heavy for him. I need your help to send letters to all our friends."

Frances assured Pere Albert that many people would send donations.

"The doctor told me that he will be able to clean the pancreas with the chemotherapy. I put everything in God's hands. Now I will write my message for your newsletter."

"Pere Albert, you don't need to do it. Just get your rest."

"No, Mrs. Frances. It will be good for me. It will be good for all of us."

The phone call ended, as usual, with Pere Albert getting his way.

As Pere Albert endured chemotherapy, he wrote his column for April's *Haiti Happenings*.

> Isn't that a miracle to see how deep is the love you have in your heart for our mission work in Haiti and specially for your brother Jean-Wilfrid Albert. I want to thank all those who were touched by my problem and sent letters of encouragement.
>
> Let me share a little history I lived while I was in the hospital. A man with pneumonia was put in the same room with me. One day, I tried to approach him to let him know that God loves him. I can tell you that this man did not accept his sickness. He was so angry with God that I left him and went to my bed. I said to myself, "God is so good with all that he gives to us, but we love it more than we love him. God gave life to that man

203

and he was so happy to enjoy his life that when he got sick, he blamed God." The attitude of that man was an encouragement to me. If men love life on this earth so much where there are all kinds of bad things, I wonder what kind of life we are going to live in the Kingdom of God.

I tried to approach the man again to let him know that God will never abandon him. He said to me, "And what about your cancer?" I told him that I know God loves me with my cancer. It is He who advised me to come to U.S. for treatment. I told him that I am not afraid because God loves me so much that all decisions He will make will be good for me.

It may happen that one day in our life, we will have to face some difficult moments. It is important for all of us to keep communion with God so that we may have peace forever in our souls. If we believe that God loves us so much that He died for us and if we trust Him, we will never feel hopeless.

Our GOD is a faithful GOD. If we keep on doing His will on this earth, there is no sickness, no death, and no problem which can make Him abandon us. He is preparing a room for all of us so that we all may be with Him in His house. AMEN!

Pere Albert understood that this was the final letter he would write to his many friends across the United States.

A month after Frances's eighty-eighth birthday, Medical Benevolence Foundation held a conference in Arizona. Bishop Duracin was one of the speakers. Frances, who had never met him, was intrigued.

She told Pere Albert she planned to attend. He wrote, "The bishop loves the work we do there in the mountains. The extension of the Episcopal Church in that area pleases him very much but he doesn't like you and me because we don't let any door open for him to fill his pocket."

Frances reminded herself to be on guard.

Ann Smith, Gretchen Jacks, and Frances flew in from Arkansas. John McDaniel arrived from Tennessee. Anne Wuerker, my husband Don, and I came from California. We were all there because of our interest in better health care across Pere Albert's mountains.

Besides, Don and I wanted to see Frances again.

We seven sat at a round table in the dining room of Scottsdale's First Presbyterian. Nearby, Bishop Duracin, in his clerical collar, chatted with others. Not a tall man, he exuded power and control.

Frances stood up, smiled, and spoke to us.

"Pray for me. I am going to meet the bishop."

She walked up to the Episcopal leader of Haiti. Poised and postured, she held out her hand.

"Bishop Duracin. I am Frances Landers. It is so very nice to meet you." She stretched out the word *so*. He gave a small smile in return.

After a brief conversation, she returned to our group, thanked us for our prayers, and did not say what she and the bishop had talked about. But she never again mentioned a concern about the ten percent administrative fee.

On April 12, Pere Albert returned to Cherident, but not to his little room in the vocational school. Evelyn Howell had funded a small home for the priest, at the top of a hill across the road from his church.

With a green knit cap over what little hair chemotherapy had left him, Pere Albert greeted Haitian friends and a sizable group from the United States.

Chris McRae, trained on the filtration process used by Living Waters for the World, wanted to assess the water situation in Cherident. On a return trip, he and Wil Howie would install a water-purification system.

Dan Hardie and two other Michigan doctors opened Cherident's clinic doors. With J. P. Bell's help, they treated hundreds of patients daily. One day the doctors rode with Clement, a revered Haitian community health worker, to the village of Bejin. Bob Sears went along. He was overwhelmed by the immense need for medical care in the region.

The rest of Bob's southern California team had spent the day working on solar power. That evening he told them, "The doctors vaccinated hundreds of children today. We are right to want to focus on health care."

On April 26, Pere Albert had a long conversation with Bob and his teammates: Ben Small, Don Miller, Dick Thompson, and Alex Lang.

"We want to create a nonprofit called Haiti Healthcare Partners," Bob said to the priest. "We need your advice and your blessing."

Pere Albert looked toward the road, thoughtful. Then he rose slowly from his chair. He gained energy as he walked down the hill, his arms outstretched. Bob, Ben, and the others followed. The priest reached the clinic, opened its door, walked in, and wildly clapped his hands above his head. His voice was far more robust than his health.

"Out! Out! Get out!"

Vagrants, who had settled in the seven-room clinic, scattered. When the last had gone, Pere Albert turned to the Americans. He extended his long index finger toward the dirty, largely empty building.

"This is your spot. The clinic belongs to the Episcopal Church. I give it to you. I am very pleased for you to bring health care to St. Matthias Parish."

Bob smiled, grateful but cautious. His work had just begun.

Conversation shifted. The Americans expressed concern for the future of Pere Albert's parish, his people, and the schools.

As usual, the visionary priest was way out ahead of everyone else.

"Come back to my house tomorrow morning," Pere Albert told the Californians. "We will talk about the leadership of my villages."

After breakfast the men returned. Haitian men sat in straight-backed chairs, lining Pere Albert's small living room. The Americans knew Pere Irnel, Ancy, Jean-Robert, and Harry Theodore. They were introduced to the others.

"I want you to meet our leadership board," Pere Albert said. He explained that several years earlier he had started to plan his succession.

"God trusts these men. I trust them. They represent the churches, schools, principals, teachers, parents, and your clinic. They will be in charge of my communities."

Legal Haitian nonprofits were not common. But Pere Albert had formed one. The group was called OCDES (pronounced oak-des). Its Creole name translated to Christian Organization for Community Development.

The priest held up a typed document. It was the OCDES bylaws.

Pere Albert had been at this for some time.

"He spent most of the time in his house," Don Miller said. "But he came out to give us his customary big hugs and good-byes. We had a sense that we had seen him for the last time."

In May Susan Turbeville, her husband Joe, and John Reed visited schools in Cherident, Bejin, and Moreau. Susan was also glad to get to Lamothe so she could report progress to St. John the Divine. Construction neared completion, the workmanship was good, and the children were thankful that soon they would have a new school.

Susan gave abundant thanks too for a final visit with Pere Albert.

Frances was grateful that her busy schedule helped keep her mind off of Pere Albert's struggles. When HEF supporters learned of his cancer, they increased their giving. Daily, Frances spent hours writing her donors.

Mike and Susan Landers drove Frances to Lake Charles, Louisiana. It was "Haiti Day" at Church of the Good Shepherd. Frances spoke to the congregation and returned with large donations and a larger smile.

Withstanding complaints from her family about being gone on Father's Day, Frances committed to "give the sermon" on June 20 at First Presbyterian in Lake Village, Arkansas. She rationalized that at eighty-eight she could not afford to be choosy about dates.

On May 21, Pere Albert sent an e-mail to Frances through Ancy's account. "Even though I feel healed, I have to pass the test to be sure what happen inside."

Pere Albert returned to the United States and stayed with his niece Sandrine Princival in New York. From his American friends, the priest received many telephone calls, cards, flowers, donations, and prayers.

This fifty-six-year-old giant of a man learned that he was not healed.

Reverend Tom Litteer regularly visited Pere Albert at Sandrine's. Tom had been the priest's dedicated friend and ministry partner for years.

"If we are fortunate, we will meet four or five truly great people in our lives," Tom told his congregation. "Pere Albert is one." Tom felt it was a privilege to help care for Pere Albert in his final days.

In mid-June Pere Albert encouraged Sandrine to spend money on neither flowers nor burial clothes. He reassured her that he was safe in God's hands and ready to go. He wanted no tears.

He instructed Ancy to give his small personal savings to Frances for a few scholarships.

On June 22, two days after Father's Day, Josef called Frances.

"Last night my brother was taken to the hospital by ambulance. He has heart failure, fluid on his lungs, and other problems. He is on life support."

Gardner and Frances cried.

"We are grieving terribly," Sandrine told those who called. "My uncle was the leader of our entire family."

By July 1, Pere Albert was too weak to talk. To communicate, he feebly nodded or shook his head.

The next day the doctors could no longer detect brain activity.

Four days later, Wednesday, July 6, 2005, this holy man slipped quietly away and went to be with his best friend and Father.

Undoubtedly, Pere Albert was welcomed into heaven with fanfare.

He may not have wanted tears, but a river of them flowed across Haiti and the United States.

On July 10 in Brooklyn, New York, there was a viewing of Pere Albert's body. "I will send you a beautiful picture of my brother," Josef later told Evelyn Howell. "He looked so peaceful."

Pere Albert's service, in English and French, was held at St. Bartholomew's Episcopal Church. Eight Episcopal priests attended. Reverend Tom Litteer gave the homily. The church was remarkably full.

Josef brought his brother's body to Haiti. Albert siblings from Haiti and the United States gathered in Thomazeau. Their mother came down the mountain from Cherident. So did hundreds from across Grande Colline.

Early Tuesday morning, July 12, a twenty-four-hour vigil began. Pere Albert's friends sang his favorite songs, but the mood was grim. Sandrine told Frances, "People were crying and saying that he will never be replaced."

On Wednesday mourners walked twelve miles to a viewing in Croix-des-Bouquets. Then adult and children's choirs and bands with musical instruments led hundreds to St. Simeon Episcopal Church. Four choirs sang. Family and friends talked of Pere Albert's influence on their lives.

A second service back in Thomazeau followed. People poured into St. Michael's, a church Pere Albert had built years earlier. Crowds stood outside, straining to hear the service over the crying of children and adults.

"The saddest time," Sandrine said, "was when the priest asked if anyone wished to say a few words about Pere Albert. There was a long line from the altar to the rear of the church."

There were more tears at Pere Albert's burial. Several children fainted. People who had never known Pere Albert but had heard of his great work came to pay final respects.

Many stayed at the burial ground until eight o'clock that night.

Pere Albert's faith was abundant, his energy magnetic. He pastored dozens of churches and, with Frances, founded schools in forty villages. He attracted Harriet Prichard, Scott Sabin's Plant with Purpose, and Living Waters for the World. When droughts or floods struck, he saw to his people's needs. He tended the poorest of the poor. He had the foresight to create OCDES to govern in his absence.

His final gift was to entrust the health-care clinic to those in the United States who promised to give it sustained life.

Pere Albert loved serving his people, young and old. His stern discipline and bountiful laugh showed just how much. He met every challenge, knowing that God would provide. And God did, abundantly.

Frances received tributes to Pere Albert from dozens of supporters, including the young people who had looked up to him. Jean-Pierre Jackson told Frances, "Pere Albert was someone who loved everybody. He helped everybody. We found Pere Albert in all and everywhere."

Blanche Carper wrote that Pere Albert "radiated the person of Jesus Christ from his eyes, his beautiful smile, his laugh, and his demeanor."

Of Pere Albert, Pere Bruno said, "Wilfrid lived the gospel he preached. He was a man of great heart, full of love for his brothers and sisters."

And Harvey Musser said, "What a tremendous soul and heart God gave this man. Oh, to have more like him."

For a long time, it was hard for Frances to put into words how *she* felt about the loss of her dear friend—perhaps because Pere Albert was so much *more* than a friend.

Pere Albert was in so many ways a man beyond his title of father. He was a priest, yes, but also a teacher, a mentor, a disciplinarian, and a parent.

Frances had watched Pere Albert bend over the crib of a sick child and weep. She had heard him advise the young people in his villages, scold them, and goad them to make their music louder.

There were those hugs, given as a father would hold a child. There were words of encouragement. "Fight your cancer, Frances, and never give up."

He had sat by the road on weekdays, talking with his people as they came by. He'd stood tall on Sundays, preaching God's Word and making it all so very real.

Pere Albert was in so many ways Frances's brother in Christ.

She had shared with him her deepest faith and confided her deepest doubts. With her brother Pere Albert, she had discussed her health and Gardner's, and the loss of close friends. And with his sister in Christ, Pere Albert had shared his dreams, disappointments, and times of isolation.

Pere Albert was in so many ways Frances's son.

Frances smiled, thinking of Bill and Jim and Mike. Pere Albert was much more irascible, complex, relentless, and unreasonable than they were. He was a son who was open to life and full of life. He understood life—this one and the everlasting one.

He was protective, as a son would be of his mother.

Father, brother, son—this was a man of faith and great gifts, a man whom God used as a planter of vision and ideas, of churches and schools, of meals and medicine and goats.

Did Pere Albert have regrets? He never married. He had no children. Frances thought about this and smiled. When he committed his life to the Lord, he had been richly blessed with thousands of children, young and old.

Frances could not imagine Pere Albert ever using the word "regret."

Did Frances have regrets? It was not a word that she used either. But she thought for a moment and sighed, and a tear fell.

No matter the circumstance, there can be no sadder moment than when a mother's son leaves this world before she does.

In the end, Frances could not begin to tell her *Haiti Happenings* readers all that she felt. She could simply say this:

> *I deeply feel the loss of my dear friend and brother, Pere Albert. BUT, God calls us to PRESS ON, and I know that Pere Albert would have it no other way.*

Here we are, more than a decade later, doing just that. Pressing on.

Clinique Jean-Wilfrid Albert provided villagers with the
only health care within a full day's walk.

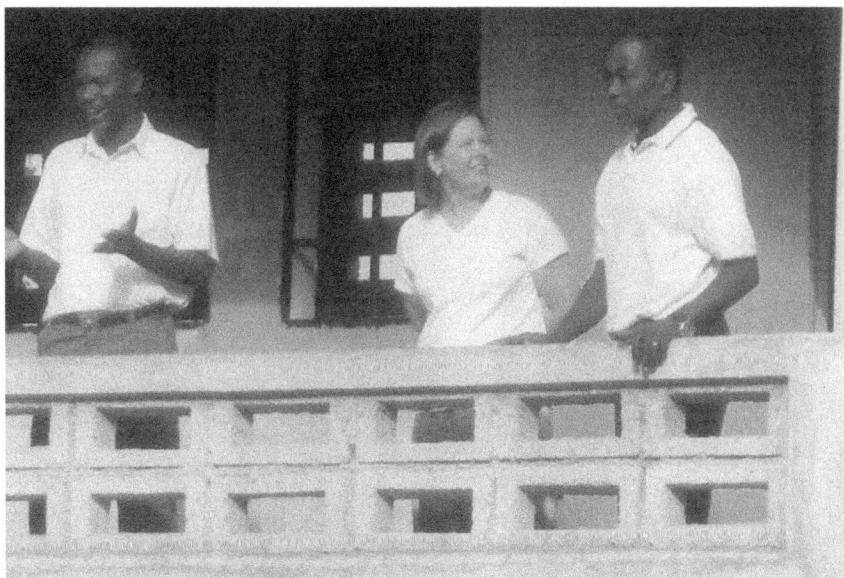

Susan Turbeville, executive director of Haiti Education
Foundation, was Frances's excellent choice for a successor.

Chapter 26

Transitions

As you know, "ME" is not the "ONE" who did all this.
—Frances Landers, El Dorado, Arkansas, 2008

Mrs. Albert returned up the mountain to Cherident, consoled by her family and friends on the loss of her son. On August 3, 2005, Pere Jean Phillippe Alphonse was installed as priest-in-charge of St. Matthias Parish.

Back in Arkansas, Frances pushed herself to move forward. Pere Irnel delighted her, and she had confidence that Pere Alphonse would too.

Every day, she pressed on.

One late summer morning, Frances went to The Spudnut Shop to buy donuts for old friends, a family of five staying with her and Gardner. Forced to flee New Orleans as Hurricane Katrina advanced, the family was sure it would return to nothing. Frances counted her blessings.

In California, Bob Sears, Ben Small, and Don Miller filed paperwork for Haiti Healthcare Partners, or HHP, and named Cherident's little medical building Clinique Jean-Wilfrid Albert. They rounded out an HHP board, hired Jean-Pierre Jackson as clinic administrator, searched for a Haitian doctor and nurses, and itemized the cost of repairs, pharmaceuticals, and equipment.

In the Shenandoah Valley, Pastor Rob Sherrard sent a letter to many people, inviting them to a remembrance of Pere Albert. "Until our own homecoming in heaven," Rob wrote, "there will be no more broad smiles, no more deep laughs, no more clap of the hands to get things going."

John Reed organized the event at Tinkling Spring on the first of October. Reverend Tom Litteer came down from New Jersey. Frances, Mary Jo Oliver, and Susan and Joe Turbeville drove up from Arkansas. One hundred people from six states shared stories, tears, and laughter, and recommitted their support.

"It was a bittersweet day," Pastor Rob said. "Most of us thought Pere Albert to have been the most exceptional person we have ever known."

The following week across Grande Colline, the schools opened.

On October 23, Ann Smith and Gretchen Jacks spearheaded an event in Dallas to share news of Haiti's mountain ministry. Frances and Susan spoke about Haiti Education Foundation. Chris McRae introduced Living Waters for the World. Ruthie McRae and J. P. Bell talked about health care.

In New Jersey Tom Litteer told his church that he had been attracted to Pere Albert's ministry because it addressed the needs of the whole person: physical, educational, emotional, and spiritual. Reverend Tom viewed the mission across Grande Colline as a model for what ministry should be.

In 2005 noted economist Jeffrey Sachs published *The End of Poverty: Economic Possibilities for Our Time*. He shared Tom's perspective, writing that the basic services required to lift a group out of extreme poverty were clean water, better agriculture, small loans, education, and improved health care.

Frances, Tom, and the priests would have added faith to Sachs's equation. But his basic philosophy—developing a community holistically—applied to Grande Colline, and especially to Cherident.

Yes, the road was inadequate and electricity sparse. But members of farmer cooperatives walked that road to their thriving church. Village women stopped at the commissary for beans and rice, and went to the Plant with Purpose office to pay down small loans. A thousand students crowded into Frances Landers Tech, the secondary school, the primary school, and the kindergarten. The water-purification system was up and running. The opening of Clinique Jean-Wilfrid Albert was just months away.

Pere Albert and Frances hadn't read Jeffrey Sachs's books, but intuitively they followed his reasoning. Sachs's writings had influenced Bob Sears's decision to take on health care, and that pleased Frances greatly.

Losing Pere Albert was still hard to accept. But in 2005 HEF had done well financially. Donations had exceeded five hundred thousand dollars. HEF's accountant advised Susan Turbeville to use the phrase, "No administrative costs are deducted from your donation" at every opportunity. "I have never seen a 501(c)(3) operate like this," the CPA said.

In February 2006 Frances traveled to Gainesville, Georgia. As always, First Presbyterian was generous. In March so was First Presbyterian of Fort Smith. Before leaving, Frances lined up overnight help for Gardner. At ninety-two, his memory was not as strong as his constant encouragement of Frances's work.

In April eighty-nine-year-old Frances packed for a speaking engagement in Fayetteville, Arkansas. Mike and Susan Landers picked Frances up for the five-hour ride. Ten miles out of El Dorado, she coughed that telltale cough.

Mike pulled off the road. "Mother, how do you feel?"

"I am tired, and I have a slight sore throat." Back to El Dorado.

The next morning Frances was hospitalized with pneumonia. She returned home after four days but needed full-time oxygen for three weeks.

Confinement did not agree with Frances. But she enjoyed spending time with Gardner and with their son Bill, who had retired and stopped by most days. Writing letters was therapeutic too, as was hearing news that Haiti Healthcare Partners was soon to open its clinic doors.

On June 14, the employees of Clinique Jean-Wilfrid Albert arrived early and posed for photographs. Haitians are formal people. The doctor, nurses, and other staff stood side-by-side, proud and solemn.

Outside, the clinic building sported fresh white and green paint. Clement, the community health worker now in his seventies, organized the many patients who gathered on the clinic's porch. Inside, the pharmacist finished sorting medications. The nurses and doctor saw the first of dozens of patients they would accommodate that day.

The seeds of improved health care would reap a lasting harvest.

Frances always had shots to prevent pneumonia and flu. But upper respiratory infections went to her lungs. Her pneumonia, twice within ten months, concerned her. So did Gardner's low energy and poor memory.

On August 7 he was hospitalized, unable to breathe easily. The opening to his aortic valve was severely constricted. Insufficient blood reached his brain, worsening his confusion.

At Gardner's age, heart surgery was risky. He decided to go forward.

The surgery was successful. A supply of small ice cream cartons from daughter-in-law Lynn bolstered Gardner's spirits. So did his round-the-clock care provider, Angie, whom he adored.

Frances was grateful that Gardner strengthened day to day and was mentally much sharper. But cancer further compromised his health.

He could not recover. His beloved family prepared to say good-bye.

On October 6, 2006, Gardner Hayden Landers peacefully passed away at home, a month shy of his ninety-second birthday. Frances lost her husband of sixty-four years exactly fifteen months after Pere Albert's death.

On October 9, Pastor Daniel Loomis led the celebration of Gardner's life. Three generations of family filled the front pews of El Dorado's First Presbyterian. Friends too honored his courageous military service, his outstanding ophthalmology career, his love for his family (and his golf game), and his unfailing dedication to Haiti.

The night of Gardner's service, Frances had a vivid dream.

> *I saw the river and he was on the other side. I saw him very plainly. The river was narrow but was full of limbs and it was rough. I called to him and said, "I am coming over." He answered, "Don't come, you have work to do." I had jumped into the river, ready to cross, but when he said that I turned around and came back. I have not seen him since.*

Frances had hit a rough spot in the river of her life. But she was not alone. She had seven grandchildren, seven great-grandchildren, wonderful friends, a good church, and "work to do."

Despite her grief, Frances also had memories that made her laugh.

On Frances and Flo's ten trips to Haiti, they always spent their final night at the Hotel Montana in Port-au-Prince. The hotel, which had expansive views of the city, bay, and mountains, offered a quality restaurant, bar, swimming pool, and tennis courts.

The women didn't need the amenities, but they enjoyed hot showers and a comfortable night's sleep. One year Frances told Flo she wanted to "fix up a bit." She came out of the bathroom, her hair rolled up in plastic strips torn from sandwich bags. "I don't want to scare Gardner when I get home," she said.

Now in early 2007, 1801 West Block Street was sadly quiet. But as long as Frances received mail, she didn't mind staying alone.

"I give Haiti the credit, as I always have something to do," Frances told Evelyn Howell. She had lunch with friends and enjoyed church and Bible study. Weekly she went to Walmart for a good walk, pushing a cart for balance.

Walking gave her time to reflect. Gardner had been unhappy his final two months. He missed being on the golf course and disliked his friends' seeing him in bed. With Gardner's passing, Frances felt that a load had lifted, and she believed strongly that he would not have wanted it any other way.

In March Susan Turbeville drove Frances to Little Rock. There they met Ann Smith, Ancy Fils-Aime, and Harry Theodore. The two Haitians had come to Arkansas to study details of Living Waters's purification process.

Ancy looked at Frances, glanced around, and said, "Where is Flo?" Frances laughed. The two women had been that inseparable in Haiti.

Frances thanked Harry and Ancy for their hard work. OCDES members had full-time jobs and lived in various villages, but the board worked perfectly.

Each month Susan itemized the upcoming month's budget by e-mail. Mary Jo made the wire transfer. Ancy or the priests withdrew funds and sent a receipt to other OCDES members and to Susan.

Ancy updated the Americans on the atmosphere in Haiti's cities. Despite peacekeepers authorized by the United Nations, the violence caused by Aristide's overthrow never totally subsided. Former President René Préval had been back in office ten months. Protests and unrest continued.

For the third straight summer, Windy Cove did not send a team.

Frances relied on correspondence far more than travel to sustain regular donations. A meaningful letter to her nephew John Young prompted him to fund a new school in honor of his parents, Ardell and Marjorie. When Frances wrote a former El Dorado resident to share local news, the man sent her ten thousand dollars.

Publicity helped too. In July 2007 Evelyn Howell sent an article to *Guideposts* magazine titled "Fantastic Frances." Evelyn told readers about this ninety-year-old woman's example of how tireless commitment can make a difference. The article reunited Frances with friends she'd known for decades—and brought her new friends as well. Many sent checks.

Pastor Dennis Falasco wrote that his church in Idaho Falls was ready to get involved with HEF. Frances called this an answer to prayer.

In August Frances spoke again to the local Rotary Club. Many left sixteen cents by their plates. To her surprise, a reporter for the *El Dorado News-Times* covered the meeting. The following morning, Frances was on the front page.

"Of course, this is a small town, and I am sure they were short on news," she said to friends.

In 2007 and 2008 Grande Colline was not short on news.

Haiti Education Foundation added Terminal II classes in Cherident. This prerequisite to college had been available only in Port-au-Prince. Now HEF funded eight qualified teachers. Young people in St. Matthias and Ascension Parishes had a convenient, safe, and inexpensive way to complete their high school graduation requirements. Soon one hundred more young men and women were in college.

Clinique Jean-Wilfrid Albert was thriving. Haiti Healthcare Partners began a nutrition program, Medika Mamba, for malnourished infants. Little lives were being saved. Papa Luc, the carpenter, happily told HHP, "Since the health-care center opened, I do not make as many coffins."

Living Waters for the World installed a water-purification system in Bainet. Harry Theodore helped Chris McRae and his team assemble parts by the hundreds and then educate villagers on how to access the water they never thought they would have. The community erupted in joy when a switch was flipped. For the first time, Bainet had clean water.

"It is a miracle," said Ancy Fils-Aime.

On March 5, 2008, Frances turned ninety-one. Haiti Education Foundation was formally transitioned. Frances was named chairman of the board, Mike Landers became president, and Susan Turbeville continued as executive director. HEF maintained its strong and active board of directors.

Though Frances kept fighting respiratory annoyances, she had energy for one more trip to Haiti. She had exceeded Pere Albert's prediction that God would grant her the health to travel there until she was ninety. This trip, her forty-third, was the most poignant. After Gardner died, HEF received thousands of dollars of memorials in his name. Years earlier, Pere Albert had told Frances he wanted a school in Gardner's honor in the village of Hess.

In April, Frances, Mike, Susan Turbeville, Flo Boggs, and Lynn Landers traveled back to the country they loved. Heather Hahn and Chris Dean from the *Arkansas Democrat-Gazette* accompanied them.

Frances weathered three airplane flights and the familiar, harrowing drive from Port-au-Prince up to Cherident. On the third day of the trip, the white Isuzu bounced its way up a steep, narrow trail to Hess.

Flo told me, "The school in Hess was not completed, just the foundation, but Frances especially wanted to see it. She knew she would not be coming back to Haiti. I remember her sitting among the children."

Mike added, "Though the school was not finished, the children were wonderful. They gathered around Mother and made her feel grand."

On May 14, 2008, readers unfolded the *Democrat-Gazette* to find a large photo on the front page. Haitian children, their yellow uniforms pristine, surrounded a ninety-one-year-old woman dressed in white.

A month after Frances returned to Arkansas, she received word that Bishop Duracin had reassigned all of the Episcopal priests.

"We might think he is trying to irritate us," Frances wrote to Flo and Harry, "but he moved everyone." Pere Fritz Desire came to St. Matthias Parish, Pere Mardoche Vil was assigned to Ascension, and Pere Fruitho Michaud went to St. Marc, which included HEF schools in the village of Trouin. Pere Irnel and Pere Alphonse were given parishes elsewhere in Haiti.

Mike, Susan Turbeville, and Chris McRae (just added to the HEF board) took a September trip to meet the new priests. They returned home right before Hurricanes Gustav and Ike dealt Grande Colline severe blows. Wind and water destroyed thousands of homes and many schools. Livestock and crops were lost, fruit trees blown to the ground.

Pere Michaud called the damage in Trouin "enormously sinister."

Frances asked supporters to fund seeds, food, goats, cows, chickens, and shelter. Donations totaled twenty-five thousand dollars, which Mary Jo added to the forty-thousand-dollar monthly school budget. The new priests and the OCDES board distributed the relief money.

Mary Jo also sent some money to Pere Alphonse and Pere Irnel; the hurricanes had hit their new parishes hard as well.

About the tremendous amount of rock that tumbled from cliffs into valleys below, an optimistic Haitian said, "At least our people will not have to carry the rock down the mountain to reconstruct their houses. It has been delivered for them."

Villagers worked together to dry out textbooks, clean debris, and get HEF's schools reopened.

In the cities, protests had stopped during the hurricane season. In early 2009 the weather cleared, and things dried out. Protests resumed.

On March 5, 2009, Frances's children treated her to a birthday lunch and a relaxed visit. The next day she wrote Flo and Harry to express thanks for the gift of scholarships. Always, scholarships were her favorite present.

Now ninety-two, Frances accepted few speaking engagements. Mary Jo and Susan were both polished presenters who enjoyed stepping in.

In July, as more than ten thousand students were wrapping up the current term, Susan went back to Haiti. She delighted in taking first-time travelers Jan Gartrell and John Lowery to Cherident.

"There is nothing like visiting classrooms," Susan wrote in *Haiti Happenings*. "As long as class is in session, every eye is on the teacher."

John, the youth pastor at El Dorado's First Presbyterian, had braced himself for the intense poverty he knew he would encounter, but he was unprepared for the paradox between it and Haiti's natural beauty.

Chris McRae was determined to harness part of that natural beauty—sunshine—to improve lives. Living Waters for the World had teamed with another American nonprofit, Solar Under the Sun, in a pilot project. In July the nonprofits installed a solar-powered water-purification system in Haiti.

At the top of Frances's stack of mail was an article Chris had sent her about Solar Under the Sun. These days, Frances went to bed about eight-thirty. By five she was awake. In the quiet of the morning, she read the mail she had not gotten to the previous day.

Already astounded at the collective work of HEF, Alternative Gifts International, Plant with Purpose, Haiti Healthcare Partners, and Living Waters for the World, Frances took great interest in Solar Under the Sun, the newest partner in Grande Colline.

In the fall of 2009, midway through her ninety-second year, Frances experienced shortness of breath. Tests pinpointed the cause as weak lungs. She left the hospital with orders to stay on full-time oxygen.

Frances didn't care for the portable tank that she used away from home. A larger oxygen system had tubes long enough to reach from her bed to her computer and to the kitchen.

"I have good days and not-so-good days," Frances told Flo and Harry in October. "But I was optimistic enough to buy a new printer this week."

The "not-so-good" days increased, requiring Frances's lungs to be drained periodically. Still, she enjoyed receiving and writing letters and listening to every scrap of news from Haiti.

Cherident's guesthouse was receiving many teams. Susan and the HEF board worked well with the priests and OCDES. Despite a weak US economy, supporters were generous.

Frances had primary schools in forty villages, with adjacent secondary schools in ten, plus the vocational school. Though many still needed repairs following the hurricanes, she knew their future was secure.

Of her home oxygen system she said, "If I could stretch the cord to my beauty shop, I would have it made."

Steel beams poked out of the ground, offering promise that the Hess school would be finished, hopefully soon. "Gardner would be so pleased," Frances said.

Chapter 27

Crumbled

"Though the mountains be shaken and the hills be removed, yet my unfailing love for you will not be shaken nor my covenant of peace be removed,"
says the Lord, who has compassion on you.
—Isaiah 54:10

In 1995 Pere Albert told Frances that Cherident's commissary needed to be built with a concrete roof to prevent vandalism.

In 1998 Hurricane Gordon ripped the tin roofs off of several schools. "We will replace these roofs with hurricane-resistant concrete," Frances said.

In 1999 Ben Small commented to teammates that Haiti's building standards did not begin to meet California's structural codes.

No one suspected a thing.

On Tuesday, January 12, 2010, ten thousand children and young adults spent an ordinary, wonderful school day in forty Episcopal villages of St. Matthias, Ascension, and St. Marc Parishes. The sun was warm and the sky cloudless. The air was clear and quiet with barely a breeze.

In mid-afternoon classes were dismissed. Students filed from first-floor classrooms and came down second-story staircases with no railings. Soon the mountains of Grande Colline were dotted with school uniforms and chattering kids. The children, so disciplined during school hours, were free to sing, laugh, and run. They forgot their hunger.

In Cherident four teachers gathered in the primary school for a meeting. Down the dusty road, a young man made repairs inside St. Matthias Episcopal Church.

A hummingbird darted. Birds sang.

Across Grande Colline, no one suspected a thing.

In Arkansas Frances was getting her late-afternoon rest. Two months before her ninety-third birthday, her lungs were weak. She still wrote short letters but was grateful that Susan Turbeville was managing Haiti Education Foundation.

HEF was in good hands. Its board provided vision and oversight. Susan was an excellent executive director. She was challenged when the priests-in-charge were rotated too often or occasionally not often enough. But OCDES helped Susan work through rough spots, and HEF's donors were faithful. The mission work was largely smooth. Frances knew that the outlook for Haiti's mountain children was bright.

Frances never suspected a thing.

The magnitude 7.0 earthquake struck Haiti for thirty-four seconds at 4:53 in the afternoon. To the millions of victims trying to outlast the catastrophe, it felt like minutes.

Buildings with inadequate steel reinforcement swayed and rocked and crashed to the ground. Children and adults screamed. The concrete roofs of homes, schools, and commissaries collapsed within seconds, crushing anyone and everything within. Upper stories of buildings pancaked the lower ones. Staircases ripped from their structures and were flung away. Humble shanties shuddered. Rocks poured down the hillsides. The air filled with dust.

On the front porch of Cherident's guesthouse, the wooden rocking chairs shattered and were reduced to sticks.

The terror of 4:53 replaced the serenity of 4:52.

This wasn't the first earthquake to strike Hispaniola. In 1751 and 1790 the southern city of Port-au-Prince was leveled. Hundreds were killed. In 1842 the last recorded earthquake and tsunami left thousands dead in the country's north. But history had done little to document Hispaniola's seismic pattern of a massive earthquake followed by decades, or even centuries, of dormancy.

Except for a few scientists and historians, no one had suspected a thing.

Reporters aren't regularly stationed in the poorest country in the Western Hemisphere to be on the spot when news breaks. There was no cadre of journalists in and around the epicenter. But Christine Webb was in Léogâne.

Christine was with a group from a Florida nonprofit, New Missions. It was her first time out of the United States. Amid the destruction, Christine weathered aftershocks and sent home the earliest reports from her cell phone. Days later, her team was rescued by the US military in Black Hawk helicopters.

News spread, first just verbal reports of the ruptured fault line beneath the surface of southern Haiti. The hundreds of thousands who gave time and money to help Haiti were stunned. The Americans who supported Pere Albert's mountain mission were speechless. Frances grieved.

Then photographs and video footage of the death and devastation began to trickle out. Hearts broke. Once again Haiti experienced an amount of suffering vastly disproportionate to its size.

The Duracins had arrived home in Port-au-Prince shortly before five. As the bishop pulled his car inside the garage, he saw his barber and stepped outside to greet him. The earth began to shake. Bishop Duracin's wife, Marie-Edith, was ejected from the vehicle and suffered a serious leg injury. The home collapsed. The car was buried by rubble.

Marie-Edith was taken to Zanmi Lasant, a hospital in Cange, up north. Bishop Duracin, uninjured, said, "I can tell you it was a miracle of God to be saved." Homeless, he chose to join his people in a tent city.

Most buildings in Port-au-Prince, including the beautiful Hotel Montana, were rubble. Homes along the hillsides were destroyed. The National Palace where Baby Doc and Michele had frolicked was heavily damaged.

Susan Turbeville posted a message on HEF's website. "It is with much sadness that we have learned that Haiti has been struck by a severe earthquake, followed by aftershocks. We are trying to contact the priests and others associated with Haiti Education Foundation. Please pray for safety and peace. We will keep you informed. A disaster fund has been established. As always, 100% of donations will go to the need designated."

Across the United States, those who supported HEF prayed fervently as they waited for news from the parishes.

"Susan," Frances said to her young friend, "God will get us through this. We did not know how we would survive the death of Pere Albert. We did. God will get us through this too."

From West Virginia, Flo e-mailed Frances. "You've heard the Haitian proverb, 'Beyond the mountains there are more mountains.' One wonders how many more mountains our poor Haitians must struggle over just to live, much less progress. My heart aches ... especially for the children."

Nearly 90 percent of Léogâne's buildings were destroyed, along with the city's power and water systems. Sainte Croix Hospital was too damaged to be of use. The epicenter of the earthquake was, in fact, just south of Léogâne, ten miles from Cherident, God's wide spot in the road.

An initial report cited twenty-five thousand lives lost in Léogâne. The government reported three hundred thousand deaths across the nation. Non-Haitian sources estimated two hundred thousand. Witness the imprecision of Haiti.

Hundreds of thousands were injured. Disease became a secondary disaster. Many who were treated in makeshift clinics survived initial injuries but died of gangrene, infectious disease, or malnutrition. A million Haitians lost their homes. Everyone was hungry and afraid.

Searching for survivors, villagers dug away rocks and mortar by hand. Within two days, mass burials began. Since most bodies were unidentified and not photographed, families lacked confirmation of their losses. They lacked closure.

On Thursday, January 14, Ancy found a way to call Susan. His family was safe in Port-au-Prince. Pere Desire had a slight leg injury. It took Pere Vil a week to find e-mail access. He reported that he was fine, but his schools and churches, like Pere Desire's, were not.

Ancy heard that the stately St. Matthias Episcopal Church in Cherident was in rubble. So were the rectory, commissary, guesthouse, kindergarten, primary school, secondary school, and Frances Landers Tech.

All were destroyed.

A few miles away in Trouin, Pere Michaud was fine. But four people had died during a church service. Five hundred people, homes destroyed, huddled in the courtyard next to the rubble that used to be the church. The schools were severely damaged. Food and water were scarce, injuries many.

With no water for the trip, Ancy set out from Port-au-Prince Thursday night, walking for hours to Cherident. He was not prepared for the devastation that greeted him on both sides of the road.

The second story of the empty guesthouse had collapsed the first story and sat on top of it, eerily undamaged, at ground level.

Though Frances Landers Tech was destroyed, several hundred people found security sleeping within its walled courtyard. Miraculously, no one died in Cherident.

Ancy heard incredible stories. The four teachers meeting in the primary school escaped with minor injuries, seconds before the walls collapsed.

As the young man made repairs inside St. Matthias Church, something (or Someone) told him to change what he was doing. As he rushed outside, the ceiling fell in. Moments later the stone-and-mortar church crumbled apart. When the tin roof crashed down into the rubble, the chiseled cross was jettisoned into the churchyard. An open Bible flew to the ground, its pages fluttering in the unsettled gray air.

The one-story Clinique Jean-Wilfrid Albert was bruised but standing. Though thousands of injuries needed tending, the doctor and nurses had not yet arrived. Dazed people milled about, hurt and homeless.

One aftershock was measured at 5.9. Structures already weakened tumbled down. The death toll mounted, and fear increased.

On January 16, Susan's daily HEF update reported that Jean-Pierre Jackson was helping recovery efforts outside Port-au-Prince. Harry Theodore was trying to locate a source of clean water in Léogâne. Jean Francois Dujour, an OCDES board member, sent a grim e-mail to Chris McRae, describing the horrific sounds of people trapped under debris, yelling for help.

The next day a rescue team maneuvered the damaged Port-au-Prince runway and reached Léogâne. More help arrived every day. Since Léogâne had no airport, an unpaved field was used for small planes. Route 9 around Léogâne was cordoned off as another landing strip. Helicopters buzzed as they made airlifts within tight quarters.

Medics, military, peacekeepers, and engineers poured in during January and February, arriving from England, Canada, the United States, Japan, Argentina, Sri Lanka, Nepal, and South Korea.

The grounds around Sainte Croix Hospital and other parts of Léogâne not covered in rubble were clogged with a Canadian medical station, a Japanese field hospital, and an American search-and-rescue unit. Haitian Boy Scouts and Girl Guides controlled crowds at food distribution sites. A United Nations team gave Haitians cash to clear irrigation channels.

Overflowing refugee camps were everywhere.

All of this swirl in Léogâne might well have been light years from Cherident, though it was only a few miles away. In Cherident and across the remote mountains of Grande Colline, rescue workers did *not* flock in from around the world.

But the earthquake further solidified the bond between established nonprofits—Haiti Education Foundation, Plant with Purpose, Haiti Healthcare Partners, Living Waters for the World, Solar Under the Sun, and others like them—and the Haitians they loved.

The HEF board knew that international aid would not soon (if ever) reach the remote mountains of Grande Colline. When Susan appealed to supporters for relief funds, donations overwhelmed Frances's mailbox at 1801 West Block Street.

There was no way for HEF to get money into Grande Colline other than to bring it. Two weeks after the earthquake, Chris McRae braved his way to Haiti. He carried a sizable amount of cash for the priests and OCDES leaders to use for water, food, temporary shelters, and assistance to new widows. Some of the money went toward Clinique Jean-Wilfrid Albert, where the respected Dr. Nesly Catolin, Ancy's wife Lorna (a nurse), and the entire clinic staff worked tirelessly to tend to thousands of injuries. Ancy somehow found infant formula and brought it to a needy orphanage, possibly saving the lives of a dozen babies.

As soon as the bank in Carrefour reopened, Haiti Healthcare Partners wired additional funds for medicine and supplies.

All forty-two Haitian staff members of Plant with Purpose survived the earthquake, though one man tragically lost his wife and newborn son.

225

Plant with Purpose supplied one hundred tons of food and seeds to forty-five villages. Anticipating the hurricane season, farmers were hired to plant thousands of trees and construct hundreds of miles of erosion barriers.

"Fifteen years ago," said Scott Sabin, director of Plant with Purpose, "I wasn't that excited about working in a nation referred to as the graveyard of good intentions. Too often Haitians are portrayed as victims. But they are the ultimate survivors."

The needs in Grande Colline were compounded by a forty percent increase in population as thousands of homeless, frightened Haitians—including many amputees—fled from the ruins of the cities into the mountains. Demand for water, food, medical care, shelter, and education surged.

The priests made the difficult journeys to their forty villages and reported back to Susan. Bejin's schools were heavily battered. In Labiche, LeBeau, and Moreau, there were slight cracks. Bainet's schools were unharmed, but Pillard's were demolished. In the end, eleven of Frances's schools were destroyed and another eleven heavily damaged.

HEF's board of directors had voted immediately to pay its four hundred principals and teachers, regardless of how long schools were not in session. When the board talked and prayed about the wisest next step, it became clear that it was paramount to get the children back in school as quickly as possible. Providing tents and other temporary enclosures became as high a priority as funding scholarships.

Susan received an e-mail from a concerned principal, which validated the board's decision. The children were running around the villages, anxious and bored, the principal told her. "They could possibly cause trouble. Please help us open the schools soon."

"That e-mail really struck us," Susan told me. "Decades ago, Pere Albert and Frances knew how important it was to have children in school. Now principals, priests, teachers, and parents—everyone in the villages—saw the difference when the children were out of school. We felt like Haiti Education Foundation's ministry had come full circle."

HEF made another strategic decision.

"Cherident's guesthouse has always been foundational to the success of our mission in the mountains," Susan said. "Replacing the guesthouse quickly was vitally important to Haiti Education Foundation and Haiti Healthcare Partners."

In March, two months after the earthquake, Chris McRae returned to Grande Colline. He sat down with the priests and showed them the plan for a fabricated steel building. He spelled out HEF's proposal to construct a hurricane- and earthquake-resistant guesthouse in Cherident that would also house Pere Desire's family. Designed by Arkansas-based Erecta Building Systems, the steel building would hold up for fifty years or more.

While the adults mulled details of temporary school shelters, a new guesthouse, clean water, food, and medical care, Haitian children simply wondered what was next.

"The school is our future," one little girl said as she sat next to the rubble that used to be Cherident's primary school. "Now it is gone."

In Trouin, through a gash in an unsteady wall of its damaged primary school, a third-grade boy saw a chalkboard. On it, beneath layers of dust, he recognized the lesson he had been taught on January 12.

"I miss what I used to learn," he said.

Susan and HEF's board of directors began to raise seventy thousand dollars for Cherident's steel guesthouse. The project would team Erecta, HEF, Living Waters for the World, Solar Under the Sun, and local Haitians.

Expecting many hurdles, everyone was nonetheless exhilarated.

Haiti's Department of Education wanted schools reopened, if possible, by April 1. The HEF board refurbished the front-end loader and a dump truck to aid in cleanup, and purchased temporary school shelters, chairs, and chalkboards.

Many schools did open by the first of April. The rest followed as soon as some sort of structure was erected in a safe place. By June all of HEF's schools had completed the 2009–2010 school year. In August amid continued cleanup, classes resumed for the 2010–2011 term.

With their children back in school, the adults in all forty of the Episcopal villages regained some ability to look forward.

Windy Cove's summer team returned to a vastly different Cherident. Pastor Rob said, "On the one hand, the devastation was terrible. On the other, there were places almost untouched. Such a jumble of emotions. My most difficult moment was when I walked to where the guesthouse had been. The Haitians were clearing away debris. I picked up a shard of the lovely red tile that had covered the floor of the porch, and I thought about standing on the site as Pere Albert declared, 'This is where we will build the guesthouse.' Pere Albert built that guesthouse. Now it was gone. I shed tears because my good friend was also gone."

Since Cherident's church was destroyed, Rob's team worshipped under a simple, open-air structure. The scene was repeated across Haiti, Sunday after Sunday. Christian congregations gathered next to piles of bricks and stone that had once been their churches.

They sang. They prayed. They trusted. They picked up the pieces, literally, and tried to move on.

Within six months, Haiti Education Foundation raised three hundred thousand dollars. Susan and the board were judicious, sending money to the priests or OCDES leaders for specific purposes. They asked for photographs to show results to donors. They reported inevitable setbacks. They shared stories of success.

Frances's supporters had every reason to feel valued. Beyond the funds raised by HEF, virtually no aid money reached the mountains.

Seven months after the earthquake, Frances talked with Susan about the struggle to rebuild.

"You know, Susan, always the situations we believed to be the worst possible in Haiti have brought about the richest blessings."

Political upheavals. Unrest. The embargo. Hurricanes. Church politics. The loss of Pere Albert. The earthquake.

Frances had seen a lot since 1977.

At ninety-three, her faith and wisdom were immense. Both were as large—or larger, Susan reasoned—than the collective challenges that Haiti Education Foundation now faced.

On January 12, 2010, Cherident's St. Matthias Episcopal Church crumbled, but the village's faith was not shattered.

The four schools in Cherident, including the two-story secondary school, were destroyed. Classes for six hundred students had ended. No one was hurt.

The guesthouse, remodeled seven years before the earthquake,
was a second home for many visiting mission teams.

After the earthquake, the second story of the
vacant guesthouse sat at ground level.

Each fall, Haiti Education Foundation, the Episcopal priests, and qualified
teachers ensure that new little boys and girls will begin their journey of education.

PART III

SUSTAINING HOPE

Chapter 28

Losing Frances

All I ever planned was to have one school with four hundred students.
—Frances Landers, El Dorado, Arkansas, 2000

Frances Lucile Maschal Landers
March 5, 1917–September 14, 2010

In 2008 Arkansas Senator Mark Pryor stood on the floor of the United States Senate to pay tribute to Frances Landers.

> It is with great honor that I recognize remarkable contributions of ninety-one-year-old Frances Landers of El Dorado, Arkansas. At a time when most people consider retirement, Frances dedicated the past thirty years of her life to making education accessible to the children of Haiti. Frances's formation of Haiti Education Foundation opened educational doors of opportunity for children who otherwise might never have learned to read.
>
> Frances visited Haiti this past April to say her good-byes, for this was her last visit. She first came to Haiti in 1977 as a medical volunteer with her late husband, Dr. Gardner Landers, an ophthalmologist. Dr. and Mrs. Landers began making two trips a year, providing surgery and eyeglasses to the Haitian people. During these visits, she met Father Jean-Wilfrid Albert, a chaplain of the mission hospital. Through Father Albert, Frances discovered that many villages had no schools and most citizens were illiterate. Impassioned to make a difference, Frances returned to Arkansas and began raising money. She soon launched one school, and over time, many followed.
>
> Because of Haiti Education Foundation, there are now forty primary schools and ten secondary schools, which are educating more than ten thousand children. Donations and scholarships provide schooling, hot

lunches, shoes, school uniforms, textbooks, Creole Bibles, milk, and goats for families. These schools set the foundation for students to enroll in universities and pursue careers to break past poverty barriers.

Mrs. Landers has lived in service to the people of Haiti and is an extraordinary example of what can be achieved when committed to a worthwhile endeavor. Today I honor and thank Frances Landers for inspiring those around her to do the same.

Senators from across the United States applauded.

Nine months later, June 2009, Frances was hospitalized in intensive care. She reflected on her wonderful life. This latest illness, she thought, might be an indication that the time had come for her to ... *go.*

Two doctors in crisp, white coats—Dr. Donald Voelker and Dr. Hanam Ready—walked into Frances's room. She told them what she was thinking.

"God sets the timing in such matters," Dr. Voelker reminded her. He prayed for Frances. The three chatted, and the doctors left.

Rounding a hallway corner, Dr. Voelker and Dr. Ready met Lynn Landers, who was just arriving.

"We came to cheer your mother-in-law but she cheered us instead."

The next morning Frances's physician, Dr. Alan Pirnique, came by. "You will be moving to the fourth floor to finish your recovery," he said. "Then you will be going home."

Frances later wrote,

I did go home on schedule. God made it clear that it was not yet time for me to GO."

No, it was not yet time. On July 10, 2009, Mike and Susan Landers accepted for Frances an Arkansas Community Service award. Governor Mike Beebe and his wife Ginger recognized Frances for her longstanding commitment to volunteerism.

After the January 2010 earthquake, Susan Turbeville stopped by 1801 West Block Street most every day. She and Frances had many conversations about earthquake damage, repairs, money, and priorities. One thing was consistent. Frances did not fret.

"I don't tend to worry," she told Susan. "Worry doesn't accomplish anything. If something bad happens, I will worry then. It doesn't make any sense to worry twice." She smiled gently. "God did not have these schools all built in one day. When God wants them rebuilt, they will be."

The first of September was a crisp fall day, the season hinting at change. Susan knocked on the door and was greeted, as usual, by a smiling Angela Narcisse, Frances's dedicated caregiver. Frances was alert and busy.

"Frances," Susan said, "I can't believe you are still writing note cards and using your computer."

"Doing my work, Susan. That's what keeps me alive."

Frances stretched her oxygen cord farther, reached up, and gave her protégé a hug.

Susan was concerned about Frances's health. But she tried to stay focused on her own work, which included planning an upcoming HUG (Haiti United Gathering) Conference. She'd set the dates: September 17–19. She'd booked the location: Ferncliff Conference Center, just outside of Little Rock. She had sent out invitations.

"This gathering will provide the opportunity for people all over the United States to learn more about our mission," Susan wrote. "A few of our Haitian friends will be present. This is a vital time in our ministry!"

Pere Desire and Pere Vil had tickets in hand. So did Ancy, whose objective assessment of the villages was always invaluable.

The Haitians were coming to Arkansas a day early to spend time with Frances and to personally tell her how much she meant to their parishioners.

When it became apparent that Frances was not well enough to greet visitors or travel from El Dorado to Little Rock, Susan added to the agenda, "A Video Message from Frances."

Frances wanted, even in a limited way, to participate.

Sadly, her health precluded her from making a recording, one that would have given all who loved her some fresh, final words of encouragement.

Tuesday, September 14 was a long travel day for the three Haitians. Ancy drove Pere Desire and Pere Vil, bouncing and jostling, down the mountains of Grande Colline to the crowded Port-au-Prince airport. They waited for their flight to Miami and then the connecting one to Little Rock.

Susan met the men at the airport. She said softly, "Frances passed away at home this morning, peacefully, while you were in the air."

"It is sad," Susan wrote to me the next day. "But she was so tired."

"Champion of Haitian Education Dies at 93" headlined the *Arkansas Democrat-Gazette* on Thursday, September 16, 2010. Frances had a huge heart, but in the end it failed. Her family and her faithful Angela were by her side.

Four years earlier, Frances had said good-bye to Gardner. Her brother John Howard and sister Marjorie had also preceded her in death.

Over five years had passed since Frances had lost Pere Albert. When he died in July 2005, Frances had sighed. "Oh, Susan, how do we sustain the work?"

By the grace of God, and with lots of energy from Frances, Susan, the board of directors, and many others, HEF had soldiered on.

Now, in a new wave of grief and loss, Frances's supporters once again said, "Oh, my." Her feet were sizes smaller than Pere Albert's. But the shoes to fill were just as large.

The challenges in the mountains seemed as large as the mountains themselves. The earthquake had affected half of HEF's schools. Across the parishes, rubble remained. Temporary shelters were inadequate.

Haiti Education Foundation was by far Grande Colline's largest employer. Ten thousand scholarships for the children funded over four hundred teachers and principals. The annual school budget was $466,000.

Though HEF wanted to raise teachers' salaries, donations had recently fallen short by forty thousand dollars, a gap that needed to be closed. These were challenges that fifty-two HEF supporters from eight states would discuss at the HUG Conference just a few days away.

But first let's pause to give thanks for the life of Frances Landers.

Christian theology sets a person's death within the larger context of everlasting life. On September 16, hundreds of friends and family gathered at El Dorado's First Presbyterian for the "Witness to the Resurrection and Celebration of the Life of Frances Landers." As he had done for Gardner, Reverend Daniel Loomis led Frances's service.

Though Ancy, Pere Desire, and Pere Vil did not get the chance to visit Frances, God's timing enabled them to enrich her service. Ancy translated from Creole to English as Pere Desire read the opening scripture and Pere Vil gave the benediction. In between, Reverend Loomis based his meditation on the twenty-fifth chapter of Matthew. Verse forty says, "And the king will answer them. Just as you did this to one of the least of these who are members of my family, you did it to me."

As the Scripture commanded, Frances indeed loved "the least of these." She gave food to the hungry and milk to thirsty children. She welcomed strangers by the tens of thousands. She took care of them.

Gardner and Frances were blessed with an outstanding family, all of whom attended her service. Their sons and daughters-in-law were of the highest integrity. From El Dorado came Dr. William Hayden Landers and his wife Lynn, and Judge Michael Richard Landers and his wife Susan. From Little Rock came Dr. James Howard Landers and his wife Linda.

Frances was blessed with seven grandchildren: Elizabeth Hayden Clement and her husband David; Brian David Landers and his wife Susan; Allison May Moss and her husband Dennington; Dr. Andrea Hayden Huntley and her husband Justin; William Jeffrey Landers; Dr. Jason Maschal Landers and his wife Laura; and Michael Bryce Landers and his wife Elizabeth.

In her final four years, Frances's great-grandchildren had increased from seven to twelve: Gardner Landers Moss, Ella Clayton Moss, Hadley Dennington Moss, Samuel Emerson Landers, Alexander Jack Landers, Davidson Paine Landers, Lilly Frances Landers, Lee Clayton Landers, Mary Hayden Huntley, Georgia Scott Huntley, James Landon Clement, and Carson Saunders Clement.

Just look at all the family names!

But Frances's *entire* family was vastly larger than this.

"God's children, all of us," Frances reminded others. She embraced thousands of Haitian children as her own. Their families and the priests flocked to her with love and appreciation. Frances's nature led hundreds in the United States to consider her part of their family as well.

"Now Frances has handed off her mission," Susan Turbeville said after the service. "It is only fitting that we continue her legacy of bringing hope through education to God's children in the mountains of southern Haiti."

A week later, journalist Steve Brawner wrote about Frances in Arkansas's *Southwest Times Record.*

"Who in here thinks they are going to change the world?"

My psychology professor asked the question. As a 19-year-old sophomore, my surprise was that I was the only student with a hand in the air. I raised my hand because I really believed it.

"I hope you make it," my professor told me.

I'm not ashamed of that moment, even though I realize how unrealistic I was. Twenty-two years later, I'm not thinking too much about changing the world. I have two kids to raise and bills to pay, and that's pretty much my world.

That's why it was inspiring to read about Frances Landers in the statewide daily.

Frances died last week at age 93. Until she was 60, she would have been described as the wife who helped make her husband Gardner's El Dorado ophthalmology practice successful, and as the mother of three sons—an ophthalmologist, an optometrist, and a judge. If that were all she accomplished, she would have lived a successful life.

In 1977, she and Gardner attended a church service where they learned about the plight of cataract-stricken Haitians and decided to lend their skills. A one-week trip turned into two weeklong trips for 12 years. She overheard a child being turned away from a mission school in 1981, and realized how limited Haitian children's educational opportunities were. They didn't just need better eyesight. They needed a vision for their lives.

So Frances created Haiti Education Foundation and began raising money to build schools. She traveled the country presenting a 12-minute slideshow and asking for help. Because of her, there are now 50 schools serving 10,000 children who otherwise would have no access to public education. In the meantime, she overcame colon cancer and said goodbye to her husband, who died in 2006.

Frances made her last trip—her forty-third—to Haiti in 2008. She traveled to the poorest country in the Western Hemisphere at age 91, and even when this year's earthquake destroyed many of her foundation's buildings, she was not discouraged.

That's playing hard until the whistle blows. Hers was a life marked by longevity and purpose, which I don't think is a coincidence. I think she lived to be 93 in part because she was traveling to Haiti at 91. The best way to keep getting out of bed in the morning is to have a reason to get out of bed.

Frances Landers made her golden years golden. She changed the world for thousands of Haitian children, and she did it all after reaching the stage of life when lots of people would say she was too old to be so idealistic.

Anyone want to follow her example? I have my hand raised.

What a great tribute to Frances!

Please browse Appendix A of this book and enjoy the list of those whom Frances inspired to raise their own hands.

Chapter 29

From Stumble to Stride

I grew up in First Presbyterian Church. I became transfixed by the passion of Frances Landers. I will be involved with Haiti as long as there is a breath in my body.
—Mary Jo Oliver, El Dorado, Arkansas, 2012

The fifty-two HEF supporters stumbled more than once during the HUG Conference outside of Little Rock. Eyes brimmed with tears after a few inadvertent references to Frances in the present tense.

Though Susan had been HEF's terrific public face for some time, it was hard to believe Frances was gone.

Mike, Frances's youngest son and president of HEF, was stoic, though his eyes were sometimes distant as he motivated the group to continue building what his mother had begun.

The HUG event was filled with shared stories, photos, and memories. The weekend was productive too. Leaders from HEF, Haiti Healthcare Partners, Living Waters for the World, and Solar Under the Sun shared plans and looked for even greater synergy.

Pere Desire and Pere Vil reminded attendees of their parishes' vast needs. They asked HEF to rebuild the schools.

Gary Hays represented the newest ministry partner, Erecta Building Systems. His Fort Smith company was constructing Cherident's new guesthouse. The design included solar power, clean water, good hygiene facilities, ample bedrooms, a kitchen, and other common spaces.

To offer tangible hope in the aftermath of the earthquake and Frances's death, Chris McRae and Gary set up a small Electra building in the parking lot. HUG attendees clustered around.

Tight windows to keep out the bugs? Clean water warmed by solar power? Electricity that would stay on? Toilets that always flushed?

Regular travelers to Cherident could not wait.

The building's steel design had no use for a concrete roof. This was significant. In Haiti a concrete roof was a status symbol. It was a devastating irony that so many thousands died when their roofs caved in.

In the cities, rebuilding homes promised to be a financial, emotional, *and* cultural challenge. "We want to go back to our old ways," Haitians said.

"Yes," a sympathetic mission worker would reply, "except that your ways fell down." Eventually many Haitians agreed that safety was more important than culture or status, and they did not put concrete roofs on their new homes.

As the HUG weekend ended, attendees were upbeat. One woman who was new to the ministry said, "I am amazed by the commitment and joy with which the HEF folks serve the Lord."

Flo Boggs agreed. "The conference was a tribute to Frances, and a charge to continue her inspirational and vital work."

Bolstered by the energy of the conference, the HEF board made a tough but necessary decision to increase the cost of a scholarship.

Over the final years of Frances's life, fifty-five dollars—promoted since 1981 as enough to teach and feed a child for a year—was inadequate. Teachers' salaries and food prices had risen. Despite the decision to look for other nonprofit partners to provide school lunches, fifty-five dollars left a twenty-dollar shortfall.

In deference to Frances, the board waited until her death to make the change, covering the gap with investment reserves. In the next *Haiti Happenings*, Mike Landers said, "Seventy-five dollars remains an unbelievable value for the education of a child."

"Please note our new mailing address," the newsletter also said, which was perhaps insignificant to first-time readers. But to those who had for years received letters from 1801 West Block Street, the post office box number was another reminder of losing Frances.

Thirteen months after the earthquake, shipments of steel, tools, and pieces and parts arrived in Cherident. So did a team of nineteen from five states. Gary Hays of Erecta and Chris McRae directed the Americans and scores of eager Haitian men. Together they leveled the soil, set a steel beam, jackhammered anchor spikes into the ground, and started to build.

John Reed was elated to learn that the plumbing and electrical specialists were graduates of the vocational school, Frances Landers Tech.

After a week of hard work, the new guesthouse was substantially complete. The Haitians, fully capable of finishing up, waved good-bye as the team from the United States rode down the mountain to return home.

In early summer a group from Windy Cove pulled up in Cherident. To a person, they smiled. There was rubble, yes, but hundreds of students were in makeshift shelters, completing the school term. The clinic was beyond busy.

The well-loved guesthouse was gone. But all heads turned toward a shimmering building of nearly three thousand square feet. The doors of the steel guesthouse, with a few odds and ends still being completed, were open.

Cherident was back in business.

Daniel Collin, a friend of many Americans, graduated from Cherident's secondary school and went on to college. He was in France, completing his master's degree in computer science, when he heard of the new guesthouse. He wrote to Susan Turbeville, reminding her that the village of Cherident needed Haiti Education Foundation.

Mirroring the word Pere Albert used so often, Collin offered a prayer that HEF's projects and dreams would be "realized."

Jean-Pierre Jackson wrote too, thanking HEF for changing young lives and calling HEF's ministry "a divine grace."

Collin, Jackson, and dozens of other college graduates were just the encouragement Haiti Education Foundation needed to climb over inevitable hurdles. And there were several.

After four productive years, Pere Vil was transferred from Ascension Parish. His replacement, Pere Soner Alexandre, was also of high integrity, but it took time and energy to adjust to a new priest-in-charge. Dispensing funds, hiring staff, and keeping records were tasks of vital importance. Pere Soner was grateful to the OCDES board for its knowledge and assistance.

In St. Matthias Parish, Cherident's new guesthouse and busy clinic required many other on-the-spot decisions and after-the-fact detailed reporting. Pere Desire and OCDES were sometimes challenged, sharing authority.

Despite the higher scholarship price, donations continued to fall short of the amount needed to operate the schools. With its investment account of a few hundred thousand dollars, HEF had resources to close the gap. But knowing this was not a long-term solution, the board made the decision in 2013 to decrease its schools from forty villages to thirty-five. Schools in Dupera, Moise, and three other villages were not funded.

Mike told supporters, "Our hope is that donations will recover and we will soon be able to educate the children attending these five schools."

Susan added, "This is not an easy time in our ministry, but we must pull back in order to move forward."

With its operating budget resized to a little over thirty thousand dollars a month, HEF today pays for four hundred fifty teachers and meets the needs of nearly eight thousand students. Susan and others continue to travel, share stories of educated and successful Haitian youth, and attract new donors.

HEF also manages carefully its budget to fund college students, vehicles, tires, and other important aspects of the work.

And what about rebuilding the schools? HEF continues raising funds, but fortunately, God's mailing list is a lot larger than HEF's, and He is tapping others on the shoulder. A few nonprofits from the United States and other countries have come almost miraculously to Grande Colline, building materials in hand. The organizations have no interest in operating a school once it is rebuilt, but Haiti Education Foundation, of course, does.

Susan, the board, and Vicki Lambert, a talented financial secretary recently hired with grant funding, are grateful for each new partner who comes alongside HEF's ministry of education.

While HEF has regained a comfortable stride, the national scene has had its usual share of stumbles. The Haitian government was roundly criticized for mismanaging twelve billion dollars of earthquake relief funds. Recovery and rebuilding efforts were, at best, sluggish.

History shows that in many cases in Port-au-Prince and other cities, international earthquake responders overlooked a glaringly obvious truth, one that Haiti Education Foundation knows well. Most Haitians do *not* want to be taken care of. They want *help* in helping themselves.

While foreign aid groups held daily coordination meetings inside locked UN compounds, many Haitians in the cities took responsibility for their own recovery. In a displacement camp housing forty thousand, for example, Haitians formed a governing committee and subcommittees to control day-to-day necessities such as security and sanitation. United Nations workers rebuffed repeated requests to assist this camp.

Too often survivors like these were pushed aside by outside authorities who believed they knew better. It is a testament to the fortitude of the Haitian people that so many millions came through the disaster so well.

Following the quake, cholera broke out. Studies traced the highly contagious strain to UN peacekeepers from Nepal. The epidemic sickened more than seven hundred thousand. Nine thousand died. The United Nations refused to hear a US-sponsored lawsuit to compensate Haitians for their losses. At this writing, cholera remains a problem.

On January 12, 2011, the anniversary of the earthquake, Baby Doc Duvalier made a surprise return from France, ostensibly to help. Authorities responded by opening a criminal inquiry into allegations of his corruption. The investigation gained no traction, and Baby Doc moved freely around his country, doing little to help the common Haitian.

That year Duvalier ally Michel Martelly became president. A former pop music star and businessman, he vowed to accomplish much. Two years after the earthquake, most Haitians were no better off.

In 2012 Haiti's deforested mountains earned the country a dubious honor. No nation in the entire world had suffered more deaths and damage from extreme weather events than Haiti.

In October 2014 investigators concluded that remains of a shipwreck off Haiti's northern coast were not Christopher Columbus's *Santa Maria*. A potential spark for Haiti's tourism industry was doused.

On January 12, 2016, six years after the earthquake, tens of thousands of people were still in temporary housing camps. Though they were a fraction of the million and a half originally displaced, the statistic was still unsettling. Other signs of the disaster remained: rubble, graves, abandoned buildings, and chronic unemployment.

The earthquake did more than kill over two hundred thousand people and damage the land and economy. It damaged emotions. In Haitian culture, discussing mental illness was taboo. Before the earthquake, Haiti had perhaps ten psychiatrists. Only in the aftermath did Haiti's medical community begin to talk about mental health. In this country of nearly eleven million, the stigma against depression, bipolar disorder, and schizophrenia is slowly lessening as education and health care options increase.

A compounding problem is vodou, which, despite Christianity, is still practiced by about half of Haitians. Those with mental disabilities often turn to vodou rituals and sacrifices. Ironically, they attribute their illness to supernatural forces, curses, or spirits from past lives.

Like most things in Haiti, progress against mental illness can be described as "a little."

"*Pitti, pitti, zwazo fe nich li.*" Perhaps this Haitian proverb, "Little by little, a bird makes its nest," prompted Pere Albert to so often use that word: "little."

Michel Martelly's presidency was marked from the beginning by mistrust between himself and members of parliament. Since many believed the electoral process to be corrupt, attempts to organize elections repeatedly failed.

Protestors commonly marched through Port-au-Prince, calling for Martelly's resignation. Haiti's debt, forgiven after the earthquake, climbed back into the billions. One citizen said, "Haiti is rotting, the lights are out, there is misery, and they are wasting public money."

The US Department of State warned American travelers in Haiti to exercise caution, citing inadequate medical facilities and poor security. They were urged to obtain evacuation insurance in case they should need a swift exit home.

As terms of sitting senators expired, the remaining body functioned even more poorly. By early 2015 the entire Haitian parliament was dissolved. Martelly ruled by decree.

Since then, prime ministers, provisional councils, and international diplomats have come and gone. Elections in 2015 were routinely delayed and then contested well into 2016.

Haiti's future president and legislature, eventually, will have much work to do in the years to come to reach and maintain a positive stride.

Has all of Haiti's news since the earthquake been bleak? No.

Mission teams from the United States and other countries continue to make a difference—one pair of eyeglasses, two orphanages, three schools, and fifty vaccinations at a time.

There are glimmers of commercial growth as well, both from foreign investment and tourism.

At the remodeled Toussaint Louverture Airport, the American Airlines ticketing area sparkles. The Marriott Port-au-Prince opened in 2015, the first American hotel in Haiti since Best Western came in 2013. Hilton Worldwide plans to open its doors in Port-au-Prince as well.

In 2014 American retailer TOMS opened a factory in Port-au-Prince. Employing forty, TOMS produced a half million pairs of shoes its first year. Pere Albert never got his shoe factory in Grande Colline, but he must have smiled from heaven when TOMS arrived.

Other entrepreneurs and nonprofits have brought shops to Haiti's cities. Workers who make small electronics, jewelry, or blankets earn eight or ten dollars a day, more than three times the national average. Economists believe technology and bioscience businesses have a bright future.

Haiti's women show increasing strength and independence. Despite long-standing taboos, more are turning to birth control to manage family size. Microcredit loans, like those offered by Plant with Purpose, help women start small businesses, increase their income, and boost self-esteem.

In 2015 the average per capita income in Haiti rose a little to four hundred eighty dollars a year. Literacy crept upward to fifty-three percent.

Pitti, pitti.

Little by little.

Each time Haiti Education Foundation's supporters, the priests, and OCDES work together to open a new school, hire a principal, attract good teachers, and enroll hundreds of students, a village lights up with hope.

But oh, how a mountain village fully transforms when an American group *sponsors* its school. By mid-2013 nine churches from eight states had committed to sending to HEF, each month, the funds to pay the teachers and feed the kids.

Mission teams regularly come to *their* village to watch their money at work and learn of successes and needs. Side by side, Haitians and their sponsors build, paint, and plant. They enjoy Bible studies, kids' programs, and music camps. Relationships grow, ones that last a lifetime.

After perhaps a week, Americans return home to update their congregations and neighbors on their Haitian friends.

In 2012 Jackie Kossin of Johnson City, Tennessee, was part of a team that was taken aback by a ramshackle primary school near collapse in the mountaintop village of Bellevue. The group convinced its church, First Presbyterian, to adopt Bellevue's ninety children and build a new school.

The next year, Jackie and her teammates experienced exactly what HEF envisioned. They became invested in the lives of Bellevue's people.

Bellevue's children were hungry. Could the Americans supply food? For the elderly lady toting water up the mountain twice a day, would buying a mule be of help? How much would it cost to collect rainwater? What about the sixth-graders with big dreams? Where could they go to secondary school?

Jackie told *Haiti Happenings* readers that according to God's grand plan, He has asked her church to "take hold" to help bring about what He has in mind.

In the summer of 2013 Windy Cove became the tenth church to sponsor a village. Theirs was David, a small community in the middle of a cornfield. Windy Cove brought a team of thirteen from the Shenandoah Valley.

At the airport Ancy loaded suitcases full of supplies. David's children were out of school and ready for fun. After a week of building benches, playing games, and enjoying Bible studies and skits, the Haitian children showed their appreciation through song. American eyes were misty.

Though the Windy Cove group intended to give the little school in David material blessings that might make the villagers' days easier, team member April Miller pointed out that the Haitians "blessed our team beyond measure with smiles and love."

As Susan Turbeville prepared for a HUG Conference in southern California, she was pleased to learn that Alternative Gift Markets included "Scholarships for Students" in its 2013–2014 catalog. Harriet Prichard had earlier retired from Alternative Gifts International. Within a year she gallantly passed away from cancer. But Harriet's legacy, like Frances's, lives on.

In October 2013 HUG brought together supporters of HEF, Haiti Healthcare Partners, and Plant with Purpose. The weekend was one of celebration and future planning. School sponsorship was on the agenda.

Susan explained that a church or organization is encouraged to provide at least half of a school's annual financial need. For planning purposes, the board asks for a verbal five-year commitment, and in return it promises not to increase the budget during that time.

"So often someone asked Frances to share the name of the child receiving a scholarship," Susan told HUG attendees. "This was not possible. But if an entire school is sponsored, this and more is easily done."

Rob Crittenden, whose church in Roanoke has sponsored a school for twenty years, agreed. "It's our school. We built it, and these are our kids."

Viergela Louis Valles was HUG's special speaker. In 1989 she was a little girl, watching wide-eyed as Pere Albert walked the road in Cherident, promising parents that he would build a quality school.

"I remember when Father Albert was transferred to Grande Colline," Viergela told the HUG audience. "He had so much difficulty to find someone to read a Bible verse. It was not easy for him to get started. It was such a miracle when he and Mrs. Landers started working together."

Today Viergela is well educated, lovely, and poised. Many of us had not seen her for years. We leaned in to hear her soft voice.

"I am honored to be one of the beneficiaries of HEF's program. Thank you for everything you have done for my life to be a success. The young undergraduates of Grande Colline—and even those who started and did not have a chance to complete their studies—are using my voice, my lips to thank you. HEF hired well-educated and qualified teachers for our training. The proof is huge and remarkable. You will count so many professionals."

She paused, thinking of friends who are using their Christian education in Haiti's cities. Wislande Celestin is a nurse working for a prestigious private clinic. Pauline Jean Julien is a valued secretary in a law office. Marie-Ange Nicolas is a nurse. Jean Fils Chery is a priest. Cantave Fils-Aime and Jean-Pierre Jackson are well-respected agronomists. These young adults, like many others educated in Frances's schools, landed rare positions.

Other HEF graduates work for nonprofits. Anthony Jean Julien and Jean Robert Felisier are engineers for Samaritan's Purse. Elie Chery is in Cap-Haitien, an administrator for Food for the Poor.

They are Haitians helping Haitians.

"My plans are to become a nurse practitioner and go back to Haiti and serve," Viergela continued. "I will work very hard to give something to others. I thank God for His never-ending grace, mercy, and opportunity that He gives to every single partner and supporter of HEF by stimulating them to continue with the same vision, the same mission."

Tears came easily from Viergela's long-time American friends and from those who had just met her.

On July 25, 2014, Lynn Landers mourned the death of her husband Bill, the Landerses' oldest son. Bill had taken his first trip to Haiti with his parents in 1978. An optometrist, he worked alongside his father many times, and he fully supported his mother's educational ministry.

"His service to the people of Haiti and HEF has been invaluable, and we mourn his loss," his brother Mike wrote in *Haiti Happenings*. Bill's wife, their three children, and their families miss him dearly.

Bill and Lynn's son Jeffrey now serves with his Uncle Mike on the HEF board, which also expanded nationally to include George Brandon, Rob Crittenden, April Miller, Don Miller, and Reverend Cathy Ulrich.

By the end of the 2014–2015 term, HEF's school sponsorships rose to eighteen. Marsha Long from Norphlet, Arkansas, shared her story in *Haiti Happenings*. In 2014 this "housewife, mother, and grandmother turned missioner" took her first trip to the mountains. Her Methodist women's group sponsors a little school in Cavanach, which is located "past Cherident, up an absurdly steep mountain."

Rocks are everywhere in Cavanach, manageable only because of a thriving Plant with Purpose cooperative. Marsha spent a week with the villagers.

"Being able to look in the eyes of these people and children, and for them to associate us with their support, is definitely life-changing. I challenge anyone to go and see what a difference you can make."

Long-time HEF supporters Rob and Beth Crittenden know about making a difference. The Virginia couple recently formed a group of family, friends, and business associates to sponsor the village of Petite Riviere. Crittenden Family and Friends built a nine-room school, hiring Lucson Celestin—another HEF student who has done very well—to travel to the village during the building process and report progress.

Crittenden Family and Friends funds the teachers, and partners with Tennessee-based Trinity/HOPE to supply school lunches for two hundred students. Next, the Crittenden team wants to provide Petite Riviere with a water-purification system, cistern, and kitchen.

"Creating direct relationships between Americans and their Haitian schools is a blessing," Rob said.

HEF seeks to match its remaining seventeen schools with American partners and to increase donations so the five unfunded schools can be brought back into the fold. HEF is also expanding its relationship with Trinity/HOPE. This nonprofit, which specializes in feeding Haiti's children, brings hope—through bowls of beans and rice—to thousands of youngsters across the country.

David Lechter also knows about bringing hope. In 2015 this mature twelve-year-old wanted to reach out and touch the lives of others. Research led him to HEF. He and Susan Turbeville developed a plan to supply laptop computers for Cherident's primary school. David raised three thousand dollars, purchased fifteen touch screens, and had them configured for Haiti.

Ancy drove David and his parents, Robert and Lorena, up the mountains to Cherident. They were met by the smiling priest-in-charge of St. Matthias Parish, Pere Frederick Menelas, and his lovely wife Wislande.

Cherident's children were overwhelmed with David's generosity.

Many call Pere Fred "a young Pere Albert." "He is pure love," an HEF supporter said. Pere Fred did not know Pere Albert, though he has heard the stories and sees the harvest. He never knew Frances either. But each time Pere Fred talks to HEF supporters, his gratitude is abundant. "You have to always know that you have done a great job. You must be proud of yourselves."

Traveling today across Grande Colline, one will see neither Pere Albert nor Frances Landers. Many schools are still temporary shelters. Not every village has clean water or electricity. But nothing compares to the serenity of a village in the mountains.

Listen to the farmers, working cooperatively in productive fields.

Linger outside Clinique Jean-Wilfrid Albert and experience a wound healed, a life saved, or a healthy baby born.

Savor the rich Caribbean voices, the violins and brass, lifted in song.

Walk with joyful children by the hundreds and thousands, their faces and uniforms clean, smiles wide, lessons well learned, and faith strong.

Catch a glimpse of busy teachers, too many to mention, who grew up in Frances's schools—and principals too, like Wilner Salien, who governs the secondary school in Trouin and is forever in debt to Frances and Pere Albert.

Visit with Pere Donald Methellus, Pere Goursse Celestin, and Pere Fruitho Michaud—all respected priests in the mountains of Grande Colline—who were students in Frances's schools.

Traces of Pere Albert and Frances Landers are everywhere.

The challenges are many, always. The roads are rocky. But Haiti Education Foundation and its partners are on solid footing. With the ongoing generosity of its many friends, HEF will continue Frances's legacy, helping the beautiful Haitians in the mountains to help themselves.

Chapter 30

Personifying Hope

The story of Frances Landers and Pere Jean-Wilfrid Albert is a love story,
one divinely appointed by God for His purpose.
—John Reed, Fishersville, Virginia, 2012

Frances Lucile Maschal Landers had the gift of optimism. Pere Jean-Wilfrid Albert had the gift of vision. Both had faith in the Lord, who brought them together to weave a tapestry of hope across the mountains of Haiti.

So might have begun Frances's own explanation of what she and Pere Albert accomplished.

But the tall, joyful priest once explained it a lot better. "We are two people inspired by God—one to raise money, and one to spend it."

Until she was sixty-two, Frances had no idea she was gifted to raise money.

Across her long and fruitful life, Frances radiated strength and resolve and her own abundant joy. Blessed with nurturing parents in an atmosphere of love, Frances became confident and purposeful.

At age twelve she learned to drive. At sixteen she began college. She was a teacher at twenty and had moved from home by twenty-two.

In 1941 she walked into that corner diner in Fort Worth, set her sights on the officer with the curly black hair, and never looked back.

She crisscrossed the country in the little gray Buick, while Gardner served the nation. Then, happily settled in Roanoke, she hung diapers on the clothesline and enjoyed her three sons.

In El Dorado, First Presbyterian was the family's church home for sixty years. Frances was an elder, a trustee, a Sunday school teacher, and a role model. She was a pillar of optimism and care.

The Landers home was just that—home. It was homey, comfortable, inviting, and aglow with festive dinner parties and beautifully decorated tables.

Endless rivers of ink always flowed from Frances's pen. Family, friends, servicemen, missionaries, and young people she'd watched grow up enjoyed the gift of her letters.

She and Gardner were proud, oh so proud, of their sons—Bill the optometrist, Jim the ophthalmologist, and Mike the lawyer, who became a judge. Their wives, Lynn and Linda and Susan, Frances could not have loved more. She adored their children, and then those children's children.

For sixty years Frances led a rich life that became richer in 1977. When Gardner said yes to a trip to Léogâne, the couple had been married thirty-five years. Frances was by his side on this adventure, which they thought they were only going to share once.

But God had other plans. At age sixty, Frances traded a lifestyle of entertainment for a life of service. More than thirty years and more than forty trips later, Frances was still serving. Her husband of over sixty years was her bedrock of support.

Throughout her decades of ministry, Frances had three selling points. Fifty-five dollars a year educates a child. Every penny of every dollar goes to Haiti. Education is the hope of Haiti.

Today, fifty-five dollars doesn't quite make it. But seventy-five does. Every penny still goes to Haiti. And education remains Haiti's future hope.

Does every child in Grande Colline squeeze into a primary school funded by Haiti Education Foundation? No.

Does every child, after sixth grade, go on to secondary school? No.

Do all high school graduates go to college? No.

Do all college graduates get the jobs of their dreams? Certainly not.

To provide perspective, consider that twenty-seven years ago no one in the mountainous region of Grande Colline would even consider *asking* these questions. In 1989 nearly everyone, young and old, was illiterate.

Then came Frances, following Pere Albert, who had followed God.

In HEF's thirty-five villages, thousands of children simply want their own chance. A sixth-grade education improves that chance. Siblings, parents, and extended family benefit as well.

For those who attend secondary school or college or learn a trade, the news is even better. Graduates are now radiologists, journalists, priests, engineers, musicians, computer technicians, accountants, tailors, artists, and mechanics—and more. Haiti Education Foundation places four hundred fifty principals, teachers, and administrators back into its own school system. Plant with Purpose employs agronomists, and Clinique Jean-Wilfrid Albert has hired nurses and pharmacists.

The purchasing power of each person remains in the region.

Who among these or other graduates might form a profitable enterprise or bring the next business like TOMS to Haiti? Who might serve in government? Be an ambassador? Sponsor an important law? Build a hospital? Who might simply have a Christian-principled influence on another?

These educated Haitians bring more than their skills to the workplace, for they were schooled in the values of the church. They were shepherded by godly men and women. They learned the heart of Jesus.

Frances's graduates are becoming godly future leaders of Haiti, just as she and Pere Albert began to pray for decades ago.

Perhaps one hundred thousand children and adults can read and write because Pere Albert asked Frances Landers to create schools. In all probability, only a fraction would be educated today without Haiti Education Foundation.

We are barely in the second generation of literacy in the mountains.

Think what the next twenty or thirty years will bring.

This work is hard, sometimes very hard. But do not ever believe that it is too hard. Because God *does* want schools in the mountains.

No matter our age, no matter our gifts, we can make a difference. In our neighborhoods, in Haiti, or anywhere on the globe, may we too improve the lives of others.

Perhaps we are called to leave the first footprint on a new mountainside of opportunity. Perhaps we are asked to enlarge the footsteps of others.

Either way, we can take one step at a time.

Little by little.

Pitti, pitti.

Always personifying hope.

In 1992 a little girl from Cherident handed Frances Landers a piece of paper. On it, in carefully printed Creole, were these words:

"Mèsi pou lekòl mwen-an."

"Thank you for my school."

Today this young woman is about thirty. She can read and write. She knows her mathematics and her science. She knows the books of the Bible and the Architect behind them.

God willing, her own children—a second generation of the future leaders of Haiti—are now entering the schools built by Frances Landers.

Grás a Bondye.

Thanks be to God—for the woman from Arkansas, for the priest from Haiti, and for the thousands who joined them to help change a country, one child at a time.

Across the mountains of Grande Colline,
schools have brought joy and hope to village after village.

Appendixes

Every year, Haiti Education Foundation's supporters expand
the work—begun by Frances and Pere Albert—of helping
young Haitians take giant steps out of poverty.

Appendix A

Travelers and Partners

Enclosed is a gift of $1,950 for the children in Haiti. Sharing helps us heal.
—Youth of St. Phillip Lutheran Church, following the tragedy
at Columbine High, Littleton, Colorado, 1999

Frances Landers could not have asked for better ministry partners. She would have studied this appendix for hours. Pere Albert would have bubbled over with laughter while reading these very long lists. His effusive "thank you" would echo that of his parishioners, especially the children, as they clutched a pencil and paper, a stub of chalk, and a Creole Bible.

This appendix would evoke smiles from the other Episcopal priests, parish community leaders, principals and teachers, and Haiti Education Foundation's board of directors, for the work that began in 1981 continues today.

To compile the lists below, I used source documents and interviews. I apologize for the many HEF supporters whose names I did not come across and therefore unknowingly omitted.

Initially, the mission destination was Léogâne's Sainte Croix Hospital, with side trips to Mercery, Collin, La Colline, and Jean-Jean.

In 1989 Pere Albert went to the mountains of Grande Colline. Americans climbed the mountains too: an ophthalmologist and his wife from Arkansas, pastors, church teams, youth groups, teachers, doctors, nurses, dentists, missionaries, families, and friends.

The climb continues.

Were Frances with us today, she would most certainly have wanted to write one more note of thanks to each person who gave to Haiti Education

Foundation the gifts of prayer, encouragement, skill, energy, and resources—all messages of hope.

Her final personal note might have ended with "Blessings." Then, in black ink and with a slight flourish, her grateful signature ...

Frances

Travelers

(Where known, the year of the first or a subsequent trip is included.)

Ack, Billy (1989)
Adams, Margie (1986)
Adkins, Lee (1991)
Alexander, Beverly (2012)
Anderson, Sara (2015)
Arn, Nancy (1983)
Arner, Gary (2013)
Atkinson, Jesse (2011)
Ault, Cynthia (2001)
Ault, Patricia (2001)
Austin, Ellen (2014)
Baldwin, Bill (1989)
Barden, Kathleen (2015)
Barr, Gary (1993)
Barrick, Judy (2000)
Belch, Alan (1991)
Bell, Candy (2003)
Bell, J. P. (2002)
Benedict, Kathryn
Bethell, Lander (2005)
Black, John (2001)
Blackburn, Phillip (2014)
Blake, Billy (1993)
Blankinship, Dick (2002)
Blankinship, Phyllis (2001)
Blose, Ellen (1999)
Blumenthal, Emily (2012)
Boggs, Flo (1985)
Boggs, Harry (1992)
Boward, Emily (2011)
Boward, Ken (2011)
Bowen, Roger
Bowman, Amy (2015)
Bowman, Michael (2015)
Boxley, Doug (1993)
Bradley, Charlotte (2011)
Brady, Sylvia (1998)
Brandon, George (1999)
Brash, Doug (2002)
Brash, Nick (2001)
Bridgeforth, Bill (2013)

Brockenbrough, Ann (1996)
Broome, Rex (1989)
Brown, Charles
Brown, JoAnne
Brown, John (2001)
Brown, Judith (1993)
Brown, Laura (1997)
Brown, Michelle (2012)
Brown, Richard (1993)
Bryant, Sue Ann (2000)
Burlington, Molly (2014)
Butler, Fred (1989)
Byrd, Carla (2012)
Byrd, Cheryl (2015)
Calloway, Caroline (2011)
Campbell, Marge (1996)
Carlisle, Chris (2002)
Carlisle, Jennifer (1985)
Carlton, Mike
Carper, Blanche
Carper, Day
Carr, Jeff (1998)
Cashatt, Ty (2003)
Catlin, Pete (1991)
Chappell, Bill (1999)
Cherry, Pauline
Clark, Charlotte (1984)
Clark, Donna (1984)
Clarke, Suzy (2005)
Clayton, Nora
Clayton, Tom
Cobb, Chuck (1985)
Cobb, Lloyd (1985)
Cobb, Ray (1984)
Cohee, William (2014)
Conyers, Betsy (2011)
Conyers, Josh (2011)
Conyers, Sarah (2011)
Cook, Biff
Corbin, Andy (2014)
Core, Jacquie (2003)

Corell, Cindy (2011)

Cornish, Homer (1996)

Cornish, Larue (1996)

Covert, Edie (1995)

Cox, Mary Lou (1991)

Cox, Mary Rebekah (1991)

Craft, Vickie (1998)

Cranford, April (2010)

Cranford, Reed (2010)

Crittenden, Beth (2013)

Crittenden, Rob (1998)

D'Amico, Judith (1987)

Daniels, John (1997)

De Feo, Sherry (1997)

Dean, Chris (2008)

Desmarattes, Gerald (1999)

Dietz, Krystal (2000)

Donovan, Bill (2015)

Douglas, Robert

Downie, Trevor (1992)

Duke, Jackie (1993)

Ealy, Dave (2001)

Earls, Lori (2013)

Edmondson, Ann (2003)

Edmondson, Steve (2002)

Edwards, Melinda (1993)

Edwards, Randy (1993)

Entsminger, Brandon (2002)

Eppenstiner, David (1999)

Evans, Layton (1989)

Ewell, Davis (2001)

Eye, Harvey (1985)

Falasco, Becky

Falasco, Dennis (1998)

Fang, Fiona (2012)

Favor, Craig (2013)

Fielder, Jason (2000)

Fisher, Mary Louise (1995)

Flanders, Charlotte (2003)

Flanders, Dudley (2003)

Folta, Wayne (1985)

Forbes, Jean (1985)

Ford, Gary (2000)

French, Barbara (2000)

Fry, Sharon (1985)

Garcia, Eldon (1995)

Garden, Tupper (2000)

Gartrell, Jan (2008)

Gilchrest, Betty (1990)

Gilchrest, Brian (1985)

Gilchrest, Cliff (1985)

Gilchrest, Jill (1985)

Gilliam, Betty (2002)

Glass, Bill (2005)

Goode, Jerry

Goodman, Kay (1984)

Gordon, Ashley (2010)

Gordon, Sherry (1999)

Gortner, Cindi

Gray, Dick (2001)

Gregory, Randy (1999)

Griffith, Livia (2011)

Grist, Vicki (1997)

Grizzle, David (2001)

Groome, Rex (1989)

Gruelich, Beth (2014)

Guilbert, Shelby (2015)

Gunther, Bob (2011)

Gunther, Christopher (2012)

Gunther, Geoffrey (2012)

Gunther, Kathy (2011)

Guthrie, Weston (1992)

Hahn, Heather (2008)

Hall, Carol (2003)

Hall, John

Hall, Larry (1999)

Hallis, John (1993)

Hander, Skip (2003)

Hanna, Jack

Hansard, Elise (1996)

Hardbarger, Tom (2000)

Hardie, Dan (2004)

Harris, Norm (2000)

Harris, Paul (1984)

Harrison, Sandy (1985)

Hass, Derek (1998)

Hass, Kirk (1998)

Hastings, David (1998)

Haynes, Criss (1993)

Hays, Gary (2010)

Hayter, Scott (1986)
Hearn, Page (2011)
Heizer, Kay (1998)
Henderson, Bruce (1986)
Herrara, Armando (2015)
Herscher, Angela (2010)
Herscher, Traci (2003)
Hess, Greg (1999)
Hileman, Daniel (1999)
Hill, Jennifer
Hobbs, Fran (1982)
Hobbs, John (1986)
Hobbs, Pete (1992)
Hodges, Dawkins (1984)
Hohnke, Lyle (2006)
Holbrook, Philip (2002)
Holbrook, Rebecca (2001)
Houser, Jordan (2000)
Housman, Kevin (2006)
Howell, Evelyn (1998)
Howell, Paul (1998)
Howie, Wil
Hundley, Steve (1985)
Hunter, Tully (2012)
Hutton, Helen (1984)
Jacks, Gretchen (2002)
Jacks, Louis (2002)
Jackson, Marc (1999)
Jacob, Katherine (2006)
Jennings, Chris (1989)
Johnson, Hazel (1995)
Johnson, Myrna (1978)
Jones, Tara (2012)
Jordan, Edna (1984)
Jordan, Scott (1984)
Julian, Paul (2000)
Justiss, Marie (2000)
Kaled, Sue (2001)
Keith, Jane (2003)
Kessler, Rief (2014)
Kessler, Susan (2014)
Kimmel, James (2015)
Kimmel, Jenny (2015)
King, Calvin (1997)
King, Emily (2000)

King, John (2005)
King, Sam (1997)
Kinner, Heidi (2006)
Kosak, Brad (2003)
Kossin, Jackie (2012)
Krain, Benjamin (2012)
Kreuger, Sue (2006)
Lamar, Shannon (2000)
Lambert, Vicki (2013)
Lancaster, Alyson (2003)
Lancaster, Jason (1998)
Lancaster, Kim (2000)
Lancaster, Paul (1995)
Landers, Allison (1996)
Landers, Andrea (1998)
Landers, Bill (1978)
Landers, Frances (1977)
Landers, Gardner (1977)
Landers, Jason (1999)
Landers, Jeffrey (2013)
Landers, Jim (1977)
Landers, Laura (2004)
Landers, Lynn (1978)
Landers, Mike (1999)
Landers, Susan (1982)
Landes, Betty (1989)
Lang, Alex (2005)
Langevin, Barbara (1988)
Langouet, Luc (2011)
Langsdon, Phillip (1999)
Larkman, Victoria (1999)
Lechter, David (2015)
Lechter, Lorena (2015)
Lechter, Richard (2015)
Leidersdorf, Donna (2013)
Linkenhoker, Chris (1984)
Lipscomb, John
Litteer, Tom (2001)
Little, Jessica (2015)
Little, Scott (2000)
Lloyd, Georganne (2003)
Lloyd, Jeanne
Lockridge, Bobby (1995)
Logan, Dan (2007)
Logan, Karen (2007)

Long, Marsha (2014)
Lopes, Joe (2000)
Lovell, Brittany (2009)
Lovell, Eli (2002)
Lovell, Josh (1999)
Lovell, Katie (2009)
Lovell, Seth (2002)
Lowery, John (2008)
Luther, Jim (2000)
Lynn, Alice (2001)
Maliwauki, Grace (2000)
Manion, Keith (2000)
Marcum, Lara (2011)
Martin, Glenn (2011)
Martin, Mary Ann
Martin, Nancy (2011)
Martin, Paul (2015)
Mase, Christine (1997)
Matheny, Shirley (2008)
Mathes, Ben
Mathias, Jennie (2000)
Mattox, Ginnie (2000)
Maykopet, Richard (2000)
McCaffety, Keith
McCall, Jo (2004)
McClerkin, Connor (2014)
McCord, Charles (2001)
McDonald, Mark (1990)
McDonough, David (1988)
McGraw, Lee (2011)
McGregor, John (2000)
McGrew, Gary (1995)
McGrew, Stephen (1995)
McKay, Bob (1997)
McKinney, Ramona
McRae, Chris (2002)
McRae, Ruthie (2007)
Meddaugh, Julie (2014)
Meraz, LeAnne (2000)
Merian, Bob (2000)
Miles, Bob (1995)
Miller April (2001)
Miller, David (2011)
Miller, Don (1999)
Miller, Doris (1991)

Miller, John (1992)
Miller, Martha (1999)
Miller, Mikayla (2010)
Moffett, Julia Ann
Monroe, Jennifer (1999)
Moore, Percy (1999)
Morgan, Stephany (1997)
Morikawa, Bob (2000)
Morrone, Jennifer (1999)
Moulton, Gail
Moulton, Randolph
Mower, John (2000)
Murphy, Mike (1998)
Murphy, Sylvia (1998)
Musser, Doris Ann
Musser, Glenn (1991)
Musser, Harvey
Musser, Marshall (1985)
Naber, Mary (2005)
Nabers, Drayton
Nelson, Ashley Kyle (2013)
Nelson, Ciara (2013)
Nelson, Donna
Nelson, Isaac (2013)
Nelson, Phil (2008)
Newmarker, Heather (2001)
Norsworthy, Brenda
Oeschli, Mark (2010)
Oleson, Jim (2010)
Oliver, Mary Jo (1998)
Orndorff, Debbie (1985)
Parker, John (1989)
Parker, Logan (2011)
Paul, Rosita (2014)
Payne, Heather (2015)
Pennington, Jerry (1992)
Pinkner, Joe
Platamone, Nick (2014)
Plecity, Doug (1998)
Plecity, Frank (2001)
Poindexter, Sarah (2001)
Porter, Amy (2001)
Porter, Kim (1999)
Prichard, Harriet (1989)
Quillen, Daniel (2009)

Williams, Ben (2011)
Williams, Brent (1998)
Williams, Jim (2013)
Williams, Mollie (2003)
Winalski, John (2015)
Winfrey, Eleanor (1991)
Wood, Tyler (2009)
Woodzell, Russell (2011)
Woodzell, Ryan (2015)

Wooten, Carole Sue (2007)
Wuerker, Anne (2007)
Wycoff, Linda
Wycoff, Rollin (2011)
Wylie, Bob (2000)
Wysor, Haley (2012)
Yancey, Katie (2009)
Yosko, Caryl (1995)
Young, John (2015)

Partners of Haiti Education Foundation
(Alphabetized by State, then City)

Cathedral Church of the Advent, Birmingham, AL
Community Foundation of Greater Birmingham, Birmingham, AL
Unnamed Episcopal church, Birmingham, AL
First Presbyterian Church, Birmingham, AL
South Highland Presbyterian Church, Birmingham, AL
Unnamed Presbyterian church, Foley, AL
Spanish Fort Presbyterian Church, Spanish Fort, AL
Unnamed church, Stapleton, AL
Unnamed church, Arkadelphia, AR
Lyon College, Batesville, AR
First Presbyterian Church, Bentonville, AR
First Methodist Church, Camden, AR
First Presbyterian Church, Camden, AR
Tates Bluff Presbyterian Church, Chidester, AR
First Presbyterian Church, Conway, AR
Hendrix University, Conway, AR
First Presbyterian Church, Crossett, AR
First Presbyterian Church, De Queen, AR
Unnamed Baptist church, El Dorado, AR
Boys & Girls Club of El Dorado, El Dorado, AR
Civitans, El Dorado, AR
Dumas Memorial United Methodist Church, El Dorado, AR
First Baptist Church, El Dorado, AR
First Presbyterian Church, El Dorado, AR
Holy Redeemer Catholic School, El Dorado, AR
Homemaker's Council, El Dorado, AR
Kiwanis Club of El Dorado, El Dorado, AR
Murphy Oil Corporation, El Dorado, AR
Pilot Club, El Dorado, AR
Quest Club, El Dorado, AR
Rotary Club, El Dorado, AR
St. Mary's Episcopal Church, El Dorado, AR
Westminster Presbyterian Church, El Dorado, AR
Unnamed church, Eudora, AR
First Presbyterian Church, Fayetteville, AR
Pediatric Dental Associates & Orthodontics, Fayetteville, AR
Central Presbyterian Church, Fort Smith, AR
First Presbyterian Church, Fort Smith, AR
Spring River Presbyterian Church, Hardy, AR
First Presbyterian Church, Hope, AR
Westminster Presbyterian Church, Hot Springs, AR
Presbyterian Kirk in the Pines, Hot Springs Village, AR

First Presbyterian Church, Jonesboro, AR
Scotland Presbyterian Church, Junction City, AR
First Presbyterian Church, Lake Village, AR
Dr. James H. Landers, MD, Little Rock, AR
Presbytery of Arkansas, Little Rock, AR
Pulaski Heights Presbyterian Church, Little Rock, AR
Second Presbyterian Church, Little Rock, AR
Trinity Presbyterian Church, Little Rock, AR
First Presbyterian Church, Lonoke, AR
First Presbyterian Church, Magnolia, AR
Rotary Club, Magnolia, AR
First Presbyterian Church, McGehee, AR
First Presbyterian Church, Mena, AR
First Presbyterian Church, Monticello, AR
Rotary Club, Montecito, AR
First Presbyterian Church, Morrilton, AR
First Presbyterian Church, Mountain Home, AR
Norphlet United Methodist Church, Norphlet, AR
First Presbyterian Church, Pine Bluff, AR
First Presbyterian Church, Rogers, AR
First Presbyterian Church, Russellville, AR
Ebenezer Presbyterian Church, Strong, AR
First Presbyterian Church, Texarkana, AR
Unnamed church, Walnut Ridge, AR
Sylvania Presbyterian Church, Ward, AR
First Presbyterian Church, Warren, AR
Apple Valley Presbyterian Church, Apple Valley, CA
Church of the Valley Presbyterian, Apple Valley, CA
Alternative Gifts International, Lucerne Valley, CA
Plant with Purpose, San Diego, CA
Chapter TS, P.E.O., Westlake Village, CA
Haiti Healthcare Partners, Westlake Village, CA
Westminster Presbyterian Church, Westlake Village, CA
St. Phillip Lutheran Church, Littleton, CO
Unnamed church, Boca Raton, FL
Community Presbyterian Church, Deerfield Beach, FL
Eastminster Presbyterian Church, Indialantic, FL
Palmdale Presbyterian Church, Melbourne, FL
Fort King Presbyterian Church, Ocala, FL
Presbytery of Central Florida, Orlando, FL
Trinity Presbyterian Church, Satellite Beach, FL
Presbyterian Church of Seffner, Seffner, FL
First Presbyterian Church, Titusville, FL
St. Luke's Presbyterian Church, Titusville, FL
Northeast Georgia Presbytery, Athens, GA

Unnamed Presbyterian church, Athens, GA
Unnamed Presbyterian church, Atlanta, GA
First Presbyterian Church, Gainesville, GA
First Presbyterian Church, Griffin, GA
Church of the Holy Family, Jasper, GA
Presbyterian Church of the Redeemer, Lithonia, GA
St. Francis Episcopal Church, Macon, GA
Presbyterian Church of the Redeemer, Snellville, GA
Unnamed Methodist church, Valdosta, GA
Presbytery of Boise, Boise, ID
Southminster Presbyterian Church, Boise, ID
First Presbyterian Church, Idaho Falls, ID
Motorola, Inc., Schaumburg, IL
Grace Presbyterian Church, Wichita, KS
The Presbyterian Church of Bowling Green, Bowling Green, KY
Episcopal Medical Missions Foundation, Alexandria, LA
First Presbyterian Church, Bastrop, LA
Graceminster Presbyterian Church, Bossier City, LA
Alabama Presbyterian Church, Choudrant, LA
First Presbyterian Church, Ferriday, LA
Belcher Presbyterian Church, Gilliam, LA
First Presbyterian Church, Homer, LA
Church of the Good Shepherd, Lake Charles, LA
Unnamed Presbyterian church, Lake Providence, LA
Minden Presbyterian Church, Minden, LA
Covenant Presbyterian Church, Monroe, LA
First Presbyterian Church, Monroe, LA
Graceminster Presbyterian Church, Monroe, LA
First Presbyterian Church, Natchitoches, LA
Presbytery of the Pines, Ruston, LA
Broadmoor Presbyterian Church, Shreveport, LA
First Presbyterian Church, Shreveport, LA
John Calvin Presbyterian Church, Shreveport, LA
St. Paul's Episcopal Church, Shreveport, LA
Unnamed church, Tallulah, LA
Wilchins, Cosentino & Friend, LLP, Wellesley, MA
St. Luke's Episcopal Church, Portland, ME
Binda Foundation, Battle Creek, MI
Haiti Hiawatha Work Group, Marquette, MI
First Presbyterian Church, Rochester, MN
Lakeside Presbyterian Church, Brandon, MS
Lakeside Presbyterian Church, Jackson, MS
First Presbyterian Church, Leland, MS
Unnamed Presbyterian church, Oxford, MS
Unnamed Episcopal church, Asheville, NC

Two unnamed Presbyterian churches, Asheville, NC
St. Peter by the Lake Episcopal Church, Denver, NC
Triangle Presbyterian Church, Durham, NC
Almanac Presbyterian Church, Greensboro, NC
Farmland Presbyterian Church, Greenville, NC
First Presbyterian Church, New Bern, NC
Shallotte Presbyterian Church, Shallotte, NC
Calabash Covenant Presbyterian Church, Sunset Beach, NC
First Presbyterian Church, Waynesville, NC
Unnamed church, Wilmington, NC
Reynolds Presbyterian Church, Winston Salem, NC
First Presbyterian Church, Sparta, NJ
Christ Church Riverdale, Bronx, NY
North Rose-Wolcott Middle School, Wolcott, NY
First Presbyterian Church, St. Clairsville, OH
Collinsville Community Church, Collinsville, OK
Unnamed church, Norman, OK
Unnamed church, Ponca City, OK
First Presbyterian Church, Sand Springs, OK
The Goldie Frances Campbell Trust, Sand Springs, OK
First United Methodist Church, Roseburg, OR
Abington Presbyterian Church, Abington, PA
Bakerstown Presbyterian Church, Bakerstown, PA
Westminster Presbyterian Church, West Chester, PA
Ocean Drive Presbyterian Church, North Myrtle Beach, SC
Grace Episcopal Church, Chattanooga, TN
Rivermont Presbyterian Church, Chattanooga, TN
Living Waters for the World, Franklin, TN
The Outreach Foundation, Franklin, TN
Germantown Presbyterian Church, Germantown, TN
First Presbyterian Church, Johnson City, TN
St. John's Episcopal Church, Johnson City, TN
First Presbyterian Church, Jonesboro, TN
First Presbyterian Church, Morristown, TN
Bellevue Presbyterian Church, Nashville, TN
Frontier Logistical Services, LLC, Nashville, TN
Austin Theological Seminary, Austin, TX
Episcopal Seminary of the Southwest, Austin, TX
First Presbyterian Church, Bastrop, TX
Unnamed church, Bay City, TX
Unnamed church, Commerce, TX
First Presbyterian Church, Corpus Christi, TX
First Presbyterian Church, Corsicana, TX
Westminster Presbyterian Church, Corsicana, TX
Crosby Church, Crosby, TX

Covenant Presbyterian Church, Dallas, TX
Episcopal Medical Missions Foundation, Dallas, TX
Northridge Presbyterian Church, Dallas, TX
Preston Hollow Presbyterian Church, Dallas, TX
St. Andrew's Presbyterian Church, Denton, TX
Westminster Presbyterian Church, Fort Worth, TX
First Presbyterian Church, Graham, TX
First Presbyterian Church, Granbury, TX
Clear Lake Presbyterian Church, Houston, TX
Elva J. Johnston Foundation, Houston, TX
Emmanuel Episcopal Church, Houston, TX
Episcopal Diocese of Texas, Houston, TX
Episcopal Medical Missions Foundation, Houston, TX
Grace Presbyterian Church, Houston, TX
Howell Family Foundation, Houston, TX
John Knox Presbyterian Church, Houston, TX
MD Anderson Hospital, Houston, TX
Medical Benevolence Foundation, Houston, TX
St. John the Divine Episcopal Church, Houston, TX
St. Martin's Episcopal Church, Houston, TX
Solar Under the Sun, Irving, TX
First Presbyterian Church, Jasper, TX
Unnamed church, Johnson City, TX
First Presbyterian Church, Kerrville, TX
Unnamed church, Kingman, TX
First Presbyterian Church, Longview, TX
Longview Presbyterian Church, Longview, TX
Unnamed family foundation, Lufkin, TX
First Presbyterian Church, Mount Pleasant, TX
Bulverde Elementary School, New Braunfels, TX
Unnamed Presbyterian church, New Braunfels, TX
Unnamed seminary, New Braunfels, TX
Unnamed church, Pittsburg, TX
Holy Trinity Presbyterian Church, San Antonio, TX
Northwood Presbyterian Church, San Antonio, TX
Covenant Presbyterian Church, Sherman, TX
Grand Avenue Presbyterian Church, Sherman, TX
TAS Commercial Concrete, Spring, TX
Presbyterian Church of the Redeemer, Texarkana, TX
United Methodist Church, Texarkana, TX
Four unnamed churches, Texarkana, TX
First Presbyterian Church, Tyler, TX
Unnamed church, Victoria, TX
Bethel Presbyterian Church, West Columbia, TX
Unnamed church, Woodville, TX

Summer Productions, Alexandria, VA
Altavista Presbyterian Church, Altavista, VA
Bridgewater Presbyterian Church, Bridgewater, VA
United Methodist Church, Bridgewater, VA
Olivet Presbyterian Church, Charlottesville, VA
Unnamed Methodist church, Covington, VA
Unnamed Presbyterian church, Covington, VA
Craigsville Presbyterian Church, Craigsville, VA
Crittenden Family and Friends, Daleville, VA
Dayton United Methodist Church, Dayton, VA
Dinwiddle Presbyterian Church, Dinwiddle, VA
Dublin Presbyterian Church, Dublin, VA
Tinkling Spring Presbyterian Church, Fishersville, VA
Augusta Stone Presbyterian Church, Fort Defiance, VA
Front Royal Presbyterian Church, Front Royal, VA
Unnamed church, Harrisburg, VA
Presbytery of Shenandoah, Harrisonburg, VA
Hot Springs Presbyterian Church, Hot Springs, VA
New Monmouth Presbyterian Church, Lexington, VA
First Presbyterian Church, Lynchburg, VA
Rivermont Presbyterian Church, Lynchburg, VA
Massanutten Presbyterian Church, Penn Laird, VA
Unnamed Episcopal church, Mechanicsville, VA
Windy Cove Presbyterian Church, Millboro, VA
First Presbyterian Church, Moundsville, VA
Mossy Creek Presbyterian Church, Mount Solon, VA
Presbyterian Church of Radford, Radford, VA
Crestwood Presbyterian Church, Richmond, VA
Raleigh Court Presbyterian Church, Roanoke, VA
Covenant Presbyterian Church, Staunton, VA
First Presbyterian Church, Staunton, VA
Second Presbyterian Church, Staunton, VA
Spring Hill Presbyterian Church, Staunton, VA
Trinity Episcopal Church, Washington, VA
St. Margaret's Episcopal Church, Woodbridge, VA
Woodstock Presbyterian Church, Woodstock, VA
Berkeley Springs Presbyterian Church, Berkeley Springs, WV
Bloomery Presbyterian Church, Bloomery, WV
Burlington United Methodist Women, Burlington, WV
Unnamed church, Falling Springs, WV
Falling Waters Presbyterian Church, Hedgesville, WV
Connections Community Church, Inc., Inwood, WV
Grace Episcopal Church, Jackson County, WV
St. John's Episcopal Church, Jackson County, WV
Kearneysville Presbyterian Church, Kearneysville, WV

Calvary United Methodist Church, Keyser, WV
Emmanuel Episcopal Church, Keyser, WV
Keyser Presbyterian Church, Keyser, WV
Lions Club, Keyser, WV
Lewisburg Rotary Club, Lewisburg, WV
Old Stone Presbyterian Church, Lewisburg, WV
First Presbyterian Church, Morgantown, WV
St. Frances De Sales Central Catholic School, Morgantown, WV
Trinity Episcopal Church, Morgantown, WV
First Presbyterian Church, Moundsville, WV
Mt. Storm Presbyterian Church, Mt. Storm, WV
Petersburg Presbyterian Church, Petersburg, WV
Grace Episcopal Church, Ravenswood, WV
St. John's Episcopal Church, Ripley, WV
Romney Presbyterian Church, Romney, WV
Ronceverte Presbyterian Church, Ronceverte, WV
Roney's Point United Presbyterian Church, Roney's Point, WV
Slanesvlle Presbyterian Church, Slanesville, WV
Upper Ohio Valley Presbytery, Wheeling, WV

Other Partners Frances Mentioned in Her Letters

Sam Allen, Julie Anderson, Rodney and Sharyn Babe, Betty Ballard, Shirley Bushong, Katharine Church, Walter Compton, Josie Corning, Gary Elia, Nancy Elia, Nate Evers, Bob Gage, Laura Grubbs, Timothy Hawkins, Ed Hurley, Douglas Jackson, Don Johnson, Jane Keith, Ivory Kinslow, Carl Luthman, Ed Magee, Margaret Marsh, Jim Matheney, Cynthia McCaffety, Michael Means, Dottie Medlin, Paul Morris, Glenn Myers, Bill O'Neal, Sandrine Princival, Allison Robinson, Barbara Schmader, Amy Stewart, Julie Trimble, Maria Villegas, Chotsie Ward, Suzanne Werkema, Paul White, John Wilson, Heather, Linda, Robin.

Frances Landers, slide tray in hand, arrived at Flo Boggs's West Virginia church to speak about the Haitian children she loved.

Appendix B

Schools in the Mountains

I would ask Mrs. Frances if we could build another school and she would say no,
there is no way we can support another school.
Then I would pray to God and ask Him.
He would say, "Sure, she can support another school."
So I would build another school, and more and more would be enrolled.
—Pere Jean-Wilfrid Albert, Cherident, Haiti, 2005

The villages of Grande Colline bear secular names, many with varied spellings (for example, Bejin or Begin, Moreau or Moro). The Episcopal churches and schools share the same religious name. This book refers to the names of villages rather than the names of schools.

Many generous American churches and organizations funded the initial construction of Frances Landers's schools. Haiti Education Foundation continues to provide schooling for thousands of children in the mountains of Grande Colline by funding the salaries of qualified principals and teachers.

HEF schools are located today in thirty-five villages, listed below. Half of the villages enjoy being sponsored by a specific church or organization. These sponsorships create a lasting bond between a Haitian community and the Americans who help care for it.

Please see haitifoundation.org for up-to-date information on total enrollment in HEF's primary and secondary schools, as well as a listing of sponsorships.

Village	School	Parish
Bainet	Ascension	Ascension
Barreau	St. Barthelemy	Ascension
Bejin	St. Mathieu	St. Matthias
Bellevue	St. Innocents	Ascension

Village	School	Parish
Bras-de-Gauche	Bon Samaritan	Ascension
Cavanach	St. Andre	St. Matthias
Chemin-a-Boeuf	St. Esprit	Ascension
Cherident	St. Matthias	St. Matthias
Corps	Transfiguration	St. Matthias
Daneau	Bon Berger	St. Matthias
David	Notre Dame	St. Matthias
Denard	St. Jacques	Ascension
Detete	St. Thomas	Ascension
Duny	St. Simon / St. Jude	Ascension
Duvillon	Transfiguration	St. Matthias
Gazou	St. Croix	Ascension
Grandou	Epiphanie	Ascension
Hess	St. Jean Evangeliste	St. Matthias
La Brezilienne	St. Luc	Ascension
La Feuillade	La Touissant	Ascension
La Revoir	St. Timothy	Ascension
La Vallee	St. Barnabe	St. Matthias
Labiche	St. Cyprien	Ascension
Lamothe	St. Etienne	St. Matthias
Lavanneau	St. Thomas	St. Matthias
LeBeau	Bonne Nouvelle	St. Matthias
Marigot	St. Esprit	St. Matthias
Monchil	Christ Roi	St. Matthias
Moreau	St. Jean Baptiste	St. Matthias
Morin	Epiphanie	St. Matthias
Petite Riviere	St. Jacques/St. Philippe	Ascension
Pillard	St. Jos. D'Arimathee	St. Matthias
Sorel	Incarnation	Ascension
Trouin	St. Marc	St. Marc
Venant	St. Nom de Jesus	Ascension

A nutritious noon meal improves dramatically the children's ability to learn.

Appendix C

Opportunities

We had a blessed trip. The weather was great,
eighty-five degrees with a light breeze. No bugs.
—*Raleigh Court Presbyterian Church, Roanoke, Virginia, 2014*

You can be part of this ongoing miracle in Haiti's mountains.

Consider spreading the good news of this ministry and praying for it.

Consider joining a mission trip to Grande Colline. Cherident's guesthouse is waiting. So are the children.

Consider a financial gift. One hundred percent of your donation goes directly to this work, as you designate. Seventy-five dollars sends a child to school for a year. Once children begin school, Haiti Education Foundation ensures that they receive a scholarship each year until graduation. If you give scholarships, HEF encourages you to renew them by September.

To continue bringing hope through education to Haiti's mountains, please contact HEF:

Haiti Education Foundation, Inc.
PO Box 10775, El Dorado, AR 71730
870-862-1252
haitifoundation.org

Consider learning more too about HEF's partners in Grande Colline:

Alternative Gifts International: altgifts.org
Haiti Healthcare Partners: haitihealthcarepartners.webs.com
Living Waters for the World: livingwatersfortheworld.org
Plant with Purpose: plantwithpurpose.org
Solar Under the Sun: solarunderthesun.org

Trinity/HOPE: trinityhope.org

These nonprofits work holistically to bring education, health care, clean water, agriculture and microcredit loans, solar energy, feeding programs, and more. The organizations share the commitment to help the villagers in southern Haiti help themselves, with Jesus Christ as their guide. Check out this Facebook page, too, and see how HEF graduates are honoring their priest: Fondation Jean-Wilfrid Albert.

And should you decide to "just come and see," the following packing list will be helpful!

Duffle or backpack, preferable to checked luggage
Money belt and about seventy-five dollars per day (cash) in small bills
Cash for entrance tax at Port-au-Prince airport
Credit card for use in airports
Paperwork: passport, copy of birth certificate, tickets
Writing and study materials: journal, paper and pens, Bible
Snack food: power bars, dried fruit
Packs of moist towelettes ("Use the Wet Ones!") or hand sanitizer
Plastic travel pack of sixteen washcloth-sized wipes
Plastic bags for trash you will accumulate
Toiletries, towel and washcloth, soap and shampoo, razor
Water bottle, filled when departing United States
Hat, sunscreen, sunglasses
Good insect repellent, hand mirror, brush or comb
Work clothes: jeans, thick gloves, sturdy shoes, absorbent socks
Casual clothes: shorts, T-shirts (fresh every day), waterproof sandals
Church clothes for men: button-down shirt, tie, slacks
Church clothes for women: dress or skirt and blouse with sleeves
Lightweight pajamas
Swimming attire for trip to the beach
Poncho or water-repellent jacket
Flashlight and extra batteries
Camera
Needle and thread, tweezers, adhesive bandages
Medications: Cipro, Imodium, Neosporin, antimalarial, ibuprofen
Watch, GPS
A kind and flexible attitude
Expectations for a wonderful experience!

Appendix D

Sources

The material in this book is taken from three broad sources: published works, unpublished works, and personal communications. I am grateful to all who shared their knowledge of Frances's ministry, as well as to the authors of excellent books and articles on the storied history of Haiti.

Published Works: Articles, Books, Newsletters, Pamphlets

"A Report from Haiti and the DR." Medical Benevolence Foundation, Woodville, TX, 1991.

Abbott, Elizabeth. *Haiti: The Duvaliers and Their Legacy.* New York: McGraw Hill Company, 1988.

"About Collinsville." City of Collinsville, Oklahoma, http://www.cityofcollinsville. org/About_Collinsville/History (accessed January 5, 2012).

Adams, David and Amelie Baron. Reuters, "Tension Mounts in Haiti as Clock Ticks on Electoral Impasse," http://news.yahoo.com/tension-mounts-haiti-clock-ticks-electoral-impasse-003727687, December 9, 2014.

"Arkansas Community Service Award Given to El Dorado Woman." *El Dorado News-Times,* July 29, 2009.

Association Hotelicre et Touristique. Map of Haiti. Office National du Tourisme et des Relations Publiques, Port-au-Prince, undated.

Barnwell, Carol E. "Medical Mission Grows to Ministry of the Heart." *The Texas Episcopalian,* May 1999.

Brandon, Phyllis D. "High Profile: Frances Maschal Landers." *Arkansas Democrat-Gazette,* December 2, 2001.

Brawner, Steve. "One Woman Did Change the World." *Southwest Times Record,* September 22, 2010, Fort Smith, AR.

Bringing Hope through Education. Brochure of Haiti Education Foundation, Inc., El Dorado, AR, 2012.

"Building a Sustainable Shoe Industry in Haiti." TOMS, http://www.toms.com/stories/giving/building-a-sustainable-shoe-industry-in-Haiti, January 21, 2015.

"Camp Blanding." Wikipedia, http://en.wikipedia.org/wiki/Camp_Blanding (accessed April 10, 2013).

"Caribbean." Wikipedia, http://en.wikipedia.org/wiki/Carribean (accessed March 12, 2013).

Clayton, Tom and Nory. *The Clayton Crier.* Newsletter, Fort Lauderdale, FL, December 1996.

"Code Noir." Wikipedia, http://en.wikipedia.org/wiki/Code_Noir (accessed March 12, 2013).

Compact Edition of the Oxford English Dictionary. New York: Oxford University Press, 1971. Twenty-seventh printing in the United States, April 1988.

Cooper, Helene. "Mountain to Climb: For Haiti, Corruption, Crime and Depravation Hobble Economic Plan." *Wall Street Journal*, November 4, 1994.

Dor-Ner, Zvi. *Columbus and the Age of Discovery*. New York: William Morrow and Company, Inc., 1991.

"Dragon Ladies Under Siege." *People Magazine*. March 3, 1986.

Dubois, Laurent. *Avengers of the New World*. Cambridge, MA: The Belknap Press of Harvard University Press, 2004.

"Episcopal Bishop in Haiti Living in a Tent City." St. Paul's Memorial Church, http://spmcrector,blogspot.com/2010/01/episcopal-bishop-in-haiti-living-in. html, January 18, 2010.

Falasco, Dr. Dennis. "Ministry in Haiti." *First Presbyterian Connections.* Newsletter of First Presbyterian Church, El Dorado, AR, June 1998.

French, Howard W. "Ferry Disaster Underlines Haiti's Everyday Needs." *New York Times*, February 21, 1993.

"French Revolution." Wikipedia, http://en.wikipedia.org/wiki/French_Revolution (accessed March 12, 2013).

"General Wade Haislip," http://www.combatreels.com/General_Wade_Haislip.ctm (accessed February 20, 2013).

Goodman, Kay, Dawkins Hodges, and Rob Sherrard. "The Bleak Landscape of Haiti." *Shenandoah Seeds*, newsletter of Shenandoah Presbytery, Harrisonburg, VA, November–December 1984.

Granitz, Peter. "Haiti's Political Crisis is About to Get Worse," November 24, 2014, http://foreignpolicy.com/2014/11/24/haitis-political-is-about-to-get-worse/.

Hahn, Heather. "Arkansan Builds School in Haiti." *Arkansas Democrat-Gazette*, May 14, 2008.

"Haiti." Wikipedia, http://en.wikipedia.org/wiki/Haiti (accessed March 12, 2013).

"Haiti Crisis: Anti-Martelly Protest Turns Violent." December 16, 2014, http://www.bbc.com/news/world_latin_america.

"Haiti: Consular Information Sheet." US Department of State, January 21, 1999, http://travel.state.gov/haiti.html (accessed March 16, 1999).

"Haiti Education Foundation," www.haitifoundation.org.html.

Haiti Happenings. Newsletter of Haiti Education Foundation, Inc. (originally the Haiti Fund), Vol. 1, No. 1, September 1993, to Vol. 23, No. 2, Fall 2015, El Dorado, AR.

"Haiti Population Clock." Country Meters, http://countrymeters.info/en/Haiti/ (accessed September 28, 2015).

"Haiti Public Announcement." US Department of State, January 9, 2004, http://www.travel.state.gov/haiti_announce.html (accessed January 19, 2004).

"Haiti Travel Alert." US Passports & International Travel, August 7, 2015, http://travel.state.gov/content/passports/en/alertswarnings/haiti (accessed September 28, 2015).

"Haitian Revolution." Wikipedia, http://en.wikipedia.org/wiki/Haitian_Revolution (accessed March 20, 2013).

"Haitian Vodou." Wikipedia, http://en.wikipedia.org/wiki/Haitian_Vodou (accessed June 5, 2013).

"Haiti's Cholera Outbreak Tied to Nepalese UN Peacekeepers." NPR, http://yahoo.com, August 13, 2013.

Hall, John. Trinity/HOPE, http://www.trinityhope.org/our-mission (accessed November 9, 2015).

Hanson, Aprils. "Champion of Haitian Education Dies at 93." *Arkansas Democrat-Gazette*, September 16, 2010.

"Hispaniola." Wikipedia, http://en.wikipedia.org/wiki/Hispaniola (accessed March 12, 2013).

"History of Haiti." Wikipedia, http://en.wikipedia.org/wiki/History_of_Haiti (accessed March 12, 2013).

Holler, Larry. "Haiti: A People's Struggle for Hope." Background paper no. 107, *Bread for the World*. Washington, DC, September 1988.

Hope for Haiti. Newsletter of the Haiti Fund, Vol. 1, No. 1, August 2000, to Vol. 2, No. 1, August 2001, El Dorado, AR.

"Hospital Ste. Croix: Léogâne, Haiti." Episcopal Medical Missions Foundation, http://www.emmf.com/hscroix.htm (accessed June 15, 2012).

Kane, Thomas S. *The New Oxford Guide to Writing.* New York: Oxford University Press, 1988.

Katz, Jonathan M. "Haiti's Absolute Scarcity of Agricultural Land, Its Multiplying Effect, After Efforts to Halt Deforestation Falter." February 16, 2000, http://www.wehaitians.com/haiti%20absolute%20scarcity%20of%20 agricultureal%20 land.html (accessed March 12, 2013).

——. "The Clintons' Haiti Screw-Up, As Told By Hillary's Emails," http:// www.politico.com/magazine/story/2015/09/hillary-clinton-email-213110, September 2, 2015.

——. "How the World Came to Help Haiti and Left a Disaster." Excerpt in *Scientific American,* November 7, 2014, http://www.scientificamerican.com/article/ how-the-world-came-to-help-and-left-a-disaster/

"Leonard's Department Store." Fort Worth Culture, www.fwculture.com/ leonards_museum.html (accessed February 5, 2012).

Lightner, Jill. "Simple Acts of Compassion: Frances Maschal Frances's simple acts make a profound impact on the education of Haitian children." *Quill of Alpha Xi Delta,* Summer 2002.

McCaffety, Cynthia. "A Hunger to Learn." *Arkansas Times,* October 1989.

McFadden, David. "Haiti Better Off 5 Years After Quake, Though Still Troubled." The Associated Press, January 10, 2015, http://news.yahoo.com/haiti-better-off-5-years-quake-though-still-050224121.html.

McIntyre, Janice. "Hope for Haitians." *El Dorado News-Times* (AR), April 3, 2000.

"Missionary to Speak." *News-Tribune-Keyser* (WV), March 12, 1987.

"Missionary to Visit." *News-Tribune-Keyser* (WV), February 22, 1994.

Moloney, Anastasia. "Voodoo Priests, Doctors on Front Line of Mental Healthcare," January 9, 2015, http://news.yahoo.com.

Morales, Kristen. "First Presbyterian Church's World Mission Conference." *Gainesville Times,* Gainesville, FL, January 31, 2008.

New Revised Standard Version Bible, 1989: Division of Christian Education of the National Council of the Churches of Christ in the United States of America.

Ng Cheong-Lum, Roseline and Leslie Jermyn. *Cultures of the World: Haiti.* New York: Marshall Cavendish Benchmark, 1995. Second edition, 2005.

Obituary of Gardner Hayden Landers, National Obituary Archive, http://www. arrangeonline.com/Obituary/obituary.asp?obituaryid=69639006&info=vs (accessed December 15, 2010).

Obituary of Harriet Prichard. *Wichita Eagle* (KS), November 2, 2014.

"Officials in Haiti Celebrate Completion of Marriott Hotel Built by Telecom Company Digicel." Fox Business, February 24, 2015, http://www.foxbusiness.com/ markets/2015/02/24/officials-in-haiti-celebrate-completion-marriott-hotel.

Patterson, Carolyn Bennett. "Haiti: Beyond Mountains, More Mountains." *National Geographic*, Vol. 149, No. 1, January 1976.

Penn, Sean. "News Flash: Haiti Is on the Upswing." *Wall Street Journal*, June 18, 2014.

"Presbyterians Making a Difference." *Presbyterians Today*, June/July1998.

Reed, John. "Finding the Silver Lining in Haitian Earthquake." *News Leader* (Staunton, VA), January 17, 2010.

Rincher, Deslande. *Franse Ak Angle: San Traka e San Dlo Nan Je*. Forest Hills, NY: Rincher and Associates, 1986.

Robbins, Carla Anne. "Face of Defiance." *US News & World Report*, February 17, 1986.

Roberts, W. Adolphe. *The Caribbean: The Story of Our Sea of Destiny*. Indianapolis and New York: The Bobbs-Merrill Company, 1940.

Sabin, Scott. "Under the Rubble." *To the Source*, January 21, 2010, http://www. tothesource.org/ 1_20_2010/1/20/2010_printer.htm.

Sachs, Jeffrey D. *The End of Poverty: Economic Possibilities for Our Time*. New York: Penguin Group, 2005.

Sanon, Evens and Danica Coto. "Hundreds Attend Duvalier's Funeral in Haiti." The Associated Press, *Summerland Review*, October 11, 2014, http://www. summerlandreview.com/national/278899541.htmlă.

Saying Yes to Haiti's Children. Brochure of Haiti Education Foundation, El Dorado, AR, four undated versions.

Saying Yes to Haiti's Children. Brochure of the Haiti Fund, El Dorado, AR, undated.

Saying Yes to Haiti's Children. Brochure published by Medical Benevolence Foundation, Woodville, TX, undated.

Saying 'YES' to Haiti's Children: The Story of the Haiti Education Foundation. Brochure published by Bellevue Presbyterian Church, Nashville, TN, undated.

Schlesing, Amy. "Hope Rises for Haiti Schools." *Arkansas Democrat-Gazette*, March 12, 2010.

Schmidt, Hans. *The United States Occupation of Haiti, 1915–1934*. New Jersey: Rutgers University Press, 1971. Second printing, 1995.

Sherrard, Robert L. "Mission, Haiti," *Shenandoah Presbytery News*, Harrisonburg, VA, Fall 1984.

Simmons, Tracy. "An Interview with the Episcopal Bishop of Haiti, the Rt. Rev. Jean Zache Duracin." The Episcopal Diocese of Connecticut, https://www.ctepiscopal.org/Content/Interview_with_Bishop_Duracin.asp (accessed December 5, 2013).

Spencer, Christopher. "Local Resident Continues Mission." *El Dorado News-Times* (AR), February 23, 1998.

The Sower. Newsletter of Plant with Purpose (originally Floresta). San Diego, CA, March 1998–Summer 2015.

Taft-Morales, Maureen. "Haiti: Prospects for Democracy and US Policy Concerns." Foreign Affairs and National Defense Division, United States Government, March 20, 1992.

Webb, Christine and Margaret Kavanagh. "Hope for Haiti, 5 Years Later." January 12, 2015, http:www.baynews9.com/content.

Zarin, Michael. "The Battle for Democracy in Haiti Just Got Tougher." *Wall Street Journal*, June 25, 1999.

Video Recordings

"Haiti Education Foundation," First Presbyterian Church, Gainesville, GA, 2008.
"Haiti Education Foundation," St. John the Divine, Houston, TX, 2000.

Unpublished Works in the Author's Possession

Conference Materials

HUG (Haiti United Gathering), El Dorado, AR, March 23–25, 2000.
HUG (Haiti United Gathering), Little Rock, AR, September 17–19, 2010.
HUG (Haiti United Gathering), Fishersville, VA, October 5–7, 2012.
HUG (Haiti United Gathering), Westlake Village, CA, October 12, 2013.

Correspondence

Albert, Pere Jean-Wilfrid. Collection of eighty-nine letters and e-mails to Harry and Flo Boggs, David Grizzle, Paul and Evelyn Howell, Gardner and Frances Landers, DiAnn Shamblin, Bob Stinson, and many supporting churches, 1987–2005.

Byrd, Senator Robert to Flo Boggs, May 7, 1991.

Hathaway, Colonel George J. to Commanding General, XV Corps, APO 436 US Army. Subject: Recommendation for Award for Lieutenant Colonel Gardner H. Landers, May 15, 1945.

———. to Commanding General, XV Corps, APO 436 US Army. Subject: Recommendation for Award of the Legion of Merit for Lieutenant Colonel Gardner H. Landers, August 3, 1945.

Howell, Paul and Evelyn. Collection of thirty-six letters and e-mails between the Howells and David Grizzle, Reverend Larry Hall, Charles McCord, Bob Stinson, and Fannie Tapper, 1999–2006.

Landers, Frances. Collection of eight hundred letters and e-mails between her and Pere Kesner Ajax, Pere Jean-Wilfrid Albert, Harry and Flo Boggs, George Brandon, Pere Jean Monique Bruno, Pere Jean Mathieu Brutus, Day and Blanche Carper, Pere Jean-Elie Charles, Edie Covert, Pete and Fran Hobbs, Paul and Evelyn Howell, Emily King, Phillip Langsdon, Reverend Tom Litteer, Don and Martha Miller, Marshall Musser, Mary Jo Oliver, Harriet Prichard, Sandrine Princival, Scott Sabin, Barbara Schmader, Pastor Rob Sherrard, Ruth Standefer, Fannie Tapper, and Suzanne Werkema, 1990–2009.

Landers, Frances and Susan Turbeville. Annual Christmas letters and other updates to Haiti Education Foundation supporters, 1996–2015.

Miller, Don and Martha. Collection of twenty letters and e-mails between the Millers and Simon Archile, Claude Belanger, Celestin Lucson, Pere Fred Menelas, Franz Saintilma, and Viergela Louis Valles, 1999–2015.

Sainte Croix Hospital staff and missionaries. Collection of eight letters to supporters from Dr. Richard and Dr. Judith Brown, Scott and Edna Jordan, and Dr. David McNeeley, 1982–2000.

Thomas, Captain Henry C. Military Records and Report of Certificate of Service of Gardner H. Landers, January 5, 1946.

Turbeville, Susan. Collection of eighteen e-mails to Haiti Education Foundation supporters, 2010–2015.

Journals, Memoirs, and Reports

Adams, Margie. "In Haiti, One Makes a Difference," July 1986.
Clear Lake Presbyterian Church, "CLPC's Adventures in Haiti," May 2000.
Evans, Layton. "Mission Team Fulfills Law of Christ," July 1989.
Gilliam, Betty. Trip report, January 1999.
Hobbs, Fran. Journals, September 1984 and August 1986.
Landers, Gardner Hayden. Memoir, November 2004.
Landers, Frances Maschal. "Dear Gardner," November 2004.

———. Diary of first trip, November 1977.

———. "Gardner Hayden Landers Died October 6, 2006," 2008.

———. "Haiti Education Foundation, Inc.," 2002.

———. "Hospital Happenings," July 2009.

———. "Memories at Ninety-Three," 2010.

———. "My Friend, Jean Monique Bruno," 2002.

———. Untitled memoir, June 2004.

Mathias, Jennie. "My Testimony of Haiti," July 2000.

Mattox, Ginny. "Thoughts on My Haiti Experience," July 2000.

McRae, Chris. Journal, March 2002.

Miller, Martha Abbey. Journals, April 1999, April 2000, March 2002.

Reed, John and Anne. Trip report, April 2008.

Sears, Bob. Journal, March 2002.

Tapper, Fannie. Mission Report, St. John the Divine, March 2004.

Windy Cove Presbyterian Church. Trip report, July 1986.

Windy Cove Presbyterian Church. "Our Haiti Homecoming," September 2011.

Worship Bulletins

Augusta Stone Presbyterian Church, Fort Defiance, VA, March 15, 1988.

First Presbyterian Church, El Dorado, AR, January 3, 1993 and September 16, 2010.

First Presbyterian Church, Jasper, TX, March 8, 1998.

First Presbyterian Church, Staunton, VA, March 25, 2001 and April 27, 2003.

Keyser Presbyterian Church, Keyser, WV, March 15, 1987 and July 23, 1989.

Romney Presbyterian Church, Romney, WV, March 24, 2001.

Westminster Presbyterian Church, Westlake Village, CA, June 2, 2002.

Windy Cove Presbyterian Church, Millboro, VA, June 7, 1998.

Woodstock Presbyterian Church, Woodstock, VA, February 11, 1990.

Personal Communications

I am grateful for my discussions with and the support of many people, including Flo Boggs, George Brandon, Steve Brawner, Pere Jean Monique Bruno, Rob Crittenden, Dennis Falasco, Ancy Fils-Aime, Nancy Hall, Fran Hobbs, Tom Holmes, Michael Landers, Chris McRae, Dottie Medlin, Pere Fred Menelas, Wislande Menelas, April Miller, Don Miller, Christine Moore, Mary Jo Oliver, Harriet Prichard, John Reed, Scott Sabin, Bob Sears, Tony Steiner, Susan Oliver Turbeville, and Viergela Louis Vallee.

Image Credits

Flo Boggs: cover and pages 91, 101, 107, 125, 126, 135, 142, 172, 211, 240.

Harry Boggs: page 271.

Pastor Dennis Falasco: page 172.

Ancy Fils-Aime: pages 229, 230.

Haiti Education Foundation: pages xii, 83, 84, 258, 288.

Landers Family Collection: pages 2, 178, 234.

Frances Landers: page 116.

Dr. James Landers: page 33.

Judge Michael Landers: pages 178, 220.

Susan Landers: page 152.

Don Miller: page 230.

Martha Abbey Miller: cover and pages v, vii, viii, x, 18, 44, 72, 102, 116, 143, 144, 184, 192, 199, 231, 254, 256, 272, 275.

Bob Sears: pages 91, 211.

Pastor Rob Sherrard: page 61.

Maria Villegas: page 115.

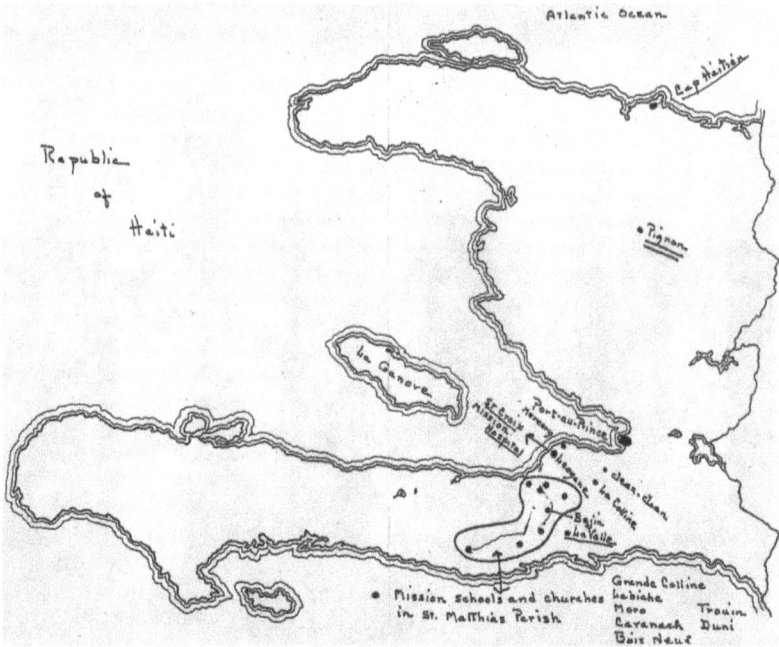

Frances Landers took great care in the hand-drawn maps she shared with her supporters. Above, she circled the first schools she and Pere Albert built in the mountains. Within a few years, her schools tripled, as illustrated below.

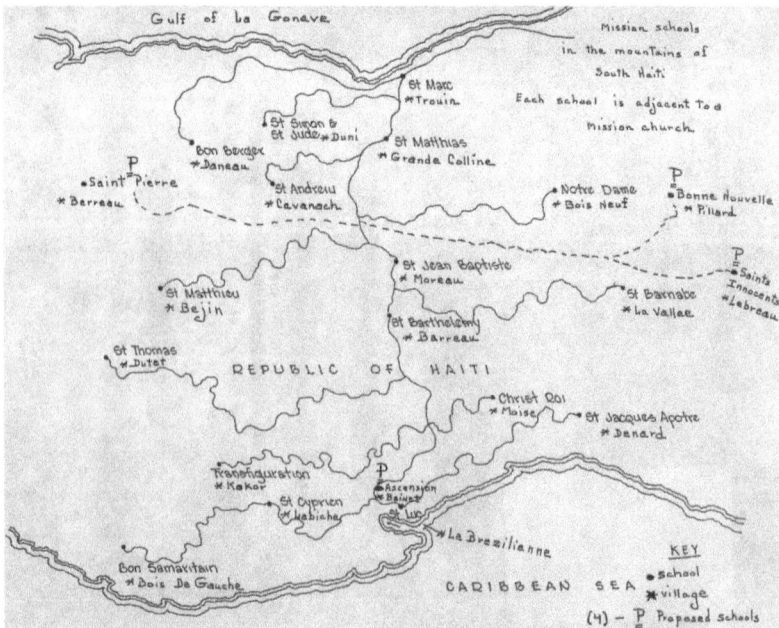

Printed in the United States
By Bookmasters